Stout, Robert Joe.

The blood of the serpent :
Mexican lives

DATE DUE			

THE BLOOD OF THE SERPENT

THE BLOOD OF THE SERPENT:

Mexican lives

Robert Joe Stout

Algora Publishing
New York

ISBN: 0-87586-215-2 (softcover)
ISBN: 0-87586-216-0 (hardcover)

Library of Congress Cataloging-in-Publication Data:

Stout, Robert Joe.
The blood of the serpent : Mexican lives / by Robert Joe Stout.
p. cm.
ISBN 0-87586-215-2 (soft cover : alk. paper) -- ISBN 0-87586-216-0 (hardcover : alk. paper)
1. Mexico--Social conditions--1970- 2. Social problems--Mexico. I. Title.

HN113.5.S76 2003
306'.0972--dc21

2003001949

Printed in the United States

Table of Contents

Preface

In our favorite Mexico City hangout, a huge bustling bar called Sep's, not far from the entrance to Chapultepec Park, half a dozen of us were hoisting steins of dark beer, laughing and lying about our G. I. lives before we'd become Mexico City college students, when we saw one of our professors working his way among the crowded tables. We invited him to join us. His presence brought several others to our table — National University of Mexico graduate students, some of the professor's teaching colleagues, I don't remember who all was included or how large the group got to be.

But I do remember how animated our conversations became as we challenged each other's political assertions and amended each other's historical viewpoints. *Mestizaje*, the Revolution of 1910, Maximilian's interlude and protective tariffs aroused curiosity and controversy. So did Pancho Villa's buried treasures, the Virgin of Guadalupe, the myth of Cuauhtemoc and why and how the mysterious Toltecs disappeared. And we talked about the founding of Mexico City on an island in a lake that had formed in the crater of an extinct volcano. There, on a cactus, the Toltecs had seen the fulfillment of a promise: an eagle clutching a serpent in its claws.

"The Mexican eagle," one of our group commented.

"The eagle," our professor repeated. "And beneath it, when it flew away, the serpent's blood that flows through our veins today."

Introduction

I was only twenty-one, naive and self-centered but reasonably sure of my own capacity to do what I wanted to do, when I embarked on life as an ex-G.I. undergraduate in Mexico City. I had been in large cities before — Los Angeles, Denver, London, Copenhagen — but never had lived in one for any length of time. And none of them was like the Mexico City I stepped into as the quiet '50s were becoming the turbulent '60s.

I didn't speak Spanish well at the time, but I felt the city — the culture — pull me into new awarenesses, new feelings. The outer shell of my being opened to admit impulses and emotions that until then had been confined to dreams. On a powerful psychic, subconscious level, I identified with this Mexico that I was experiencing.

I identified with it, but as the outsider — the foreigner — that I was. On the surface, I always would be a *gringo* — blue-eyed, awkwardly stumbling over pronunciations and verb endings, constantly being thrown off by contradictions and idiosyncrasies — but in that part of me from which dreams arise and where spirits dwell, a bond was forming that never would be erased.

Now, forty years after that process — that merging, that love affair — began, the bond still exists. I still live in Mexico whenever I can, and I still find the country and its people perplexing, fascinating, strange. This series of portraits, images, adventures and conversations will, I hope, convey both the bond I feel and some of the many facets of the Mexican personality, countryside and psyche.

In *The Blood of the Serpent* I have tried to render a Mexico mosaic that is "true" both perceptually and emotionally. To achieve this I have taken a number of liberties.

I have reproduced a number of the interviews from memory. Though they are not verbatim accounts, they accurately re-create the conversations that I describe.

In some cases, these conversations occurred over the space of a few days, or weeks or months, as I've indicated in the narratives. In most instances, they were held in Spanish. In reproducing them, I've focused on the spirit and intent of what was being said, rather than attempt to achieve literal translations. By letting the individuals depicted have their say without authorial injections or mind reading I hope to have achieved a frankness that otherwise would not have been possible.

I've followed both geographical and cultural boundaries in choosing the section and chapter divisions. The groupings are to some extent arbitrary, and I've made no attempt to equally balance one region against another, one state against another or rural Mexico against urban Mexico. I have, however, tried to put together events, observations and conversations for each of the three sections that dramatize life in the separate regions.

With few exceptions, the names given are the names of the people involved. Where there was uncertainty about names, I've tried to indicate the vagaries and inconsistencies. (In most cases, I've assumed that the names, locations and opinions given me by the various people involved were accurate.)

Despite a common boundary over 1,000 miles long, an American population living in Mexico that exceeds 1 million persons, an estimated 20 million Mexican immigrants in the United States, commercial transactions in the billions of dollars and active tourist industries, most Americans seem to know relatively little about Mexico. Their contact with our neighbor south of the border all too often has been confined to the border cities and/or beach resorts like Cabo San Lucas and Cancun.

Misconceptions about Mexico have been a burr under my saddle for the past forty years, and I have little faith that much will change in the forty years to come. (Change, as those of us who were '60s idealists have learned all too well, is more window dressing than structural in most societies and for most governments.) I do hope, however, that *The Blood of the Serpent* provides fresh insights and new perspectives and opens a few little corridors to understanding and appreciating both the dark and the light sides of the love affair that is my Mexico.

Portions of this manuscript have appeared, some in slightly altered form, in the following magazines: *Aim, Catholic Digest, Commonweal, Focus, Kit-Kat Review, Mexico West, Rosebud* and *Toward Freedom*.

The proximity of Mexico has brought new words into use in the U.S., some of them more widely known than others. In the following pages, as I share the "local flavor," I have sought to balance linguistic accuracy with readability.

PART I

THE URBAN CORE

No city in the world has grown as rapidly in recent times as Mexico City has. And no area in the world has created so many problems for itself and the plains, hills and arroyos that surround it than the ancient capital of the Aztecs. Seven-thousand-plus feet above sea level, situated in the crater of a long extinct volcano on shifting subsoil undercut by earthquake faults, Mexico's urban core lacks almost everything that a 21st century city would desire: adequate water sources, drainage, natural ventilation, proximity to transportation, room for expansion.

It wasn't always that way. Seventeenth-century reports describe constant fresh breezes, moderate temperatures and magnificent views of snow-capped mountains that made life relaxing and gardening easy. Even so, the quaint capital was accessible only by torturously winding roads, and its residents frequently incurred plagues, suffered respiratory problems and had to contend with periodic shortages of food and building materials.

Hernando Cortez, the Spanish conqueror of the Aztecs, made Mexico City his capital despite the advice of both local and Spanish notables, who warned that the city's mountainous location would impede accessibility to other parts of the country and would handicap growth. Sporadic attempts to de-centralize both industry and government over the four centuries that followed never succeeded and the capital of Mexico-the-City has remained. Nearly 40 million people — over one-third of the country's population — live within its urban area and thousands more pour in, intending to become permanent residents, every day.

It is the center of Mexican life, culture, business, government, education and entertainment. The country's great art treasures are there. The country's huge Roman Catholic cathedral is there. The movie industry is centered there. The major newspaper and television outlets are there. Every airline that flies into the country lands and takes off from its airport. Virtually every decision, whether involving the takeover of unfarmed land in Tabasco or counting gray whales off the coasts of Baja California, is made there.

Every politico aspiring to higher office, every surgeon hoping to become famous, every writer dreaming of being published, goes there. The mayor of the city wields more power than any elected official except the president himself.

It is more than a city, it is a dynamic organism that has overwhelmed natural boundaries and spread across the countryside that surrounds it. A federal *diputado* (Congressman) labeled this growth "a contagious disease."

Cities that have formed in its shadows — Netzahualcóyotl, Iztapalapa, Chimalhuacan, to name only a few — wreathe the capital city with equally dense congestion, competition and crime. Despite all the problems, despite its reputation (well enough earned!) for unbreathable air, unmoving traffic and intolerable vice, it remains a mecca for the poor, the disenfranchised, the opportunistic and the starry-eyed.

No urban area like it exists anywhere in the world.

"Thank God for that!" many say.

CHAPTER 1. CITY OF LIFE, CITY OF DEATH

NUEVOS RICOS

Floor-length drapes opened onto a view of tiled patios and terraced gardens, cobble-stoned driveways and stained glass windows. Beyond them, "on a clear day," Teresa Carballo smiled, one could see the skyscrapers of downtown Mexico City six miles away.

The windows, she confirmed, were a 1980s remodeling of the late 19th century home's third-floor living room. They extended from floor to ceiling, wall-to-wall, and were so unmarred and spotless that, looking through them, my back to rooms filled with glisteningly efficient computers and state-of-the-art medical research equipment, I felt momentarily transported into the genteel, aristocratic rhythms of colonial Mexico.

"It reminds me that, after all, I have antecedents, that I am Mexican, that this was part of my heritage," the 45-year-old millionairess nodded as she crossed the room to stand beside me. On the rooftop across the street, a chubby maid was hanging print bed sheets and brightly colored pillowcases on a line strung in front of a cable television receptor dish. Two houses further down a young man, hose in one hand, sponge in the other, busily scrubbed the undersides of a black BMW's fenders. Sudsy water trickled across the sidewalk into the gutter.

Everywhere, on stairways, around doorways, lining the carports visible through locked wrought iron gates, ancient brown *ollas* cascaded azaleas, geraniums, palmiras and cacti. Past the corner of a rooftop tennis court visible just beyond a tile-roofed turret, I could see treetops above a little park where old men gathered to smoke and talk, and crisply dressed kindergartners teased their middle-aged *nanas*.

"But it's not much more than a reminder," Carballo continued, a smile teasing the corners of her mouth. "Like Christmas parties that still are called *posadas*, or the *salsa* that we add to our food, a little bit of seasoning."

She spoke Spanish with the clear, practiced diction of someone used to talking to foreigners — someone for whom exactness was both a virtue and a persona.

"We, after all, are the '*nuevos ricos*.'" Her lips twitched inward around the phrase. "We are *pepenadores* — garbage pickers — who got rich on the leavings of others."

I bit back the impulse to contradict — Mexican satirists delight in cartooning the *nuevos ricos* as voracious Uncle Sam-shaped coyotes and/or assassins of Mexico's traditional old guard oligarchy. I sensed nothing of that in Carballo's attitude. She obviously took personal delight in the irony of her own rise to "comfort."

If she was what I had expected — a straightforward, alert, attractive woman whose outer briskness veiled a Mexican tendency towards flirtatiousness and sentimentality — the residence she shared with her life and business partner, Carlos Geraldo, was not. Although its exterior emulated the old colonial mansions around it, with its wrought iron banisters and spiral staircases, inlaid tile and servants' quarters on the roof, inside it was a James Bondian marvel of neatness and simplicity.

Even the living room was spare — Spartan; the lone superfluous piece of furniture was a 19th century portrait photographer's hooded camera on a tripod, placed so carefully a few feet from the windows that it resembled a museum piece. Posters from art openings, political benefits, rock concerts — many of them autographed — hung in metal frames on the walls. From what had been designed as a parlor behind it, I could hear the chatter of a Fax machine bringing reports and messages.

"Can I offer you something to drink? A glass of wine, perhaps?" Her own *savoir faire* seemed to amuse her and she laughed. I expected a servant to appear, but she brought the glasses herself.

"What would you like? Chardonnay? Bordeaux? I have a very nice Greek wine, actually. Or would you prefer American?"

Without waiting for me to announce a choice, she half-filled the two simple but expensive crystal glasses and offered one to me.

"You have to understand," she lifted a precise, but understated, toast, "that I wasn't born into luxury. I still get quite amused to find myself where I am."

The austere house, with its icy lack of ornamentation, chattering Fax and panoramic view, was not an ivory castle from which Carballo, in antiseptic detachment, controlled her domain. The roads that led from the view of maids sweeping tiled patios and rooftop tennis courts veered quickly into arterial traffic and swerving delivery trucks, dented Volkswagens and grimy buses.

Carballo drove her year-old Toyota with the same determined self-irony that characterized her conversations, speeding around older vehicles, honking as she accelerated through amber-turning-red streetlights, shortcutting down narrow residential streets to avoid congested intersections. Crossing Insurgentes, the ancient serpentine-like thoroughfare that still is one of Mexico City's main traffic arteries, she circled glistening all-glass office buildings, braked, and tapped the horn twice with a curved forefinger.

A figure came suddenly alive in the front seat of an old Ford Mustang parked at the curb. Its muffler rattled and a burst of exhaust smoke shot into the already murky air as a trimly mustachioed chauffeur lifted forefinger to his forehead, winked and cranked the old hardtop away from the curb. Immediately Carballo twisted her Toyota into the parking place it had vacated and the Mustang roared off.

"A convenience," Carballo smiled. "It's worth it to pay him to find and hold parking places."

She touched the tip of her thick-rimmed glasses and shrugged. "We *nuevos ricos*," she explained, "have to be ingenious."

On the sidewalks leading past the offices and businesses that bordered Insurgentes, Teresa Carballo struck a commanding pose. There were others like her, women with the quick, authoritative pace of success in a demanding, difficult world: impeccable business suits, *Mademoiselle/Elle* coiffures, articulate simple gold and platinum jewelry, a liberated *don't-touch-me* determination squaring their jaw lines.

Sidewalk traffic seemed to part to let them slice through to obviously important destinations. Here and there people would turn to look — corpulent businessmen with the practiced scowls of professional assassins, young clerks spooning yogurt out of plastic cups, uniformed schoolchildren chattering over book satchels and magazine pictures of their favorite movie stars.

Like most of these women, Carballo seemed to have a sixth sense about everything happening around her. She seemed able to process an incredible amount of detail instinctively, maintaining our conversation without being distracted by the horns, screeching brakes, engine roars and shouts of traffic.

Others got caught up in the pedestrian surge past the hundreds of makeshift stalls lining the passageway between the center of the sidewalks and the curbs, but she glided through, virtually untouched. The carnival of colors and smells and sounds emanating from policemen, beggars, *taxistas*, food vendors, tourists, *borrachos*, commuters and *chilango* housewives shopping for their husbands, children and friends, even the cement-dust coated construction workers knocking a section of curb apart with jackhammers, did not seem to faze her.

"Who was it who wrote, 'This is a city of eighteen million, seventeen and a half of whom are destitute and the other half a million afraid of becoming that way.'? It doesn't matter, it's true. Look, there's the business I was telling you about. We owned it only for two days.

"'*In-si-der in-for-ma-tion*,'" she pronounced carefully, in English, tilting her head back and laughing, her fingertips touching her glasses. "We made more on it than I made the whole year working for *Seguro Social*.

"Excuse me a moment." She sidestepped two men propelling a huge old wooden desk along the sidewalk and disappeared between two kiosks.

I squeezed through after her and saw her crouching to negotiate the purchase of two fresh calla lilies from a wide-eyed, fine-boned girl who couldn't have been over eight or nine years old.

"Here, *chica, gracias*. As I was saying...." she resumed our conversation, darting a warning glance at a tousled passer-by who, accidentally or intentionally, had fingered her purse.

Carballo and her partner, Carlos Geraldo, never intended to purchase real estate, she explained. As a university student in Aguascalientes, she had studied to be a *maestra*, and as a young secretary-turned-administrator in Mexico City, had left a state-run medical processing department with two of her young, ambitious supervisors to set up one of the first firms providing computer-generated processing of doctors' claims in the capital.

Money borrowed from her father, a retired Mexican Air Force general, allowed them to expand just before the 1982 stock market crash and subsequent devaluation. Overnight, she explained, her hands framing her small, hyper-attentive face as she readjusted her glasses, they converted all their liquid assets to dollars and thrust them into American banks.

"I was left with stacks of paper — bills I couldn't pay, receipts I couldn't collect on. I had nothing — but neither did anyone else. My father — he comes from the old school, Puebla, pay cash for everything, don't trust anybody — persuaded me to hold onto the business. I told him I couldn't even pay the rent and he laughed and said the landlord probably couldn't pay his mortgage either.

"That turned out to be true. The landlord was going to lose the building. I went to work — as a secretary [for one of Mexico City's largest automobile dealerships], essentially — to make payments to purchase it."

Her father, she explained during a later telephone conversation, negotiated an escrow settlement and put the property in her name. The man with whom, at the time, she had had the longest and most intimate personal relationship, Carlos Geraldo, became interested in her dealings; together, they managed to obtain title to a number of medical-related businesses and real estate holdings.

"To acquire them — legally — we needed to go through a government office that was processing bankruptcies and other defaulted properties. Everything there was chaotic: They had ten times more than they could handle; not only were there delays, but a lot of the titles weren't valid, or the paperwork had been lost." Coincidentally, through social contacts, they met someone who worked in that government office who was interested in acquiring some property of his own.

"He was about our age; the three of us had many similar interests. Through his job, he had access to businesses about to go into bankruptcy. Without too much difficulty, we were able to work out an arrangement whereby he would help us quickly complete all the legal details for the purchases if we would give him a share of the purchases when he left government employment.

"Thousands of properties were available. For a year, literally, we didn't know whether we had anything [financially] or not.

"We tried to confine ourselves to businesses that we knew something about, but during that time we wound up with a chain of homeopathy supply houses, the land and buildings of what had been a private university, a bunch of resort homes on a lake in Tabasco, a pipe tobacco importing company. Both Carlos and I were working [a geneticist, Geraldo taught at a medical school in Mexico City]; we tried to be careful, to analyze what we were acquiring and to listen to the advice our partner from the government office was giving us."

As the economy began to improve — or as it appeared that the economy was going to improve — competition among the *pepenadores* grew more intense. Many speculators and small-time wheeler-dealers over-extended themselves and lost everything they had. Others had only tenuous title to many of their real estate and business acquisitions.

Carballo and Geraldo, still linked to their contact in the government office, continued to buy and trade, focusing as much as possible on medical-supply and medical service businesses. In the process, they also acquired a hillside retreat in Guanajuato, a time-share on the Caribbean, and investments in Cuba, the United States and France.

"I live well," she admitted. "I have more than I need — more, to tell the truth, than I ever wanted."

Despite her commanding presence on the street, her ability to deal quickly, efficiently — and caringly — with professional equals, politicians, journalists, employees and waifs vending flowers, she did not see herself ever becoming a major player in the business world.

"There's too much against it," she confided, "including my own personality." The look I gave her must have surprised her; peering directly at me, her fingertips adjusting her glasses again, she continued:

"I think we were lucky, Carlos and I. Because of the [economic] situation, there was room for us. The powerful families, the PRI families, the entrepreneurs who own and control everything, waited out the collapse: They knew they could. But a lot of the smaller players didn't. Or couldn't. They sold. Or crashed.

"We were outsiders, we '*nuevos ricos*,' — opportunists; we just happened to be there. Most of us didn't have political connections or family connections. The collapse [of 1982] was like an earthquake that shifted the layers of controlling order: For that brief space of time, we had opportunities that never had come up before. We jammed our way in.

"But, *entiende*, the big families never lost control. The political system is the same. Only a few of us ever will get big enough to join them — maybe by marriage, maybe by appointment to public office. We will keep our money — our American contacts — and they will keep theirs.

"Carlos and I — our motives are different from theirs. We're not trying to build dynasties. I'm never going to have children — it would be too late for that..." she let a little, self-teasing smile play across her lips "...even if I wanted to.

"So I enjoy my money. My life. I like going to the Caribbean. To Europe. I like..." For a moment, her features seemed to soften, then the self-determination — the control — returned.

"I like making money — I like it a lot. I don't think God helped me — I don't believe in God. I believe in *Ahora* — Now. I believe in what I control. The rest..."

Again she smiled and adjusted her glasses to squarely frame her dark, determined eyes. As though amused by her own eloquence, she extended her hand. "And *now*," she nodded, a touch of laughter insulating her voice, "it is time for my workout.

"*Adiós, Señor* Journalist, I hope that I have not disappointed by who I am."

Special Services

Nowhere is the contrast between rich and poor greater than in the condominiums visible from the clogged downtown streets of the central business section. Condominium living in Mexico City has increased by several thousand percent over the past 8-10 years.

"The condominiums rise like luxury ships among the teeming, rat-infested wharves of the inner city," an *Uno Más Uno* correspondent wrote several years ago. Condominium managers supervise corps of workers to do everything from trim shrubbery and wash windows, park cars, go grocery shopping, run child-care nurseries, instruct classes in English and, as armed security guards, patrol the hallways and entrances. For many of these employees, working for the condominiums is a second or third job, for which they receive under-the-table (and sometimes less-than-minimum-wage) payments.

Condominium residents not only pay for these services but also shell out for garbage pickup, street maintenance and sewer service that the government theoretically provides. Mexico City's explosive growth long ago outstripped the city's ability to provide basic services; under-paid city work crews rely on *morditas* to supplement their wages. As one of these workers, Juan Antonio Soberanis, explained:

"I have five children. Do you know what I pay for a tiny *vecinidad* in my *tugurio*? For it alone, I pay more than I earn in three weeks. What would the children eat if I did not get money on the side?"

The truck that Soberanis drove lumbered along the rutted streets like a wounded triceratops. One front fender was missing and the passenger-side door was splayed open, almost off its bent hinges. Steam hissed around the radiator cap. "Don't worry!" Soberanis shouted over the grinding gears, "I have water here!" and he kicked a grimy 10-gallon container next to the seat. Diesel smoke billowed through the window beside him as he accelerated; the mechanical crane that scooped garbage into the truck's smelly main bin clanked and rattled.

"*Échale!*" A smudged round face appeared beside mine as one of Soberanis' helpers swung onto the running board. He pointed towards the curb, where a man lay sprawled against a stack of green plastic garbage bags that had been thrown against a light pole.

"Throw him in and leave the bags!" a second helper shouted.

"Leave them both!" I heard from behind us, where a third collector, the youngest of four men Soberanis supervised, was hurling a dripping cardboard box into the bin.

"*Chinga!*" Soberanis cursed, "Leave him alone, the poor son-of-a-bitch!"

"*Mételo!*" At the shout, the round-faced worker beside me twisted to grab two five-foot lengths of new rebar that one of his *compadres* had thrown towards us. He tossed them into the space behind the seat that already was half-filled with similar collection items. Recycling in Mexico City is the proprietorship of garbage men, who make a few extra pesos selling what they find on the streets. Other scavengers establish rights to areas of the huge garbage dumps outside the city and those that twist through the shantytowns around Netzahualcóyotl and Ixtalapa.

As they worked, Soberanis and his crew told stories about their finds — or finds that garbage-collector friends had made, especially in the more wealthy areas: jewelry, tuxedos, baby cribs, suits of armor, wallets filled with $10,000 peso notes. Less rare — and more quickly disposed of — were beer cans, cigarette packs and bottles of tequila.

But as we neared the condominiums, the finds were fewer and the streets were cleaner. Here the collectors worked in pairs, one hurling everything bagged and boxed into the truck, the other behind him scooping up cans, plastic and paper that had toppled out of the containers. "After us," Soberanis laughed, "come those with brooms to sweep even the dust away."

Outside the condominiums' parking garage entrance, Soberanis tapped his horn. Two overall-clad workers shoved a sliding metal door open to expose half a dozen huge cast-steel dumpsters. Soberanis cranked his big truck around and backed into the passageway. His helpers hooked the dumpsters to the truck's cranes and with much banging, shaking, clanking and cursing, emptied them, one by one, into the bowels of the truck.

Lurching through streets stacked with garbage put out for collection ("We'll get them on the way back — if we have time," Soberanis coughed), the square-faced driver told me that the condos paid the equivalent of $18,000 dollars a month for the "special services" he and crews like his provided.

I challenged the figure: "A month, *mano*! but the city is paying you, too! You must be richer than they are!" and I waved at the structure behind us, with its gardened balconies, tinted glass windows and private parking garage.

"Do you think I get it all?" he questioned, then explained that, like all "such business" in the capital, the fees trickled down from the top. The condo owner or manager arranged with a government official to get the "special services"; each condominium resident contributed an equal share. The government official (who, Soberanis noted, probably had paid a substantial amount to get appointed to his post) then "arranged" with his subordinates — for a fee — to effect the pickup.

His base salary, paid by the city, provided only 15-20 percent of his actual income, Soberanis noted: The rest came from his share of the *cuotas*, all of which was paid in cash and none of which was taxed.

It is little wonder that *Seguro Social* (Mexico's social security system, which provides for medical care and unemployment as well as retirement) was in such bad shape, he added. Everything in the capital functioned outside the system, rather than within in.

"Do you think it is any different with the *correo* (mail service)? Or the sewers? Or the telephones? Or, for that matter, the police?"

He glanced at his watch, a Timex with luminous dials that, he grinned, he had not found in the trash, but had purchased from an *ambulante* (peddler), and shouted for his helpers to hurry — they had other "important buildings" to clear out before daybreak. His hand clasped mine in a complex three-part Mexican handshake and I jumped out of the drafty cab and waved a "Take care, *amigo*!" as the lurching triceratops careened eastward around a corner.

Soberanis' helpers waved, too, "*Qué vaya bien, guero!*" The last to leap on the lumbering monster grinned and hurled the contents of a garbage bag he had ransacked behind them on the street.

YOUNG EYES, OLD BRAINS

"Those Catholics, those who believe in Church, don't understand that they're already in Hell," 17-year-old Manuel Gonzalez snorted over a soft drink at a corner *miscelenea* in an old barrio near Chapultepec park. Gonzalez derided both the government and the press for focusing on "horror" stories like the Chiapas insurrection and shootings of *indocumentados* on the northern frontier when daily, on the streets of the city, hundreds (he said thousands) of men, women and children were being shot and mutilated, were starving to death or dying from disease or were being kidnapped or abandoned or raped.

"There's death everywhere — everywhere in the city," he insisted.

While three of his school friends and I listened, he described accidentally knocking over a 50-gallon garbage drum while chasing through an alley and dislodging a still-warm child's cadaver. Less than a year before that, his voice rose sharply, only a few blocks from where we stood an eight- or nine-year-old child had stumbled out of a street car choking on her own blood and vomit, her livid eyes gyrating wildly and her wiry arms shaking so violently she couldn't hold on to him when he tried to catch her.

He'd eased her to the sidewalk and screamed for passers by to help him but "they pushed me aside — they didn't care." He'd rushed home to bring back his mother, brother and sister; the child was dead by the time they'd gotten to the street car stop. There had been a few people huddled around the dying child, but most simply had avoided the scene and rushed on by.

Such things happened so frequently, Gonzalez insisted, that no one reported them.

"*Mire!*" he nudged his companions, "ask them, *señor*. Their parents, do they listen? Do they believe? Never! Like everyone else, they see only what they want to!"

For one so young, Gonzalez has experienced more than his share of adult adversities. His father, a struggling young doctor, died when Manuel was 11. Two years later, he, his mother, his sister and his brother moved from their cramped house on the outskirts of Polanco to an apartment closer to Chapultepec Park.

When he was 16, his sexual relations with a young neighbor resulted in her becoming pregnant. The girl's father threatened to chop both Manuel's balls and head off; the devoutly religious mother insisted that the girl bear the baby.

Finally, after protracted and acrimonious negotiations, Manuel's mother worked out a financial settlement with the girl's parents.

"I would have run away, gone north to the United States, done something — who knows?" Manuel spit. But his mother's paying his way out of marriage indebted him to her even further.

He had no choice, he told me, but to force himself through school, into a profession. He did not know whether or not he could make it. Every day, he said, he felt such a need to have sex with women that he couldn't think about anything else, yet he was afraid to seek out prostitutes because the police might arrest him or someone might beat him up. He especially thought about it at night, he said, returning home from his three-hours-an-evening job washing laboratory glasses and equipment at a university four miles away.

He did not, he added, ever expect to be happy — in all his experience, he did not know anyone who was happy. Everyone he knew, everyone he met, just like him was wading through death. Constantly the city hurled its dying children into the arms of the living, as it had done to him.

He did not know, he said, whether or not he might be the next to be thrust, dying or dead, into some stranger's arms.

"Perhaps it doesn't matter," he shrugged. "Perhaps there is no need for me to worry about obligations. How can I know that this *pinche* city will let me stay alive?

"There is death everywhere. Everywhere. Surely you, *señor*, also can smell its stink?"

If everything in the city was dying, insisted Manuel Garcia, then it was filling every dark corner, every alley and housetop and doorway and deserted lot with ghosts and spirits. They howled and yowled and infected people's minds: the madness in the city was their doing, the violence was their doing; they were unhappy and becoming vengeful because the people had turned against them, had chosen a way of life that was destructive and illusory, that pulled them away from the truth of their spirits, their roots.

The rush of words — and the intensity of feeling that generated them — belied Garcia's smooth, eager features, the bright curious animal eyes. A year younger than Gonzalez, Garcia aspired to become a *curandero* — healer, shaman — and fantasized a return to the old ways of communal caring, natural living and love.

From the bus on which we met — a groaning, ancient vehicle whose windows were so coated with grime one couldn't see through them — he led me to a little hillside *cabaña* on the western edge of the city where he lived with his *enfermera* — "nurse." The rebar pillars of inexpensive multiple-room apartments under construction pushed through a shantytown of lean-tos and sheds niched into a steeply stubbled slope littered with garbage that had been dumped from the hilltop above them. A winding network of rutted streets forked off a larger, semi-paved thoroughfare where the bus lurched to a stop — the end of the line before it turned around to descend again towards the winding Mexico-Toluca highway.

Garcia opened the heavy wooden shutters to a vista of rooftops and television antennas as he brewed us two mugfulls of native herb tea. From Yucatan, where he was born, he told me, his grandparents had taken him to Chiapas, then, a few years later, other relatives had brought him to Mexico City. Their living situation had been so congested, he said — four or five adults and eight to eleven children, depending upon who was staying with them at any given time — that he had left soon after he'd entered *secundaria* and gotten an evening job at a munitions factory.

Though he'd slept on the streets "only as a last resort," he'd bounced from living arrangement to living arrangement until he'd met his "*enfermera*," a woman ten to fifteen years older than him, who'd taken him in and become his lover, teacher and friend.

She had experience, he explained, as a *curandera*, though she did not understand the darkest and most important secrets of the ancient healers. He hoped to learn as much from her as he could, he said, then go to Yucatan and apprentice under some great master. But first, he added, he had to finish school.

"It is important that I know things of this world as well."

I asked if it bothered him that his life was so different from that of his schoolmates, and he shrugged.

"It is not so different. Many, like me, work. In factories. In shops. Selling on the streets."

A smile skittered across his mouth. Again, for an instant, he seemed sixteen — naive, mischievous, a-sparkle with youthful enthusiasm. Then the prematurely-forced-into-adulthood half-averted stare returned.

"I am lucky. Many do not stay in school. Many..." he shrugged, his hands groping as though trying to shape something physical in the space that separated us.

"There are dark forces in the world that reach out to clutch us," his eyes flashed as he tried to bring the vision closer. "In the city, many fall into their grasp. They lose their spirits. Though their hearts still beat, they are dead inside. They have no way to resist. They are flung this way and that way, like things caught in the wind. Or the tide. Finally they crash. They have desolation.

"You see them everywhere. They have no brightness. The dark forces control them. Their life is worse than death. The good spirits do not speak to them."

Suddenly the teenager again, he pulled back into self-conscious awareness of me and of his presence in the room with me. He explained that he wanted to become a *curandero* in order to open his own being fully to the good spirits and show others, young and old, how to do the same.

After leaving him to catch a bus back to the western edge of the city, I remember silently voicing a hope that he would succeed in his attempts to become a *curandero*. Between a gap in the construction tangle I could see the roof of his dwelling, a minute pyramid, the home of one teenager and his teacher/nurse/mistress, one among thousands of better and worse dwellings that I knew housed thousands of youths his age and younger, youths already adult in experience and tribulation. And I felt myself shiver as I turned back towards the city again — the huge, congested crater where unhappy and vengeful creatures lurked ready to devour the spirits of those who could not, as Garcia seemed to have done, rise above their dark, carnivorous munching.

A Witch's Pit

A gigantic gray stone, Huitzilopochtli grimaced from its perch on sagging pallets in the center of the second-story apartment's living room. Candles flickering in containers shaped like the bellies of ornamental Buddhas flung lacy shadows across walls lined with bookshelves thrown together from 1' x 10's and concrete blocks. *"Pasa! Pasa! Es tú casa!"* Gerardo Yañez guided me past a cracked *olla* filled with rolled up political and advertising posters, "let me introduce you to — "

He jammed both hands against his forehead. *"Ah! My friend!"* he laughed, and in garbled English apologized, *"Excuse me, but I don't the half of them know myself!"* He touched my arm, a pantomimed "what-can-I-tell-you, what-can-I-do?" and shrugged towards the twenty-some people laughing and talking above the beat of recorded indigenous music emerging from speakers hidden among the books. "Don't — *let it worry you...*" I intended to continue but, "Ah! Gerardo! *Your American friend?*" interrupted us. The intruder shook my hand and apologized for the group invasion: One of those present, he explained, just had had some drawings accepted by a gallery and they were throwing a little celebration.

"But then," he added, in colloquial English, "you know how we are, we celebrate everything!"

Gerardo started to introduce us; then, realizing that he had offered me the house, but nothing to drink within it, gestured that he'd be right back and disappeared behind the statue toward what I presumed was a kitchen. I watched him skitter away, his thin arms jerking with the same curious exuberance that I remembered had characterized his movements when I'd first met him twenty years before. Laughing, I remarked to my new acquaintance how little Gerardo had changed.

He looked up at me, his dark eyes blinking as if to exclaim *Oh! americano! How little you know!* Between anecdotes from those university days, when Gerardo and I and young students like us — intense, naive, filled with ourselves and what we could do for the world — had written and painted and drank and talked, my new acquaintance described how Gerardo's parents had reacted to his coming out of the closet, his being fired from essentially meaningless — but salaried — jobs, and telephone calls from an emergency ward after a gang of police ruffians had raided a gay bar and beaten Gerardo so badly that he had had to spend two months "whimpering about injustice" through a wired-together jaw.

"It's better now! It's better now!" Gerardo insisted, his shoulders twitching as though an inner vitality was trying to fling itself through his thin frame and escape into the atmosphere.

From somewhere among the cluttered bookshelves he extracted a softback, square-bound volume of Mexican gay writings. The cover, a stark, black-and-white photograph, silhouetted a dozen young men lined along a street leading towards the blurred illumination of a lone streetlight. I looked for Gerardo's name among the contributors but, his hands going in separate directions with their flutterings, he explained — apologized — that he hardly wrote poetry anymore; for several years he'd been immersed in ecological movements; he'd done some sketchings, some wood constructions; he'd made a number of trips — pilgrimages, he called them — to the old Mayan cities in Quintana Roo, in Guatemala and in Belize.

Two musicians had moved in front of Huitzilopochli. One, shirtless, tapped at native drums. He was a big man; his flesh seeming to hang in half-moons from his shoulders and neck and his long gray hair was tied in a huge bun over one ear. The other, thin, with quick, nervous coatimundi-like movements, piped at a variety of native flutes. Although no one gathered around them to listen to them, everyone seemed to accord them a certain deference.

As conversations veered from recollections of past persecutions to commentaries on newspaper reactions to capital artistic events, I surveyed Gerardo's home; the walls, I could detect now that my eyes had grown accustomed to the wavering candlelight, were one gigantic mural: hundreds of Cupidesque bodies woven together among thick-leafed vines, some of which duplicated the Cupidesque figures and were woven into their sexual connections.

Seeing me inspecting them, Gerardo jumped to his feet. He moved so quickly, and with so much surplus energy and seeming lack of coordination that he seemed to be trying to fly and to turn cartwheels at the same time. Hand clasping mine, he led me around the room, explaining as he did that his older brother Adrian had painted the mural. Adrian, he told me, had become a Satanist — a *brujo*; he had illustrated a number of books and hundreds of *misas* had been read denouncing him, one in the National Cathedral.

Our circumnavigation of the room led us to the artist whose painting had been accepted by a gallery. He was a few years younger than Gerardo, a small man with a severe, expressionless face; his stance and presence enervated physical strength. To be accepted by that particular gallery was not a big deal, he explained in terse, informative Spanish — in the long run it would bring him very little money, and no recognition to speak of.

While Gerardo fancified the artistic production of our college years, the artist snorted and shrugged that art in Mexico City never had been based on production, but on cults of personality. From the gala openings around the Bellas Artes to storefront exhibitions in Colonia Napoles, dilettantes and hangers-on flocked to a succession of parties — "Look around you, like this one!" — to argue endlessly about politicization and aesthetics that, in the long run, he claimed, meant nothing.

Of 20 million people in the city, only a few thousand cared about art — the rest pinned Holy-Mary-Mother-of-God prints to their walls with thumbtacks and the closest to poetry they came were the verses on bus commercials. He defined art as a "sub-culture that opened its arms to outcasts, perverts and earring-wearers."

Gerardo, arms flailing like a puppet being manipulated by someone undergoing an epileptic fit, defended artists and poets as the standard bearers of culture in a threatened age.

"*Chingada!*" the artist exploded, "look around you on the streets! What the f— good does art do for those millions who eat garbage and sniff glue in order to live! All we are are parasites clinging to the undersides of the rich elite!"

His limbs a dance of kinetic confusion, Gerardo screeched that art was the best pathway to the masses.

The argument drew a gradually increasing medley of opinions and refutations as, singly and in clusters of three and four, party-goers edged in to listen and kibitz. I edged away, aware that other voices were crowding my own participation, voices insisting that artists and poets in Austin, in San Francisco, in New Orleans, in Los Angeles were the forefront or the scum or the prophets or the con artists of a culture that over-exalted the importance of money or over-commercialized the successes of innovation. And I laughed — privately — and tried to clear my mind and listen again to Gerardo and his friends attack and defend these impressions — and values — that, to them, felt as important as life itself.

From the street outside the apartment, where the party, though subdued, seemed determined to continue until the last of the celebrants either drifted home or fell asleep, Gerardo Yañez took my hand and wished me a good trip back to California.

"We didn't get to talk enough about the '*good old days*,'" he twitched, flicking at his receding hairline with nervous fingers. He let his arms flop against his sides as he shook his head and forced his thin lips into an imitation of his once ever-mischievous grin:

"Wish me well, friend," he murmured. "And pray that when you visit again I am here to receive you. That I have not fallen into a witch's pit. Or been thrown in jail.

"Or..." he hesitated, his arms flopping again, unable to repress the energetic force within "...become sick — one never knows. I am careful now, I..."

He thrust his hand into mine and I shook it vigorously.

"Please! Please, do not worry!" he called as I turned towards the corner to hail a cab. "I have gods to protect me!"

On the ride back to my hotel I thought about what his artist friend had told me about Gerardo's life. And I prayed that those gods, be they Huitzilopochtli or others, take good care of him.

A Margin of Respect

It was a sad day for Edgar Jesus DeBurgh Mendoza. Hat in his hand, his sloped shoulders twitching slightly as he peered past the newly painted exteriors of the walls that lined the suburban Satellite City street, he licked the loose hairs of his thick, graying mustache with the tip of his tongue and repeated, slowly, that his son, whom he had raised to be an honorable, God-fearing Catholic, not only was an ingrate, but an infidel.

"And I am not," he added, "returning to his home to live with him. I will die on the streets instead!"

His appearance a marked contrast with his surroundings — black rayon shirt, bolo tie, wide belt, slacks tucked into gray, scuffed but well-maintained boots — he turned slowly, little flicks of expression moving the flesh on his firm, if slightly pouchy, cheeks. A couple herding two school-aged children into a VW Rabbit that just had emerged from a narrow, paved driveway diverted his attention; he scowled at the boy's pressed *Charlotte Hornets* sweatshirt, Batman lunch box, Nike shoes, at the woman's business suit, at her dark hair lightened by a blonde rinse, at the *Alumnus-U of Texas* logo on the car's windshield; and the flicks of expression grew more intense.

"Infidels!" he repeated through gritted teeth, his mouth moving as though trying to gather saliva in order to spit.

"It is a hard life," I resorted to cliché, hoping to get him to talk to me.

"It is crime!" he retorted, in physical pain as he forced himself to his full height and placed his wide-brimmed hat firmly on his thinning — but neatly trimmed — gray hair. "You would not understand!" he burst, "you could not. You are *norteamericano!* Like — like *them!*"

The outburst served my purpose: He had obliged himself, as an honorable *patron* of the old order, to describe what I could not understand and why. And, as he had done the night before, in his son's home, where I had been a guest, he renounced not only the son — and his son's wife and children — but the suburb and the metropolis to which it was attached.

Don Edgar Jesus DeBurgh Mendoza, proud patriarch of Tabasco, where he had apprenticed to a printer as a teenager and later owned his own shop — "The best," he declared proudly, "in the entire state!" — against his will had come to the capital to live with his son and his son's family. His wife, *la bella doña Griselda*, he gallantly called her, had fallen ill and, in his advancing years, he no longer had been able to take care of her and maintain his shop. Of all his children, it was his eldest son Jesus who most conveniently could take them in, so he and *la bella doña Griselda* had sold their possessions and come to Mexico City.

"I did not know it would be this way!" DeBurgh Mendoza insisted. "I would not have come. It did not keep her from dying. Better that she had died there, than..."

Instinctively he reached for his hat to doff it in respect for her memory. Despite constant medical attention, *la bella doña Griselda*'s health had worsened. Without his shop to keep him occupied, Don Edgar Jesus had sat at her side, his eyes hardly seeing the boxed azaleas and rhododendrons that his daughter-in-law had carried in and out of the adjoining patio with its plastic Walt Disney swing-and-slide set and fold-up aluminum lawn furniture.

When they could, DeBurgh Mendoza's other children had come and stayed for a day or two — a week at the most — and his daughter-in-law uncomplainingly had accommodated them. Long before *la bella doña Griselda* had breathed her last, Don Edgar Jesus had begun to plan her funeral. Many times in his 70-plus years he had marched behind the caskets of loved ones and friends, wept copiously and composed encomiums that adulated, exalted and inspired: He knew how satisfying a good funeral could be.

But his son — the ingrate! the infidel! the named-after-the-Lord Jesus first offspring of his loins! — would spend nothing — nothing! — on the funeral.

"There is no reason to rent a church, have a procession," the son had said the night before as he tried to explain why he had scheduled only a quiet graveside ceremony. In temperament, Jesus DeBurgh Castro was a lot like his father: ambitious, a bit defensive, proud. Through hard work — constant work — he had developed a good business installing radio equipment on private aircraft, purchased his suburban Mexico City home, and limited his family to the son and daughter who were attending private primary schools.

"No reason!" the old man had shouted, thrusting trembling, thick fingers through his thinning hair. His eyes glazed with moisture — not tears, mind you, for none fell — and his mustache trembling, he had turned to me.

"'*No hay de que!*' Can you believe, *señor norteamericano*? His own mother. '*No hay de que!*'? She bore him, she fed him milk from her breasts, she loved and cared for and prayed for him! Prayed, mind you, to Jesus, his namesake! Prayed that he might be valiant and marry a good Mexican woman, bear sons like himself — many sons! Make money, yes! To her prayers he owes who he is!

"And how does he show his respect? Is there a funeral? No! Are there tamales? No! Is there a statue? No! Do we follow to the cemetery? No!"

"Who would come?" the son had argued. "There are only a few of us. The priest will come to the cemetery. We will buy a mass."

It's not the same... the old patriarch had insisted. Because the house was small, son Jesus had arranged for most of the family coming from Tabasco to stay in a Satellite City motel. At that, too, the old patriarch had railed.

"Arrange! Arrange!" he had quivered. "For one's family one does not arrange, one embraces! *Embraces!*"

Failing to enlist support — or even attention — from the anyone else in the room, he'd flung open his wallet to show me that in it he carried mementos, snapshots, old newspaper clippings and money — pure money — but "no *Carnet!* no *Visa!*" No credit cards!

To his dismay, both grandchildren had scurried out of the room, the lad further upsetting don Edgar Jesus with an exiting *"Okay, Dad?"* in English as he left.

In Tabasco, the old man said, turning to me, a funeral was an important event. Who could forget the funeral when his own sister, *doña Maria*, had died? From the church they had obtained the biggest statue of Christ, so big it took four men to carry it. Through the streets they'd gone — the major streets, mind you! the thoroughfares! — hundreds of people following, millions of tears shed, thousands of prayers whispered, hundreds of embraces given.

All day they had mourned — and then all night! His brothers and sisters, his brother-in-law's family, his sister's children, had brought food and drink — had hired caterers so none of the mourners would go hungry or thirsty!

The next day — ah! the next day! — *there* was a festival! They had bought thousands of tamales! Thousands! Musicians had played — the best musicians! — and they had brought barrels of *caña* — barrels, mind you! — and the best brandy and rum.

That was a funeral! *That* was what a funeral should be! It was important to show respect. It was important to honor the dead.

"To honor the dead," he repeated, as I stood beside him on the street corner in Satellite City. As it had the night before, his resolve to leave his son's house and never return was beginning to waver. Clumsily, in my imperfect Spanish, I agreed that the world was changing for all of us — and not changing for the better. He lifted his hat and replaced it, securely, over his wide-browed face and, in a voice devoid of bravado, sighed that he and his beloved *la bella doña Griselda* had lived too long.

"What funerals we would have had," he sighed, the tremors returning to his cheeks, "if only we had stayed in Tabasco!"

Later that night, after don Edgar Jesus had washed down what little of the untraditional pasta and vegetable meal he had eaten with big double shots of good brandy, his son Jesus thanked me for my attentions to his father.

"He is a difficult man," he shrugged, pulling a jacket over his shoulders — he had radios to install that he could not put off until the next day, even though it was the night before his mother's funeral. Then, his head tilting to reveal glistening, slightly crooked front teeth, "Do not tell him, please, that we only have the grave for seven years.

"Then we have to dig up the bones and cremate them."

Chapter 2: Problems! Problems!

The Sprawling Suburbs

Welcome to Neza

The pathway — broken chunks of concrete wedged together and kept in place with bits of metal and cracking stakes — descended into a mucusy bog in front of the concrete wall that separated Enrique Ortiz' Nezahualcóyotl dwelling from Calle de los Rufianes. At first glance, the street — alley, really, although it connected to equally narrow and putrid byways leading further into the shantytown — seemed to be an ugly stream of clay, plaster and sewage slithering towards the intersection few houses away.

"Cuidado," Enrique warned, touching my shoulder. I turned and let him navigate a route past a wall like the one front of his house, graffiti splayed and topped by a ridge of broken glass and two feet of barbed wire. Beyond it, a heavy plank splattered with concrete bridged us past a ramshackle collection of corrugated metal huts arranged around a huge Frigidaire propped upright by poles deeply embedded in the muck.

Although the sun only had been up for a quarter of an hour (dawn over Nezahualcoyotl is a gradual inflammation of the smog), the neighborhood was alive with workmen, children, vendors, transients and dogs. Across the street from where Enrique signaled that we should stop to wait for a bus, a barefooted woman sat in a wheelbarrow scooping gobs of *masa* from a plastic pail and patting them into bright yellow tortillas.

"*Quiere?*" she asked abstractly, offering the sale instead of saying "good morning" to a man she saw at this time every day — and who yet had to buy anything from her.

If Calle de los Rufianes ("Street of the Ruffians" — or "Pimps") was an impassable miasma, the *avenida* into which it flowed was a raging sewer. Constant traffic had gouged deep ruts through the center of the unpaved thoroughfare. Water the color of diesel oil collected in these ruts, some of which were double-sized truck-tires wide and a foot or more deep.

An ancient Volkswagen bug, its engine compartment an oily black from inefficient exhaust, spluttered and creaked as its driver tried to swerve along the ridges between the ruts. In front of us, the little car failed to negotiate a dip. The driver jerked at the gears and the VW lurched backwards, splattering black mud across the wall we just had passed; then its engine stalled and it sank to its floorboard into the trough it had tried to cross.

The driver cursed and tried to open his door, but couldn't get out. Four T-shirted teenagers scrambled out to offer their assistance — for a price. The driver, a youngish man with thinning black hair and a mustached upper lip that seemed not to fit over large upper teeth, cursed them but nodded and watched them jam sticks and flattened cans under the wheels, then grab the car's window struts and push while he gunned the car's engine.

The VW lurched forward, its wheels spewing mud, but again it stalled and sank back into the furrow. The teenagers shouted at the driver and he shouted back. A handful of bystanders, most of them, like us, waiting for buses to take them out of Netzahualcoyotl, called out criticisms, encouragement and advice.

The driver again got the car started and the teenagers shoved as he pulled forward, the car vibrating as one of the engine's four cylinders temporarily cut out. Suddenly the wheels caught and the little vehicle careened out of and back into the furrow, muck flying from beneath its wheels. The driver managed to keep the engine running and the car moving forward.

The four teenagers, their faces and T-shirts splattered with mud and their legs black to the knees, scurried after him, demanding the payment he had promised for their assistance. Forced to a stop by converging traffic, he gunned the VW's temperamental engine, cursed the teenagers through his open window and flung a handful of bills into the street.

The teenagers plunged after them, one of them stopping traffic while the others scooped up the money. Their laughter a medley of opportunism and profanity, they headed for a narrow passageway between two pieced-together corrugated metal shanties. An exchange of words escalated into a shouting match between the young men and a person inside one of the shanties, then subsided as quickly as it had started. The tallest of the teenagers disappeared momentarily from view, then reappeared with a Coca-Cola bottle filled with bootleg brandy.

Grimacing as they drank, then laughing and coughing and wiping their mouths with the backs of their hands, the foursome slid back through the passageway into the street. From a pocket in his worn jeans, one of them produced a little parcel of tobacco and laboriously rolled a cigarette, which he lighted and, after inhaling, passed to the youth next to him. From where we stood, I could hear the diminishing crescendo of their conversation curse the morning, the month, the city and the buses that never got to their destinations on time.

"Welcome to Neza," Enrique Ortiz whispered in my ear. "There is nothing like home."

Ortiz and his family have lived in Neza for nearly four years. Like many of their neighbors — and like many undocumented immigrants in the United States — they left homes in the highlands of Michoacan because they could not get land to farm or jobs to support themselves and their families.

Just twenty-four, a cordial young man with thick eyebrows, thin nostrils and black hair on the verge of rampaging over his ears, Enrique Ortiz built his one-room cinderblock house on half of an already tiny lot that he purchased from an acquaintance. A fold-up table and *petates* that can be rolled up and stored in a corner enabled Enrique, his wife and his two infant children to transform their night-time sleeping quarters into a daytime living room-kitchen.

Unless his two children woke him earlier, Enrique pushed himself off his *petate* at 5:30 a.m. He had a bite to eat — usually tortillas or *bollilos* left from the night before — and held and played with one child while his wife fed the other and packed Enrique a lunch (tortillas, cheese, perhaps an orange or banana).

He had to leave his house by 6:30 in order to catch the first of four or five buses (depending upon connections) that he had to take to reach the glass and crystal factory in an industrial section in the northwestern part of Mexico City. The job paid him the equivalent of $6.20 U.S. dollars a day for eight hours work.

Nothing in Nezahualcóyotl functions the way it should, Ortiz commented after the VW had bumbled out of sight. Hydrants don't work because the water pressure is so low. Thousands of wildcat hookups not only drain the electrical system but cause frequent shorts and brown-outs. Clogged drainpipes and gutters backwash raw sewage through the streets, where it dries and evaporates, infecting the air.

Butane explosions caused by faulty attachments and leaking gas wipe out entire blocks. The paved streets are falling to pieces, making them as impassable as the unpaved ones, and there isn't a berseem tough enough to grow in the postage stamp-sized yards.

Nearly a dozen men were standing around us; they agreed and added their own complaints about law enforcement, the postal system, and the lack of government offices, repair services and banks in Nezahualcóyotl. Suddenly, Ortiz elbowed me.

"*Da prisa!*" His hand against the small of my back, he shoved me through a cluster of men, women and schoolchildren onto the front step of a bus just as it stopped in front of us. As we stumbled inside, I heard the driver shouting at people behind us to form a line. Enrique pulled me into a cramped seat — the next to last one available — and folded his hands over his chest. The first, difficult step of the commute had been accomplished.

Past him, through the bus window as the overloaded vehicle wallowed through the muck, I saw Neza take shape in the gritty dawn. Vendors clogged the spaces between the right-of-way and the cinderblock and corrugated metal buildings. Tamales, tortillas, slices of coconut doused with chilis, *pandulces*, oranges, thick coffee in little paper cups, popsickles — one could buy anything, even popcorn and fresh-roasting ears, newspapers and chewing gum, guava candy and little statuettes of the Virgin of Guadalupe. This constant commerce continued for miles.

Quite a few of the vendors boarded the bus. Like the factory workers, they were on their way to downtown Mexico City. They laughed and wrangled and bumped each other with their boxes and trays, cursed and complained about sore backs and numb fingers and bad food and lottery tickets that never paid off.

But through the push and clamor of the street life, I caught glimpses of grimmer sides of Nezahaulcóyotl from my window perch. Rag-wrapped children squatted beside shanties, picking at things in the mud. Young men still in their teens leaned against cinder-block walls, their torn T-shirt-clad torsos jerking spasmodically as they dry-retched, blind to the world around them.

"*Hay que cuidar*," Enrique warned, nudging the pocket into which he'd seen me tuck my wallet. Pickpockets, he said, abounded on the buses.

He had seen, he said, a thief slip a knife underneath the leather band of a wristwatch, slit it and be gone before the wearer realized that his watch had been stolen. He had seen a teenager wearing a Catholic girls' school uniform stumble into the commuter crowd, apologizing as she tried to make her way towards the back of the bus, and suddenly disappear through the rear door, a briefcase or purse or box of salable goods in her grasp.

Yet as I looked around us, I sensed neither danger nor hostility. As far as I could determine, the bus riders all were duplicating Enrique's daily hegira, part of a multi-million-person flow that struggled by bus from Neza into Mexico City and back again every day of the year: vendors and factory workers and office clerks and kitchen wallahs, beggars and errand boys and nannies and security guards.

Often, Enrique told me, he had to stand, clinging to the steel baggage-rack bar, for an hour-and-a-half or two hours each way to and from the place where he worked. Because his employers docked his pay if he was late, he gave himself fifteen or twenty minutes leeway, and sat — with hundreds of worker-commuters like him — outside the plant until it opened.

He almost got fired once, he said, because the bus he was riding crashed into a state limousine and he and dozens of other passengers were forced to stay until the authorities questioned them. Another time, when the driver momentarily hopped off the bus to buy a soda, a young "*ebrio*" impetuously leaped into his seat, slammed the bus into gear and took 60 passengers for a careening joy ride that ended when he smashed into a wall trying to make a turn.

From the Nezahualcóyotl local we transferred to a larger, but even more crowded, exhaust belcher — an "express" that actually got up to speeds of 20 miles an hour as it took us through the outskirts of Mexico City. Watching faces and listening to the voices around me, I realized that here was a real melting pot, a merging of thousands of years of individual traditional identities — Nahua, Tzotzil, Tarascan, Seri, Mayo, Huichol, Maya, Otomi, Mazateco, Zapotec, Tzetzal, Yaqui, not to mention countless combinations of *mestizo*, African, European and Central American — into a demanding urban routine of schedules and paychecks and machines.

"Yes," Enrique Ortiz agreed as we rocked back and forth with the buses' braking and accelerating, "on the bus, and in the factories, there are no traditions."

A Nezahualcóyotl pundit, quoted on street corners but unidentified by name, described this creation of a new, poor, urban populace as the "*chorizo* culture." (*Chorizo* is a chili-laced hot sausage made by grinding up the entrails, snouts, etc., of butchered hogs.)

The immigrants themselves cling to as many of their traditional ways as they can, but their children, growing up in urban squalor, cease to be Tarascans and Zapotecs and become children of the shantytown and reflect its problems, manners and mores. Many of them state an allegiance to the old ways but in reality they have little or no connection with their parents' rural roots and memories.

"We only have time to try to earn a living," Enrique Ortiz admitted. "Everything else is...." His fingers flitted about his ears as though confronting a concept that was too complex for his vocabulary to untangle, "is, is *far away*," he blurted, his mouth twisting around his prominent incisors as he tried to deal with what obviously was emotional as well as spatial distance.

As the express bus veered through the honking and exhaust of morning commuter traffic to make its first stops, passengers twisted out of their seats and shoved their way towards the exits. Those who had later stops wedged themselves through the debarking crowd towards empty seats, creating inside the bus a microcosm of the traffic outside, where vehicles swerved towards exits while others crisscrossed towards the throughways, hundreds of thousands of lives converging into the one purpose that Ortiz described: "*earning a living.*"

Not all who earn a living in the city, however, do it by commute and paycheck. Both the express bus and the Mexico City locals that would take us away from the center of the city towards the industrial areas to the northwest carried hustlers of diffuse talents and energies.

A burly, mustached fellow with a shovel chin urged us to buy tickets for a Neza school lottery that offered, as a grand prize, a Moped. Enrique's fingers pinching my sleeve pulled me from temptation. Never was there a real payoff, he warned: When drawings actually occurred, the winner always was a friend of the sponsors, or a shill who exchanged the prize for a few thousand pesos.

A few steps behind the burly lottery seller, a chunky *indio* with thinning hair and a determined, innocent face squirmed along the aisle, asking if anyone knew where he could find work. I asked him where he came from, and how long he had been in the city. Through his closed fist he mumbled that he was from the state of Aguascalientes, had been in Mexico City for nearly four months and had gotten a series of jobs by asking bus passengers if they knew where he could find work.

Within the next fifteen to twenty minutes, I was proselytized by a slender woman with bleached hair who was selling watches that she begrudgingly claimed were stolen. ("She says that," Enrique whispered, "to make you think they're valuable"), a short retiree wearing strong after-shave who bypassed me but urged Enrique to commit himself to Christ, a destitute grandmother, a pair of pantomime actors, a wedding ring salesmen, several drunks and a transvestite.

The hustle diminished somewhat when we debarked and caught a fourth bus that would carry us the last mile or so to the factory where Enrique worked. He had spent 1/10 of what he would earn that day at the factory on fares.

The scene outside the bus window as we traversed an old, industrial corner of the city was not drastically different from Nezahualcóyotl. Graffiti-splattered walls and cast-iron fences separated industrial plants from each other and from intrusive residential peninsulas that jutted into them. Small manufacturing and processing plants crammed crannies and alleys. Anything that couldn't be repaired or reissued was melted, mulched or ground into a different form.

A barbed wire fence kept mountains of car hubcaps from toppling across the sidewalk. Blow torches hissed in an unlighted cavern piled with steel slabs. Bare-chested workmen stripped rubber from steel-belted casings. Sheets of furniture veneer slipped through wide-flanged old machines inside an open doorway. Workers piled them together and hoisted them onto their shoulders, then trotted away, the stacked sheets bouncing as they carried them to a furniture manufacturer eleven blocks away.

One after another, the bus on which we were riding geared past offset printers, automobile distributor re-builders, plastic bag manufacturers, match factories, commercial tile plants and hundreds of other small and large production and repair establishments. Trucks of every age and description cut into and out of the traffic, honking their horns and emitting black plumes of exhaust.

Automobiles jammed every available parking space. Men wearing makeshift uniforms guarded some of the cars, or forced the drivers of others to move on and not block their access. Food smells mingling with industrial smoke thickened into an acrid aerial clay.

"*Ya estamos!*" Enrique called, and we scrambled to the exit, leaping off the bus while it slowed down but did not stop at an intersection two blocks from the glass and crystal factory where he worked.

In front of a huge auto dismantler, we stopped as we prepared to go our separate ways. "You see, it is not so bad," he started to say about the commute, then shrugged. "*Ni modo, mano,* thus is life. Pray to God that it no get worse!"

Arms around each other, we laughed, boasted, thanked each other and promised eternal friendship. Then, "*Ay! De prisa!*" Enrique slapped my shoulder again, waved and headed towards the factory entranceway. I lost sight of him as he merged into a flow of workers funneling past the corrugated metal-covered gates.

There are so many like him! I remember thinking. So many stories like his repeated over and over again.

Making It in Neza

Though he spends most of his time in Nezahaulcóyotl, Abel Cauche does not live there. A ferret of a man, with a fine-boned face and large brown eyes, Cauche works for one of Mexico City's largest beer distributors.

He is at once, he claims, an independent businessman, an employee, a driver, a supervisor, an agent, an explorer and an enforcer. Though average sized, even by Mexican standards, Cauche has the trim body and agile mind of an athlete — he was once, he boasts, a championship soccer player and still, at 37, can out-run, out-jump and out-fight men several times his size.

I met Cauche in one of the older, more established Neza *barrios.* I had stopped in a little store to buy a soda and talk to the proprietor and a few of her customers when Cauche pulled up. He swung out of the truck's high cab like a parachutist landing behind enemy lines.

Two young assistants, imitating him, popped out of the other side of the cab. That he'd blocked two cars' exits didn't affect Cauche: Before their drivers could criticize or complain, he railed that they were idiots, they were blocking his way, they had androgynous ancestors and they damned well could wait.

He didn't give them time to respond. "Hey, *gringo,*" he picked me out of the crowd, "what are you doing here? You want drugs, you should go to El Centro!"

His sycophants laughed and Cauche winked. "It is no place for a *turista,*" he continued. "Even Mexicans do not come here unless they have to."

I told him I had friends in Neza — good friends. Cauche didn't skip a beat. He warned the customers that I'd been talking to that I probably was from the

CIA, bought me a beer, demanded a better placement for the rack of Sabritas he serviced and offered to cover bets for a weekend soccer game.

I tried to set him to a beer (in Neza one always returns favors) but he laughed and said he was in a hurry. I told him to name the time and place and I would repay him. He gave me a "hey, okay!' shake of his fist, barked out a place name and time that same evening, and told the proprietor to make sure I knew how to get there.

Young Luis Martinez Flores went with me to keep my appointment with Abel Cauche. Luis knows Neza well. Though only fourteen, Luis has lived in Neza all his life, speaks both English and Spanish and, from watching television, knows the names of every player in both the National and American leagues.

Somewhat to my surprise, Cauche got to the bar before we did. It was a wide-open Neza *cantina*. Just outside the patio doors, a pork shank rotating above hot coals provided meat for tacos; waiters dipped into a huge open cauldron for chicken soup. Cauche was at once belligerent, generous, maudlin and a practiced teller of stories, all of which incorporated no small amounts of exaggeration.

He was not from Mexico City, he boasted, but from the country's third-largest city, Monterrey, the son of a "candle-burning, always-in-church" mother and hard-working, hard-drinking father. He'd come to the capital as a soldier in the Mexican army, gone to college for a year, worked in a brewery, driven a delivery truck, transported trailer-loads of factory-molded *ollas* to the U.S. border and supervised a construction crew before he bought his way into a job as an assistant, then a driver, of one of the city's hundreds of beer distribution trucks.

"Hey! You have to know people, you have to be clever, right? Everywhere I worked, I made friends. I learned how things are done. I saw what a good deal the [beer truck] drivers had, so I went after it. How? Listen, I got to know some of the drivers. I went out of my way to get on their good sides. There were hundreds — thousands — of *mozos* like me wanting jobs with them. Why should one of the drivers hire me?

"Listen, I found one I could work with — a son-of-a-bitch who really liked me. I made hiring me worth his while. I bought him drinks. I offered him $170,000 [old] pesos to hire me. Not only that, I told him I would work for free for three months. I told him I would bring in new customers. Lots of them. What did he have to lose? He had my money, he had my body, if I didn't come through, *zsst!* he could send me away.

"Listen, I did it! *Chinga!* I brought in new customers. I took stores away from other drivers. How? Some store owners I bribed. Some store owners I threatened. Listen! You think I'm the only son-of-a-bitch in this city from Monterrey? I had *compadres* who would twist off a person's head as though it were a chicken's.

"I even started my own store. Why not? So it was illegal to deliver beer to it — I got around that. I got a legal store to double their order. Triple their order. Then I would buy it at a discount and sell it after hours, for double the price, in a neighborhood where there was no other place to get a beer in the middle of the night.

"I did everything. I took beer to construction sites. I took it to the garbage piles where the scavengers work. I made deals with restaurants. I got ice to taco stands. Every day, in addition to all the driving, all the loading and unloading and cleaning and repair, I got new customers. The son-of-a-bitch I worked for was very happy. He was getting rich on my shoulders, don't you think so?

"Some of the other drivers, they saw how good I was. They made me offers to come work for them. I took the best offer. Now I was getting commissions. I was a part-time driver. I went with a son-of-a-bitch who was exploiting Neza. We went to places no truck ever had delivered to before. I carried a gun. If a *tendajon* wanted beer, I would make him take *chatarras* — little packaged things — that we sold, too. Potato chips. Peanuts. If they had no refrigerator, I would find them one.

"Many times I have loaned money to someone starting a little *estanquillo* — I can't tell you how often! *Si, claro*, I charged interest when I could. I could tell you stories about daughters I've been offered, about the 'quickies' I've sneaked while my helpers stocked the coolers! *Chinga!* All part of the work!

"I learned to fix refrigerators. To buy old broken-down ones where I could find them. I hired *mozos* to help me get them working again. After all, all one needs to start a beer stand is a refrigerator, no?

"Or if not a refrigerator, an ice box. I hired boys to carry ice. The owner of the stand would pay me. He would not sell any other kind of beer except what I brought him. Nor any soft drinks that I did not authorize. I cut deals with the soft-drink truck drivers. I got good kickbacks. So much I sometimes couldn't keep track of them all.

"When the time came, I had the money I needed to pay for the right to drive my own truck. To become a *jefe*. I think I know every street, every alley, every path in Neza. I pay I-don't-know-how-many-people for all kinds of things. I pay to bring back empty bottles. I pay to get electricity put in places that don't have it. I pay young men to check on stores to make sure they sell only what I bring them, not other brands of beer. I fix it up so they can have signs over their stores with the names of their stores on them — you know, good signs, professionally done, that the company makes to advertise our beer.

"Believe me, my friend, I work hard. And I have done good. I have benefited many people. All these little stores, they would not exist if it were not for me. I am respected. Hey! Ask the youngster there, would he not like to be like me? To live in a good *barrio*, have money to spend?

"You see, *amigo*, he lives here, he understands. *Hsst!* Waiter! Over here! More beer for my friend here — no, señor, you cannot refuse — and a little bottle of tequila. It is hard work, believe me! There are too many people and not enough opportunities. Can you blame me that I want to live well? And keep on my toes? Listen! If I don't, there is somebody like me who would knock me over, take it all away!"

The Battleground

At night Nezahualcóyotl becomes a battleground. The mud and grime and smog coagulate into physical forms that murder and rape and steal. There are gangs — purportedly over 1,000 of them — bands of youths who've broken away from their parents' rural allegiances and income-contributing family ties. They terrorize new arrivals, run guns and glue and prostitution rings. The only protection against them, claims long-time Neza political activist Ramiro Gonzalez Chavez, are the cinder-block walls that the residents build to shield themselves from these dark forces of the night.

But it is not badness, nor violence, nor poverty that gives Neza its personality, but a pervading sameness. The sprawling suburb retains the feel of rural Mexico — a rural Mexico compacted into a million dwellings, 6 million people, an incredible repetition of itself crammed onto the dry sponge of what once was Lake Texcoco. Neza twitters rather than glows; there is too little electricity, too little diversity, too little noise.

"There is no core," rues Gonzalez Chavez, a corpulent grandfather with large drooping eyes and a toothy mouth set forward on his blotchy, dark-complexioned face. Rather, he explains, there exist hundreds of thousands of individual little cores, each one fashioned around a family or extended family unit. Each of these units, like separate entities of a multi-celled creature, functions exclusive of the units that crowd against it. This failure on the part of Neza residents to mold into a greater being, Gonzalez Chavez grumbles, severely limits Neza's ability to serve its citizenry.

It also has made community organization difficult, if not impossible. "The conditions don't anger anyone!" he complains. For all their poverty, Neza's residents seem astonishingly hopeful.

"It is from their families that they get satisfaction, and it is for their families that they live," Chavez says of the majority of Neza squatters. If they could form one big, inclusive family, "They would become powerful, they would lift themselves into a better life."

He is sanguine enough to realize that such a joining is unlikely to happen. Many of Neza's longer-term immigrants still visualize returning to their lands of origin, and the younger ones either gravitate towards better Mexico City suburbs or become casteless children of the ghetto, with only immediate and often violent short-term goals.

"They are wolves," a real estate developer and one-time publisher said of the "*Si'nombres*" (those without names — the abandoned youth of Nezahualcóyotl). He repeated the often-told saw that every family in Neza has lost at least one daughter to prostitution, and at least one son to prison. One only has to look around at bus stops, at the entrances to alleyways, at the construction sites and the borders of the huge garbage pits to confirm that Neza has absorbed immense numbers of disaffected youth.

Thousands of them are incapacitated by malnutrition, addiction (to alcohol and/or glue), diseases, and by physical and mental problems. Hundreds of thousands of others have become unscrupulous marauders.

Musician Jose Gonzalez Cortes, who had been victimized by "wolf gangs" more than once, described these youths as "cannibals" because they prey upon the poor among their own people. He declined to escort me through Neza after dark, but he introduced me to a quasi-underground group of activist organizers whose forays into some of the newer, rawer sections of the huge shantytown brought them into contact with the underside of Neza life.

These organizers called themselves "urban guerrillas." Less than a dozen strong, they had gone into Neza to create neighborhood self-help groups that simultaneously would force government agencies to serve them and that would protect new immigrants from being victimized by gangs.

"We had made previous attempts," the group's leader, a slight, hyperactive young man with a thin, sharp nose and russet complexion explained to me, "but they did not amount to much. They were part of our learning, however. This last time, when we came in, we had a plan."

He went by the name "Lencero" (fabrics dealer); any other names that he had had, he said, no longer mattered.

"We took nothing with us. Nothing to eat, no money, only the clothes we were wearing. We resolved to live off of the streets, and to teach how it could be done.

"The first thing to do was find food. On every block there were thousands of people scrambling to get enough to eat just to keep them alive. We went to all kinds of establishments and offered to trade labor for cornmeal, for sugar, for chicken parts and vegetables. Quickly we discovered that it was not worth the effort. The merchants, the suppliers, the processors wanted to get labor and pay almost nothing. Or they only wanted to offer a little bottle of *cana* for half-a-day's work.

"Around us we saw people accept, as if to get any kind of payment for doing work were a great accomplishment. We tried to explain to these people that as long as they took so little, they would continue to be exploited, but they were hungry and not in a mood to listen to us.

"So we devised better ways for accomplishing our purpose. We singled out places that seemed to be prosperous. We went in together, as a little group, and told the stores and the places that made bread and tortillas and that processed beans and rice and milk and cheese that we were setting up neighborhood support groups and asked them to give whatever work they could to people from the neighborhood group. We also asked them to donate a small portion of their products to us to distribute to the people in the neighborhood who needed it.

"In turn, we promised, the people in the neighborhood would donate labor to them or would provide them with things to sell that otherwise they would not have, like jellied candies or brooms or legging wraps made from old sacks. We told these establishments that we would get everyone in the neighborhood to patronize them, and we would give them an emblem to put in their windows so everyone would know that they were the places that the neighborhood people should patronize and support.

"At first many establishments told us 'no.' We did not argue or try to aggravate them. But we urged people not to patronize these establishments. Many of the people in the neighborhoods made a game of the boycotts, as though they were some original kind of fiesta. They'd tell friends and neighbors and even strangers not to shop at such-and-such a place, or use such-and-such a product. Sometimes they would block the entrances so trucks couldn't get in, or they would make it difficult for people to go in and out.

"Doing this did not alter many of the establishments' ways of doing things, but it did bring some of their competitors forward to work out deals with our neighborhood groups. Soon, in many neighborhoods throughout 'The Den' [that portion of the El Sol section of Neza in which the self-styled urban guerrillas were operating], we had neighborhood groups working with suppliers and merchants.

"Some of the establishments did not like what we were doing, and sent representatives out to stop us. In one place where we had a boycott, a gang came out and rampaged through the dwellings of the people we had organized. This gang tore down living structures, turned over stoves and ovens and broke everything these residents had. This gang pushed and beat some of the neighborhood men and boys, and threatened wives and daughters.

"The residents were very afraid, and wanted only to rebuild their little domiciles and abandon the boycott, but we convinced members of other neighborhoods nearby to come in and donate to them and rebuild with them. Then we organized an expedition against the establishment that had hired the gang. One evening just at sunset a group of the neighborhood people who had been boycotting raised a clamor in the front of their building, which really was several buildings that the establishment, which made sandals with rubber soles cut from old tires, had combined as they had expanded.

"All of the workers and managers rushed out to chase our demonstrators away. As they did, another group of our guerrillas broke through the back entranceway. For ten minutes these guerrillas knocked down shelves and boxes and turned over equipment and broke everything that would break. Then, before the police arrived, they ran away.

"The next day the police accompanied some of the establishment's men through the neighborhoods. They arrested people that the establishment's men said had broken into their building. Some of the people that the police arrested were not even members of the neighborhood group, and some others had not even been in Neza during the raid. It did not seem to matter to the establishment people, so it did not matter to us that we did not discriminate among employees of the establishment when we began our retaliations.

"We had people from the neighborhoods follow the establishment's employees home. Late at night we would post messages that their residences were marked for demolition. We painted warnings around the establishment listing the names of employees who were going to suffer broken arms, or whose children would suffer accidents. We did not actually break anyone's arms, or hurt any children, but many of the employees began to feel afraid.

"For a while the establishment fought back by hiring their own police to rough up anybody they caught making threats, but by now people in all of the surrounding neighborhoods had joined the boycott because they were afraid they would be hurt by one side or the other if they bought bundles of sandals to take out and try to sell. People who worked for the establishment began to quit and the drivers of some of the trucks that used to come to haul the sandals away stopped coming. The residents of the neighborhoods spit at the employees, and overcharged them for beverages and tacos and other things that they wanted to buy to eat, or the people in the neighborhoods refused to sell them anything at all.

"Finally, although they did not publicly admit it, the people from the establishment capitulated. Their workers helped rebuild the residences they had destroyed and people from the neighborhood went in to work for the establishment and began to get money by bringing salvaged rubber and leather to them.

"After we had organized as many neighborhood groups as we could, we went into areas of The Den where there were many places of prostitution. It was our intention to create groups similar to the neighborhood groups and thereby improve the conditions of the women there. It also was our intention to show them that, by organizing, they could create ways to live without having to engage in prostitution.

"There were prostitutes of all ages in The Den and they worked under all kinds of conditions. Most of the prostitutes worked along one street and the alleyways that fed into it. Near the entrance to the street, which was just wide enough that two cars could scrape past each other, we found a section filled with flimsy structures that had only hanging cords for doors. Outside of these structures — partitions really, there were perhaps 15 or 16 of them — women negotiated their prices.

"At night there always were lots of men milling around, cursing, laughing, drinking. Now and then one of the men would go into one of the partitions with one of the women. Sometimes the man's *compadres* outside would pull the curtains apart to watch. Later we found out that most of these women "from the stalls" had become prostitutes after they had been abandoned by their husbands, or they had been widowed or their husbands had been put in prison. These women drank a lot and often suffered beatings at the hands of their customers.

"One of the street's bigger bordellos stood on the corner of this alley and the dead-end street that was known throughout El Sol as a center if prostitution. A cinderblock wall surrounded the bordello; to gain admittance, one had to pull a bell cord and be escorted through the gate. The bordello itself was nothing more than a shanty made of concrete blocks, scrap wood and corrugated metal.

"The room in the center opened onto a honeycomb of little rooms that, instead of beds, simply had mats on the hard dirt floor. The women sat on one side of the room, behind a balustrade that was little more than a fence. The customer chose which woman he wanted, paid the cashier, and took the woman into one of the little rooms.

"The street behind this bordello was crowded with cantinas and places of prostitution. At the end of the street was a large establishment called 'El Pendon.' Like the bordello, it had cinderblock walls and rows of little stalls, but it also had a concrete floor and a bar well-supplied with beer and liquor. Forty or fifty women were available and customers could dance with them as well as take them into the stalls.

"At first our group did nothing but watch what was going on and talk to as many people on the street as possible. We tried to gain their trust and the trust of as many of the women as we could. Most of them seemed to be quite young and, except for the women in the alley of stalls, they did not seem to have been prostitutes very long.

"Gaining access to these women was difficult because they did not trust anyone, particularly men. We tried several strategies before hitting upon some that worked.

"After much coaxing and bargaining and urging, we got women from some of the neighborhood groups to participate with us. A *curandera* showed these women what herbs could be used for curing certain kinds of women's diseases that often afflicted prostitutes. We put these together with remedies for coughing and respiratory ailments and escorted the women from our group into The Den.

"With us we took hand tools and materials we had salvaged from various neighborhood projects. We started to clean up the street, to solidify the structures and to form a neighborhood group to deal with anyone who became overly intoxicated or abusive.

"We encountered some opposition from persons who did not want any changes in the way things were, but this opposition predominantly was verbal. Many people who made their living off the street saw that what we were doing was benefiting them. Gradually the prostitutes began to talk to us. They were afraid at first because they did not want to jeopardize their incomes.

"We were surprised to learn that many of the street-walking prostitutes envied the bordello prostitutes because the bordello prostitutes had safe places to work. For every prostitute working in that area of The Den, there were dozens who were working street corners, or who were controlled by the youth gangs and were selling themselves for virtually nothing night after night.

"Many of the younger prostitutes lived at home, or with relatives, and turned over most of their earnings to help their families survive. Many of them told us that they had become prostitutes in order that their younger sisters would not have to do so.

"Those who did not live at home lived together in little shanties near the street. Several of them joined our work effort. They talked to the women we had brought from the neighborhoods. Gradually we built a rapport that extended beyond the street and we began to develop alternate ways of survival and income. Some of these, like making lace, did not work because the market for the product was not big enough. To our surprise we discovered that making and selling tamales was much more profitable, even though many tamale vendors roamed the streets.

"We also found that a demand for the medicinal herbs existed. We not only sold and traded the herbs but developed a corps of *curanderas* from among the prostitutes. Those who were proficient literally could go from residence to residence and sell or trade or prescribe something at every one of them.

"To our disappointment, however, we found that many of the women who did well making and selling the tamales and the medicinal herbs continued to work as prostitutes at night. And we noticed that bordellos seemed always able to bring new young women, many of them still in puberty, in to replace every prostitute who left the street.

"The bordellos had contacts throughout the neighborhoods, and had to do no more than tell the gangs how many women to bring them. Several times we came across very young women trying to offer themselves around the stalls who said the bordellos had rejected them because they were not pretty enough or because they were unsuitable in some other ways.

"Other times we found young boys trying to procure customers for their sisters or cousins. We found that many of the young women who worked on the streets instead of in the bordellos were very passive and did not care about anything. Nothing mattered to them, so it did not matter that they were prostitutes. And because they did not care, they were less successful.

"They were the ones who most often were beaten or hurt by their customers. Those who joined with us did so because it was easier to come with us than to resist. They did not make good tamale vendors or *curanderas*, but some of them did do well making tamales, and those who quit the streets often became more alive after a passage of time.

"In many ways, what we have done has been good and we feel that we have been successful. Some of the neighborhood groups have stayed strong, and the others know that they can reorganize to unify against some threat if it occurs. The women who stopped being prostitutes have better ways to earn their incomes and have contact with those still on the street and in the bordellos and have made their lives better.

"As long as we do not look too far around us, we see that we have been successful. But when we step back, we see that we have touched only a tiniest part of Neza. There are many, many streets like the one in The Den and many, many men and women scrambling just to get enough to eat to keep from starving, with new people coming in all of the time.

"Our dream is that the seeds we've sown will grow and a real socialist community will emerge, with equal rights for everyone.

"Our fear, of course, is that the seeds will die and all the good that we have done will be forgotten."

Choices

"I've learned — and I think this is a very Mexican way to feel — that in this life I have to make innumerable choices, weighty choices, all of which are bad.

"You smile? But just think, what did the two of us see today outside of Iztapalapa? Two-hundred-and-fifty families driven out of their homes? By...whom? Police grenadiers, dressed in black from helmets to shields to boots, like something out of a futuristic movie? Assisted by bulldozers, bullhorns, paddy wagons? Children running, women screaming, grandfathers throwing rocks? To achieve what? Clear a few hectares of dust? You come to me — you look at me, Jose Acosta, dressed as I am, wearing a suit, carrying a clipboard — and you ask, 'How can you do this to these people?' 'How can you live with yourself afterwards?'

"But if I — we, the government, the PRI — did not do it, you would come later — a year from now, two years, who knows? — and you would ask, 'How could you let those people destroy the environment? Build unsafe houses where there is no running water, no drainage, no sewers?' You would ask, 'Can't you see what contamination these people cause? What health problems they create?'

"Yes, I know, what you see here in Azcapotzalco is not ideal. Far from it. But here, I will show you around. This *colonia*, like the one that we saw earlier today, once was a squatter shantytown. But now, at least, there is some sense of order here. There even is a school nearby that the children attend. Before, like in the *predio* from which we saw all the families dislodged, there was nothing. Not even animals. Not even toilets.

"And yes, you ask — and with good reason — when we drive the squatters out, where do they go? They invade some other hillside or slope or gully somewhere else, taking nothing with them. Or almost nothing — what did those that we saw earlier have with them?

"The few things that they could seize as the bulldozers came through, no? And yes, they will build other structures just like those that you saw destroyed. They will stumble through the streets picking up old boxes of cardboard, ripped pieces of metal, strawboard, sheets of plastic, anything that they can wedge together to make walls, floors, a roof.

"You will see little children, dirty little children, with cuts on their hands and knees and bare feet, trudging along carrying chunks of cement. For what? To build dwellings with. To hold in place the cardboard walls of the structures they cram into little spaces. Until the owner of the land that they invade complains.

"Then to someone like me, someone trained in forestry, can you imagine? to some Jose Acosta is handed the paperwork and out will come the grenadiers and the bulldozers and the utility crews and we will displace them again. And again, probably, many times after that.

"Even so, doing it this way — the displacement, that is — is better than some other ways, although it brings more criticism of the government, and of the police. In times before — not distant times, just a year, two years ago — the government did not do it in such an official manner. Then everything was handled through the local political organization.

"Instead of calling in a Jose Acosta and bringing in the police grenadiers, the political organization — the PRI — would negotiate for the land in question, they would buy or rent it from the owners, and form a group of *colonos* to whom they would promise the land. They would draw it all out on paper — how this new *predio* would be, with streets, connections for water, for drainage, for electricity. Then through a type of government-backed loan that the political organization could arrange, they would offer the diagrammed little plots of living space to the members of the group.

"Only then would the group discover that the land they were supposed to get already was occupied — by squatters. The leaders of the *colonos* would go to the squatters and tell them to leave. Almost always the squatters would refuse. There would be accusations, shouts, threats, fisticuffs. Sometimes the new *colonos* would call the authorities. But very often they would take matters into their own hands. They would go in with clubs and machetes and sledgehammers. They would take over 'their land.'

"Sometimes, of course, the squatters would re-invade. Then the new *colonos* would defend 'their land.' All around them they would have put up PRI banners. That they were defending their political organization against 'outside agitators' as well as defending their land would make them feel even more important. Even more bonded together.

"Of course, very often, after they had started to build their dwellings, which often were no better, really, than the structures of the squatters that had been torn down, the new *colonos* would find that the political organization had given them lots of banners and posters but no water pipes or septic tanks or electricity. True, they had a name for their *predio*, and legal papers for their little pieces of land, but in most cases they still owed money for them.

"Look, if you follow me over here, where do you see the streets that were marked on a piece of paper when the *predio* was formed? Obviously, they do not exist. And there, what do you see? People carrying water in their plastic pails? Why? Because for this entire settlement there only exists one faucet. Everyone has to go there: They are like *campesinos, no?* Going to the river? Here, right here, in the midst of this industrialized zone? And after they've carried it, what do they have? Water that really is not drinkable!

"When it rains they put out containers of all kinds to catch the water running off the roofs of their *chozas*. The sad part is, of course, that they cannot catch it all and when it rains hard the water stands in the low places. Worse than that, what drains there are overflow for, you see, they really lead nowhere. They were supposed to connect with the main sewer system of Azcapotzalco but either they were not connected correctly or they have become stopped up and nobody will pay to fix them.

"But you can see that, as bad as it is, there exists a sense of community here. Oh, there is bickering and some hard feelings — even fights — but this settlement, like many others, was created by a group of people getting together.

"That is the way, typically, that these *predios* are formed. A tight little bunch of friends, of relatives, of neighbors get together, with one or maybe two as organizers — leaders — and they talk to many people and find some piece of land somewhere, sometimes by contacting someone with political connections, and they arrange a purchase and a loan and make the one or two organizers responsible.

"Sometimes, as you have seen, the new settlers have to call the authorities and have the black-uniformed futuristic police move squatters out before they can move in. Then in they come, as a group, with their leader.

"He — or they, if there are two or three leaders — become like village *caciques*. It is not so uncommon in these days for the leader to be a woman. This leader collects all the monetary payments for the land and the utilities and he becomes the intermediary with the authorities.

"You will see, as we walk through, that it will be the leader of this *predio* who talks to us, no one else. He will boast about how content everyone is here, then he will ask for more water spigots, drainage pipes, bags of cement, stones with which to build roads. And he will tell us, probably many times, how heartily and enthusiastically everyone here worships the PRI.

"It is not true, of course. I suppose that he, like me, is making his choices, based — wouldn't you say? — not on what is good, but what is the least of the bad."

The gradual but steady rural-to-urban migration swelled as the *milpa* agriculture in the states girding the capital gave way to commercial and export crops like cotton, coffee, sorghum and cattle after the Second World War. *Campesinos* whose families had lived on tiny plots of farmland for generations transitioned into migrant and seasonal work, then, having nowhere else to go, set up shantytowns in and around the capital. Their wives and daughters, many of them children just entering their teens, found live-in work as domestics for a parallel migration of industrial, commercial and technical workers from small towns and cities throughout central Mexico.

By the mid '60s the flow had become a flood. Government officials estimated that 4,000 people a day were coming to the Federal District seeking permanent residence. Wildcat developments wedged their way into already existent *colonias*, spread down barranca sides, jammed into lots vacated by idled factories, garbage dumps and railroad yards. Mexico City authorities demolished many such *predios* in an effort to push this human phagocytosis towards the less inhabited outskirts, particularly the dry lake beds north and northeast of the capital.

There the new settlers fell into an administrative backwash, for the Federal District, which is funded and governed separately from Mexico City, lacked both the facilities and financing to control the immigrant flow. Before water could be piped in, or sewers dug, or electricity hooked up, the new *colonias populares* had surged across land that had been abandoned, that was unfarmable or that belonged to federal or local governments.

Rules and restrictions limiting their spread onto privately owned property forced many newcomers onto the least habitable terrain, creating erosion, drainage and traffic disruptions. Attempts by District officials, and officials from the independent small cities within the District, to regulate the hordes of squatters merely rearranged where — and to some extent, how — they lived, but did not stem the continuing influx of men, women and children.

For every illegal *predio* that government or political party officials dislodged, five more appeared. Longer-term permanent residents built higher walls, closed residential streets and hired private security guards, but they could not stop the shantytown expansion. Like picadors who eventually give way to the bulls they are wounding, their wrestling with the growing numbers of *colonias populares* served only to impel the squatters to more determined expansion.

When a team of lawyers hired a militia to clear several thousand squatters from an erodent hillside near Chimalhuacan, the squatters negotiated to lease the property. Borrowing at exorbitant interest rates from a fund the lawyers set up, they acquired title to the land only to discover, three years later, that the titles were fraudulent and the lawyers had not been representing the actual owners of the property. Not only did the squatters face eviction again, but they could not recoup the illegally assessed money, for both the account and the bank in which it had been deposited had disappeared.

Other owners of barren or undeveloped land sold and re-sold the property without concerning themselves about the battles for possession that their chicanery caused. Many titles were disputed, or grabbed and resold by speculators or enterprising con men. Their attempts to collect from squatters often led to pitched battles among the immigrant groups or between the shantytown communities and police or privately-hired security guards.

Various government functions — health, sanitation, transportation and the like — attempted to provide services, but wound up being able to accommodate only a small fraction of the newcomers and lost out to, rather than gained on, the continuing rural-to-urban flow. The federal government chose to consider the migration a natural adjustment to Mexico's emergence from Third World-dependency and ignore — or simply refuse to deal with — the massive scale of the social change taking place (just as it did with the concurrent surge of *indocumentados* into the United States).

To a large extent, local government followed the federal government's lead, rushing to put out little fires along the fringes without (either pragmatically or philosophically) recognizing or confronting the conflagration within. Throughout the process, thousands of Jose Acostas, charged with "solving" individual *predio* invasions, found themselves forced to make choices, all of which seemed to be bad.

The Tiradero

The old road leading westward out of Mexico City towards the regional capital of Toluca curled along a ridge separating deep barrancas before ascending the pine-shrouded slopes of the Sierra Madres. As traffic increased and the metropolis grew, clusters of houses and businesses spread along the ridge — and along other ridges like it that wrinkled the sides of the ancient volcano whose crater had been the site of the Aztecs' capital.

Following a pecking order typical of urban expansion, the most accessible (and most scenic) locations sold for the highest prices. Developers carved gated suburbs into the hillsides. Factories and retail firms built on the crests and slopes. Multi-story apartment buildings replaced stone-walled farmhouses and adobe and cinder block *estancias*.

Where goats had grazed, mini-buses swerved along new roads winding along the hillsides, picking up and delivering schoolchildren, office workers, *amas de casa*. The old highway, widened into a four-lane thoroughfare, then widened again, hosted a constant surge of cars, trucks, buses, cranes and pile drivers. As the construction continued, new residents and new businesses moved down into the barrancas.

Hillside *ejidos* that for centuries scarcely had produced enough corn to feed a few families became residential and commercial centers. Workers and new arrivals from other parts of Mexico bought or squatted on little parcels of land in places too difficult or hazardous for commercial construction. Those without means built shanties in the barranca bottoms, or made homes of the caves niched into the steep slopes.

As more people, and more goods, poured in, the new developments overwhelmed and absorbed outlying villages, creating a complex geography of manufacturing, apartment complexes, restraining walls, rutted small-town streets, squatter towns and gully bottoms filled with garbage.

Accidents were commonplace. A landslide created when loose soil gave way beneath a bulldozer attempting to level a brush-covered slope east of Cuajimalpa crushed two dozen new dwellings staggered along the slope beneath it. A few months later, a wildcat construction crew severed a water main, sending a million-gallon torrent through houses, yards and gardens, washing away vehicles and causing a number of restraining walls to collapse.

A faulty butane hookup triggered an explosion that wiped out half a dozen dwellings, cracked walls and windows and sent dirt, stones and debris cascading onto roofs, automobiles and terraces. Flash floods periodically tore through houses and businesses and the acrid fumes from waste dumped into the barranca bottoms fouled the air and choked respiratory systems.

One of the worst of these dumps, or *tiraderos*, was located in a narrow defile that wound past the residential outskirts of San Mateo Tlalenango, near Cuajimalpa directly west of Mexico City. Josefina Castro, the wife of an old friend from my college days, told me that a delegation of neighbors finally had persuaded Mexican health authorities to investigate the illegal dump. Since her husband's retirement from the Los Angeles school system, she and he spent part of each year in the Federal District and rented a modest but relatively new house from her cousins, who lived near San Mateo Tlalenango.

The dump — and the dangers it posed — was an ongoing topic of conversation at meals and during family visits. So were the activities of both protesters and authorities, particularly when one of the protest organizers, Carlos Contreras, was involved.

Contreras was not a difficult man to get to know, even for relative strangers like Josefina and me. A squat, slope-shouldered sixty-five-year-old with thick lips and a flattened nose that gave his face the power and serenity of a carved Olmec statue, he lived alone but left his apartment early every day for long walks throughout San Mateo Tlalenango and its environs.

He addressed Josefina, politely but with obvious irony, as "Señora Chicana" and, upon meeting me, made a point of stating his political affiliations with far-left *campesino* and *indigena* rights groups. Apparently relieved that I neither challenged nor disagreed with him, he became frank and confidential and volunteered to guide us through the winding hillsides to prove to us how bad the *tiradero* had become.

"Listen to me!" he expounded with the words-rushed-together haplology that characterizes colloquial speech. "This whole area once was covered with wild growth and trees. Even pines — tall ones — deep in the barranca.

"There are peoples here — I have talked to them — who grew up on the *ejidos* that used to be here. In little gardens in spaces they had cleared they would grow corn, tomatoes — the winter nights, they get cold, but not so cold that the plants would freeze — and they would hunt and sometimes would trap the animals. There were many kinds of animals — foxes, weasels, squirrels, wild pigs — even deer and, would you believe? mountain lions. The water that ran down into the bottom of the ravine was clear and, *qué padre!* it tasted, I tell you! rich and beautiful!

"Now, from here you can see — no, we go a little farther, yes, from here señor, from here señora, see? You can tell by the *murallas* which is the oldest construction there where the ridge is terraced, right across from us, you cannot see into the bottom yet, but soon you will, just follow me.

"Over there, see? That's where the first houses were located, you see it is not so steep there and the view from there, you must admit, of this side of the barranca was very pleasant. There were first those larger houses — you can see, can't you, they have more space around them? — then others, smaller, as more terraces were leveled and more people began to build houses like those you see, there, the foundations half into the side of the barranca and the lower rooms there, with the main rooms above them.

"Many times the persons building them lived first in just the bottom room — some of them were very dark — and later they built above them. If you look closely, there, you see? Some never added on and their homes are more underground than not.

"Now, if you look, come on, it is safe, these chunks of concrete won't give way, just watch where you step as we go down. You almost can see, there, beyond that large curved wall painted with political slogans...the God-damned PRI! They will spend millions of pesos to advertise themselves and, what? do nothing about the garbage that is ruining this whole area, can you believe that? Now, here, look: Right there the barranca bends into a sharp indentation, that is where the dumping began.

"You see, because so much of the land was in brush and trees — scrub trees, not big trees — and really couldn't be farmed, when the government drew up the *ejidos* they made those split by the barranca quite large. As a result all of that, all along both sides of that deep indentation that you see there, all of that belonged to one person.

"She started the dumping. Well, not her, but persons who paid her to let them dump there. No one who lived around here objected at first — they should have, let me tell you, they should have seen where it was going to lead, but they didn't. Those using the dump built a road — not a good one, I tell you, señor, señora!

"They did not use machines, just *mozos* with machetes and picks and shovels chopping out brush and moving rocks until trucks could come in and turn around. The first to come in were from I don't know where, but nearby, and they discharged all kinds of rubble from construction down into that indentation.

"Before that, yes, there was some garbage. I have heard it said that one of the municipalities dumped into the barranca to avoid paying fees — some *priista* bureaucrat pocketed the money, of that I am sure — but it was like any other barranca, not with extensive garbage, but littered with cans and paper and bones and plastic like any other here near the city of Mexico.

"Like I said, there were trees and brush, lots of it, and the rubble just sifted through it and most of it was obscured. But there was so much construction — and so much dumping — that the indentation filled up. Look, now you can see it more clearly, how it slopes outward, like a slide, and is jointed right into the main part of the barranca.

"The weight of the rubble pushed all the small trees over and as the trucks dumped more the rubble sifted into the main part of the barranca. Then the trucks moved around to dump across there, see, where they pushed the turn-around wider.

"I cannot tell you, señor, how many [metric] tons of debris was put in there. Personally, several times, I went over there to that other side of the barranca to challenge the *camioneros*. I stopped their trucks and asked the drivers what right they had to contaminate the area.

"They laughed at me and said they had every right to do it, that they had paid for their rights. If I tried to hinder them, they said, they would call the authorities. I told them I was not afraid of the authorities and that I, personally, I would go to the authorities! That I did — exactly that — but, imagine! Who listened to me? Nobody, I tell you — that is to say, they listened, talked to their secretaries, they blew smoke up each other's fat behinds, but never did they come to investigate or send anybody to investigate.

"The newspapers, they were no better. 'How terrible!' 'What an atrocity!' 'Such things shouldn't be!' the writers that I talked to would tell me. But only one of the newspapers ever printed anything and the few words about San Mateo Tlaltenango were hidden in a piece about all the dumps like it all around Mexico City. 'A national shame!' they called these illegal dumps and described how much the environment was suffering — but it achieved nothing.

"In fact, I tell you, señor norteamericano, señora chicana, the dumping after that got worse. Peer over the edge of this *azotea*. You see? The garbage is piled to the foot of the wall here. And over there, look! It is level almost with the patios of lowest houses on the slope. What's the use of those patios? I ask you, sir, what can the people who live in those little houses do with their little patios? Why, nothing, of course! They lock their doors and windows so the smell does not sicken them when they are inside.

"You see, as the dumping got worse, what was dumped was not just construction debris. Early in the *madrugada*, where it barely was light, other trucks started to come. Big ones and also *camionetas*. Some of them, in fact, they looked like ambulances. Many of them were from the hospitals. You can imagine, can't you, what they poured in here? Rags and trash drenched with blood! Drenched with who knows what else from diseased persons! Dying persons!

"And glass and plastic and liquids and syringes — everything, everything that you can imagine — and things that you cannot imagine! Many times I have climbed down into the barranca to see what all is there. Among the things, I tell you, are tanks of fluids — I do not know what all they are, but you can see big labels in red that warn '*Precautión!*' and '*Peligro!*' And there are other containers — not just a few of them, but many, many of them, some of them sealed, but others of them leaking — and these are black with greases and oils, like motor oil, no?

"Many of the trucks that bring them — big trucks, you would be surprised how big they are and how dangerously they careen down the road along the side of the barranca over there — many of them come from different factories, who knows which ones or how many? And what do they bring? I will tell you, yes, señor norteamericano, señora chicana, they bring dangerous things.

"Broken pieces of machinery covered with rust. Pieces of smokestacks. Things soaked with chemicals — all kinds of chemicals: Their smells are so strong they burn one's eyes. They are just lying there, containers of them and lamina and cloth and paper soaked by them, and all of the time — every day, every week — more things are being dumped on top of them.

"Who knows when one of these tanks or things is going to explode? Who knows? The barranca itself could catch on fire, no? Or — let me tell you, for I have climbed down there, I have seen, yes señor, señora, I have seen an even greater danger. Beneath all of the garbage, all of the rubble, there is water. The rain, when it falls in these times, it is not soaked up by the bushes and the little trees, it just sits making mud, getting deeper, and you know, don't you, what happens?

"The rubble shifts, it slides, and the ground slides with it. Portions of the barranca fall into the garbage. Then what do you have? Some of the houses lose their foundations, am I not correct? The floors of their houses and patios crack. After that they will slide into the barranca and they too will become garbage.

"Then what will happen? Ah! The authorities, finally, they will come, they will close the road, they will prohibit the dumping and the trucks, sir, you know as well as I do, the trucks will go somewhere else, those who hire the drivers will find some other barranca farther away and they will begin to fill it. But by then it will be too late for San Mateo Tlaltenango.

"It will be too big a job to clean up this barranca that you see in front of you, that you smell, that is such a disgrace. So it will be left as you see it now, filled with dangerous things that smell and rot and burn and explode and the people living here next to it will get sick and wonder why.

"It is wrong, señor. It is wrong and it makes me angry. That's why I go to the meetings. That's why I go to the authorities. That's why I sleep in front of the door of the Civil Protection Agency, so they cannot ignore me.

"But you, and you señora chicana, have seen enough, no? Smelled enough, eh? Come, we will climb this other way out. It is steep, but not so far, and there is a school just over that rise. A school where the children learn about all the good things that come to one in this life."

Despite Carlos Contreras' pessimism, he and his group of advocates did rattle enough cages to retard continued dumping. Government officials, including a chemical engineer, investigated the site and issued health and sanitation warnings. A suit seeking damages from the owner of the property, though *lis pendens*, deterred those industries that had been paying fees to dump waste into the barranca and gave the neighborhood *colonos* the muscle to stop trucks carrying garbage and industrial residue and force them to go elsewhere.

Government funds appropriated for testing and clean up trickled away during the last financial crisis, however, and haphazard dumping resumed, although on a much smaller scale than before. But, as Carlos Contreras pointed out, "the drivers will find some other barranca farther away and start to fill it."

Of the 21 million tons of garbage and industrial waste that the Federal District generates each year, less than five million tons receives what the National Ecology Institute describes as "adequate treatment and disposal." The rest — nearly 83 percent — is dumped in places like the barranca near San Mateo Tlaltenango. At the root of the problem is the vast amount of non-biodegradable materials being discarded. (In 1950, only 5 percent of the Federal District's waste was non-biodegradable, compared to nearly 45 percent in 1996.)

As costs for collection and disposal soar, both municipal governments and industrial plants seek easier — if illegal — ways to dispose of solid waste. And create even greater problems for safety and health.

Meat for the Table

The ratchety farm truck stopped, temporarily blocking an intersection in front of an abandoned roadhouse whose battered, skewed Corona sign teetered over the rutted rural street. Then it pulled slowly forward, stopped again and began to inch backwards towards the steep edge of a barranca. I glanced at my companion, Raymon Alvarez, a Mexico City schoolteacher who had moved out of Mexico City to be near his wife's family near Chimalhuacan, but resisted asking, "What in God's name is he doing?"

Alvarez craned forward over the steering wheel of his battered 15-year-old Mazda, but he didn't seem alarmed as the cab of the truck tilted upwards, then banged out of sight between the cinder-block walls of two makeshift buildings. He shifted into lower gear and the Mazda hiccupped past the overhanging Corona sign, then stopped as he yanked the emergency brake.

"Well, my friend, now you will see." As an afterthought as he opened the door, he added, "Leave nothing in the car. This wreck, it is easy to break into."

Two denim-jacketed workmen already had climbed the trucks' tailgate by the time we squeezed through the narrow aperture. They shouted something to us but I couldn't hear them over the bellowing of the cattle inside the vehicle's canvas-shrouded interior. Another workman, a young man whose round face was half-hidden by a swirl of jet black hair, jammed rocks under the trucks' back tires. It sat nearly level, but was perched dangerously close to the side of the barranca.

Behind it and the cinder-block buildings I saw what looked like a large rectangular repair shop with a corrugated metal ceiling. The front wall and the one nearest the barranca were open; the back wall and the side away from the barranca were a pastiche of metal, plastic, tires and wood. Though it was nearly noon, all I could make out in the unlit interior were a series of metal railings and an arrangement of heavy pipes holding ceiling hooks. A dog's angry barking reverberated through the vacant enclosure.

"Oye, Alelardo! Listo?"

"*Listo!*" echoed a return shout from the back of the shop.

Raymon's arm restrained me as one of the workmen yanked the tailgate open. A wild-eyed roan-colored half-Brahma steer stumbled out, then charged past us as the workman kicked it in the rump and sent it bellowing along the corridor between buildings towards the shop.

It banged against the railings and slid to its haunches as it tried to turn. The curly-haired adolescent rushed up behind it, shouting and flailing it with a piece of board. The steer lurched along the railings into the front of the building. The adolescent shoved a gate closed behind it as another workman, apparently the "Alelardo" who'd been called, emerged from the back of the building carrying a pistol the size of a field gun.

"*Cuidado,*" Raymon cautioned. I edged up beside him beneath the shed's corrugated eave, now able to detect that the building was a slaughterhouse, not a repair shop. The steer, bawling and twisting in the tight enclosure, belted the gate with its hoofs. A smallish man with muscled arms and shoulders, Alelardo (the word means "Bewildered") hoisted himself onto the side of the enclosure, a flow of curses engulfing the animal. As the steer, foam-mouthed and exhausted, stopped kicking, Abelardo pressed the *pistolete* against the animal's skull.

The steer bolted as the shot sounded. The bullet missed the crevice between the neck and head and tore through the steer's skull, splattering bone, hide and brains against the walls of the enclosure and onto Abelardo's face and work shirt. He hurled himself off the railing, screaming curses, as the animal flung its neck back and forth, splaying everything close by with gore. Then it sagged forward, a high-pitched dying whine, like a baby's cry, siphoning through its nostrils.

"Devilment," Raymon shivered, making the sign of the cross and motioning me inside. Abelardo, mopping at his spattered face with his shirt sleeve, stalked away, *pistolete* in hand, as the curly-haired adolescent and two other workmen opened the enclosure and pulled the still-twitching steer's carcass into the building. One of them bound its rear legs and hooked the knot to a pulley contraption they had devised to pull the carcass upward.

Blood squirted from decisive slices along the underbelly as the two workmen began butchering the suspended form. The blood flowed into a trough made from corrugated metal that ran the width of the building and extended past it over the barranca. The dog I'd heard barking (actually, there were two of them) bounded past, snarling and yapping.

I whirled, startled, and Raymon laughed: The dogs weren't after us, but were stray street curs that the shot and the smell of blood had attracted. The pair and the curly-headed adolescent kept the yapping strays at bay while the butchers worked.

The older of the two, a balding fellow with paired wads of graying eyebrows overhanging his squint, piled bloody intestines into a plastic washtub while his companion slit and peeled the hide away from the carcass. Both worked deftly and without apparent emotion, grimacing as they encountered minor obstacles and speaking only occasionally, under their breath, to each other.

Within minutes, both men, the animal and the floor were covered with flies. The blood spilling into the barranca had attracted some huge ravens, one of which teetered on a railing to eye the butchering before dropping out of sight. Here and there a stray dog, having evading the house guards, darted in to grab at some scrap and was rewarded with a kick or thrown missile for its efforts.

Throughout the city's outskirts, Raymon told me, clandestine slaughterhouses like this one had sprung up after the main "Ferreria" in the city had been closed by health officials. I asked him how butchering under conditions like these could be more salubrious and he winced, squinting through his thick glasses and shaking his head. "That is the point. That exactly is the point. The officials, especially in Mexico City, never think ahead."

The balding workman with the bushy eyebrows swung the severed hide over a railing as his companion finished trimming the carcass. For a moment they paused, grimacing, as they peered at the shattered remains of the steer's head, then the older of the two knelt and with short, powerful cleaver blows severed it and kicked it aside. A little pack of mongrels, evading the snarls and lunges of the guard dogs, darted after it, yapping and whining as they scurried away with the skull piece.

"Oye! Alelardo! Don'está? Ya? Listo?"

Hearing the shout, Raymon and I turned. The curly-haired adolescent and a couple of companions were driving another steer into the enclosure behind us.

"Oye'ye! Alelardo!"

"*Listo!*" Abelardo's nasal voice shouted back. Shirtless now, the *pistolete* in one hand and a newspaper-wrapped liter of beer in the other, he pulled himself onto the railing beside the pen, where a larger steer, bonier and higher rumped than the first, struggled trying to free its horns from underneath the pen's parallel pipes.

"*Chingada!*" Alelardo gulped at his beer between bellows, the barrel of his field piece chopping figures in the air above the animal's head, as though invoking some whammy on the recalcitrant victim. "Get his head up! Straighten him out!"

It devolved upon the bushy-eyebrowed butcher to wrestle the steer upright so Alelardo, after another pull at his liter of beer, could jam the muzzle of his weapon against a spot beneath the animal's ear and pull the trigger.

This time the shot was clean. The steer's eyes flashed wide and its jaw dropped open. Then it sagged quietly forward, blood oozing out its eye sockets and nostrils.

"*Bravo!*" the bushy-eyebrowed butcher applauded in mock congratulation.

Alelardo whirled and pointed his weapon at the butcher's head. "*Pendejo!*" he whispered as the two stared at each other, android-like, neither face flinching or showing emotion. Finally Alelardo grunted, a truncated utterance deep in his diaphragm, set the weapon aside and jumped down to help truss the carcass.

Gradually, as the butchering proceeded, and the swarms of flies grew darker and the ravens and stray dogs bolder, a small crowd gathered around the edges of the makeshift slaughterhouse. Most of them, Raymon explained, were meat shop owners from Nezahualcóyotl and Chimalhuacan who'd come to haggle over the prices of the newly butchered beef.

No sooner had the farm truck that had brought the steers pulled away, groaning and lurching in its attempts to get back onto the roadway, than a panel van bearing a *carnicería* logo "ALWAYS THE BEST! MEAT YOU CAN TRUST!" backed in to load several of the carcasses. Dozens of children clamored through, begging scraps of meat — "*pa' la comida, señor, p'favor! p'favor!*" as hide buyers and chorizo makers, restaurant suppliers and taco vendors wedged in to negotiate for the remaining carcasses, heads, hooves and horns.

The workers' respite was a short one. The curly-haired adolescent made a brief attempt to sweep the concrete under the butchering sites but the little bucket of filthy water he brought to sprinkle the floor didn't dampen enough of it to make his efforts successful. The lack of a breeze gave the air in and around the enclosure a smarmy thickness permeated with the smells of rot and blood. It took all the will power that I could muster to stay with Raymon and watch the day's work continue.

Continue it did. Truck after truck brought squalling steers from Hidalgo, from Tlaxcala, from all over the Estado de Mexico; shot after shot was fired, bucket after bucket of intestines filled, carcass after carcass hung, butchered, sold and hauled away. All of the workmen now were drinking from newspaper-wrapped liters of beer, cursing, jibing, shouting and countermanding orotund orders and directions.

Their workday finally over, they trooped to the roadway, their sweat- and blood-soaked garments flung over their shoulders, their faces streaked with dirt and gore. I helped Raymon wrench a carcass into a huge plastic bag and force it into the Mazda's back seat — his brother-in-law, he said, would cook it in his little *asadero* and pare tiny strips of the meat for tacos; just as we were pulling away, Alelardo waved us to a stop.

"*Oye, muchachos!*" He coughed beer and tobacco smell into my face and he leaned against the window frame. "Remember! Come back! Tomorrow we're killing pigs! A lot, a lot of pigs!"

CHAPTER 3. WHERE THE PAST IS NOT FORGOTTEN:

THE STATES SURROUNDING THE DISTRITO FEDERAL

REASONS TO CHEER

"What regrets do I have?" an aging general named Marquez Miramon whispered from his death bed over a hundred years ago. "Ah! Only that in my lifetime there were not enough parades!"

The general wasn't alone in his passion for parades. Mexico always has accorded them a great social importance. They take precedence over jobs, school and everyday traffic, which is diverted, stopped or delayed to allow the bands, blazon bearers and *charros* to pass.

It is said that the old Spanish regional capitals host the best parades. And of those best parades, none equals those that wind their way through Queretaro, three-and-a-half hours by car or bus northwest of Mexico City and a short hop over a winding mountain road from San Miguel de Allende. The biggest, most congested and noisiest of these extravaganzas are the traditionally patriotic Cinco de Mayo, Independence Day, Revolution Day and Benito Juarez birthday shebangs.

Old-timers still remember Queretaro's great parades that honored recently fought battles and military conquests. Pancho Villa's army, under the command of General Felipe Angeles, rumbled through with hundreds of mounted horsemen, nearly 100 cannons and thousands of camp followers in 1915, less than a year after Carranza's army had staged a huge parade in July, 1914. In 1876,

President-becoming-Dictator Porfirio Díaz marched a major part of the Mexican Army through town, setting off a gigantic celebration that included hours of fireworks.

But of all of the great parades of this type that marked Queretaro's history, the greatest was that organized by (and for) the Emperor of Mexico, Maximilian I, on February 22, 1867. The grandfather of a resident named Mejia, whom I had the good fortune to meet some years ago, was there. The grandson said the old patriarch's delight in telling the story of what he saw never waned.

"Of course there was no television in those days, not even radio," Mejia explained. "Everything was word of mouth. Grandfather said that he, along with many other boys his age — I suppose he was about eleven years old at the time — ran to the fields outside of town, where a contingent of soldiers had set up camp. When the boys learned that the Emperor was on his way to Queretaro with his French cavalry and a huge number of troops, they scurried back to town to spread the news.

"You can imagine the excitement!" Mejia invoked the scene his grandfather had described. Factories closed; men and women and children on foot and in carts and on burros and riding horses streamed towards the encampment. Even those who stayed in the city knew the moment that the Emperor arrived, for a huge cheer went up from the waiting soldiers.

"It was about mid-day, Grandfather said. The Emperor, astride his huge roan stallion, returned hundreds of salutes. The generals who commanded the troops that had been garrisoned outside of Queretaro called all of their soldiers to attention. In their dressiest uniforms and best military manners, they stood stiff and unmoving as the Emperor and his be-ribboned commanders filed past them."

Mejia's grandfather squiggled under a guard's horse to get a good view. In front of the Emperor in the reviewing party he saw a host of minor officers who jerked at, slapped, straightened and scolded the soldiers being inspected. Then came the generals and finally the Emperor himself.

"He was, Grandfather said, tall, confident and handsome in his regal attire and neatly clipped mustache, but the generals were obsequious and fat."

When the inspection of the troops finally ended, the generals gave commands for the soldiers to align themselves in marching and horseback units. Much to the delight of the local citizenry, Mejia recounted, they formed columns and prepared to march through the city.

By this time, all of Queretaro was celebrating. Stores and factories had closed and people crowded into the streets. They cheered and shouted, waved *paliacates* and showered the Emperor and his troops with rose and hyacinth blossoms. Altogether nearly 10,000 soldiers paraded through the city. More than any other soldiers, the townspeople cheered the Empress's special dragoons.

"The parade started in mid-afternoon, Grandfather said, and did not end until after night had fallen. And of course that only was the start of the fiesta, which lasted until after daybreak."

I asked Mejia how the populace, having demonstrated such a fondness for the Emperor, reacted to his execution a few months later on the Hill of Bells outside of Queretaro.

"Why, of course there was a parade," he replied. "It was not as magnificent as Maximilian's, for Juarez and his troops did not put on such a show. But there were banners, and pronouncements, and much cheering and, Grandfather said, pistols being shot in the air and fireworks afterwards.

"You have to understand, *señor*, that it was not Maximilian who was important. It was his, how do I say it? the presentation, the pageant, the parade. That is why the people cheered — and why they remembered the day so well.

"It was a wonderful parade!"

Though always wonderful, not all parades were as elaborate or formal as the one that accompanied Maximilian's visit. Mexican law guarantees the right for groups to assemble on public thoroughfares, and this generates everything from *campesino* protests to truck-driver strikes to cattle drives.

One of these celebrations nearly destroyed Queretaro's open air market. As reported by newspapers at the time, and recalled in a column called "Queretaro's Yesterdays," the recently elected mayor, a big landholder making his first venture into politics, decided to celebrate his victory by staging a *charreada* — a regional rodeo featuring horsemanship, races, lots of beer and *pulque* and beautiful women to bestow gifts upon the winning contestants.

A parade preceded the *charreada* and it featured the area's best-known horsemen. Just as the procession rolled into town, cheered on by people crowding the streets and applauding from the loggias that overlooked them, the boys who were supposed to be watching a herd of young bulls strayed off their guard and the excited animals stampeded towards the square.

The *charros* charged after them as shrieking women and children fled towards doorways, climbed light poles and scrambled onto the roofs of cars.

Near the corner of an open air market, where the streets were blocked by a set of temporarily erected bleachers, the bulls turned and, snorting and tossing their heads, headed back towards the throng that had assembled behind them, upsetting carts and vendors' stands as they barged against each other.

The horse-backed *charros*, hemmed in by retreating onlookers, couldn't get through to corral them, but a group of clean-limbed schoolboys scrambled past an upset vegetable stall and launched an attack with cantaloupes and honeydew melons. The astonished animals retreated, bawling and snorting as the schoolboys splattered them with the juicy ripe fruit.

Inspired by the schoolboys' audacity, the townspeople regrouped to help round up the now more or less subdued animals and the *charros* herded them out of town. The parade continued, forever to be remembered by Queretanos for the feats performed by the melon-wielding boys that day.

RAIDERS AND THIEVES

Julio Orozco's smile twitched slightly when he said, "I'll die a contented man." Although weakened by surgeries that had shriveled his once sturdy, corpulent frame, he had not lost any of the gracious, cavalier-like charm that made visitors feel comfortable in his modern home perched on a hillside overlooking the vineyards and thermal baths of Tequisquiapan.

He always greeted me with genuine interest and teased his niece, a National University language instructor, with picaresque allusions about our relationship. She would bristle back, embarrassed but feisty, "You would rather I came to visit with a bandit? A robber and a killer like you know who?"

And he would laugh, for the reference was to his grandfather, a nasty man by all accounts, a road agent, raider and thief.

"Because of him I've had no fun in my life," Orozco would complain. "Because of him I've had only one woman all these years," and he'd lift his hands with their swollen veins towards Silvia, his wife, a reticent gray-haired woman who endured her husband's expansiveness and humor because she loved him very much.

Orozco stood by the scenario that he'd led a quiet, church-going life because of his notorious forebear, "to clear shame from the Orozco name." Then, with a wink towards his niece, "Of course, everybody was always watching, expecting me to turn out like him."

"Him," was Jesus Orozco, by reputation during his youth an accomplished horseman and hard-working rancher's son who might have inherited a reasonably large estate near Queretaro — had he not abandoned wife, children, property and reputation during the hectic years when Mexico was torn by internal feuds, Maximilian's ascendancy and revolutionary struggles for power.

"Those were turbulent times," Julio Orozco acknowledged. "The national government was not very strong and *haciendas* were governments unto themselves. I suspect that when my grandfather set out, he had a cause of some kind, a political belief, but I've never found out for sure what it was.

"Apparently he and his followers — they were peasants, *campesinos*, but good horsemen who knew all the canyons and mountains for miles around — began raiding some of the big estates in order to provide supplies to the soldiers of their cause. Then the cause changed, or the leaders changed — who knows? — but Jesus did not change. He became a cause to himself and went on raiding.

"He was a hellion, no doubt about it. If he needed horses or mules or grain or beef or, well, women I suppose, he would ride onto an estate and offer the owner or administrator a choice: Give me what I want or I'll take it by force. Well, believe me, very few opposed him, although probably they hid their most beautiful daughters, those like my niece here, wouldn't you think?

"Not that my forebear, this Jesus, was the only *chorcha* — bandit — in these parts. There were others, some as wild and even more vicious than he. One *hacendero* hired my forebear to protect him from the other bandits — like having a fox guard your hen house, wouldn't you say? Who knows what price this grandfather of mine exacted, or how often the *hacendero* had to hire someone to protect him from Jesus.

"More than once grandfather hired himself out to revolutionary armies — or to armies fighting against the revolutionaries. My understanding is that Maximilian was one of those who hired him. Now — this always has amused me — either the Army or my forebear himself fashioned a military commission and he added the title '*Colonel*' to his name.

"Not that having a title changed his habits any. I think he got to liking this life he was leading — you know, it was adventurous, he was getting to do whatever he wanted to do. He and his *labriegos*, they were terrorizing the countryside all the way from Celaya to San Juan del Río and Huimilpan. See, there were no police forces strong enough to capture them, and I imagine the army had other things to do, so he didn't have that much to worry about.

"He and his men rode about more or less openly, taking what they wanted, collecting bribes and tribute, boasting how much better off they were than the poor *campesinos*. Or, for that matter, the *hacenderos*.

"Not that there weren't risks. I mean, hell, he was getting shot at all the time. But you know, when somebody gets into leading this kind of a life, they get cocky. They get away with things that you or I, I mean, we wouldn't even think about doing.

"They also make mistakes. Now, I don't know exactly how this happened, but a brigade or regiment or whatever of soldiers surrounded and captured 'The Colonel.' Now you probably know, back then, they didn't mess around with trials. The commander of the soldiers ordered my forebear to be shot.

"Now, as I understand it, long before they came to get him at sunrise, he began shouting for the guards. There was another prisoner in the jail, some poor rail splitter picked up on some minor charge. When the guards came, my forebear screamed for them to 'take that damned bandit!' He screamed that 'that damned bandit' had conjured up the devil.

"The poor rail splitter tried to protest but grandfather was insistent. He even begged the guards to shoot him 'in that terrible bandit's place!' I don't know what else he claimed — there's a story that he shouted, you see, that 'the damned bandit' was trying to, well, you know, do something sexually to him.

"So the guards woke up a lieutenant or some other officer, see, it probably wasn't even daylight yet, and they dragged the other man out of the jail and shot him. Who knows when they found out they'd made a mistake? Or if they even cared.

"Anyway, having shot their man, they passed around a few bottles of *aguardiente* and let grandfather go. He supposedly thanked them — told them they'd be rewarded in heaven, something like that — and went right back to pillaging the haciendas again. Ruining things so that descendants like me would have to go through life and never have any fun."

That wasn't true, of course. My companion's uncle had done many things in his lifetime, and collected ample rewards, including the affection of his children, grandchildren and nieces. The only thing that disappointed him, he said, was that there was no dramatic conclusion to the story of his forebear's life: a final gunfight, chase and capture, miraculous salvation or religious conversion. The

Colonel just disappeared and nobody, his grandson said, knew where he had gone or could remember when they last had seen him.

Quite possibly, the old man opined, the Colonel was ambushed and shot — perhaps by his own men — and buried in an unmarked grave. But the grandson had other theories. The dictatorship of Porfirio Díaz brought an end to much of Mexico's banditry and "now you see, 'the Colonel,' was smart, he might just have decided that enough was enough." He could have gone anywhere — the north, which was developing rapidly, Guadalajara, even Mexico City.

"Who knows? He could have started a new life, done anything, made money, started a business, become a chief of police!"

Whatever he did, he never returned to Queretaro. At least as far as his grandson — or anyone else — ever was able to learn.

A Malicious Prank

The *farmacia* of Pedro Arturo Ruiz fifty-some years ago was not like the *farmacias* you see intruding into every street corner of every city in Mexico today. It was unpretentious, dignified, cool, located within sight of the glorieta from which the spray from the Fountain of Neptune glitters into little rainbows every afternoon. In small, stately letters a sign suspended over the sidewalk notified passers by that the FARMACIA QUERETARO was behind the doors of what once had been a 17th century mansion.

Like the enterprise that he ran with attentive and picaresque humor, Pedro Arturo Ruiz differed from the pharmacists who hide behind their shelves of prescription drugs today. There was no artifice in his manner, and if he occasionally lapsed into well-worn clichés he did so only to confirm mutual interests between himself and his customers. It was rumored that he had been a playboy during his younger years, but later in life he had married a stern widow whom he seemed to respect, if not actually fear.

Though she seldom ventured out, Ruiz went early to his pharmacy every morning and remained there until late every evening. The establishment, like his person, was tidy and clean and reflected a flare for all the little extras that typified Ruiz's personality.

Mortars and pestles perched ready for use along the counter that ran along one wall, at the head of which sat a huge cash register embossed with pewter curlicues. Two small marble-topped tables and several upright chairs gave customers a place to relax while they waited for their prescriptions. The shelves behind the counter were filled with vials and bottles, jars and bins, each marked with labels and arranged it categories that Ruiz found convenient to offer his customers: stomach cures, pain relievers, health tonics, wraps and bandages.

Set apart was a special section for women's menstrual, childbirth and change of life potions, douches and absorptive tissues. The labels on these items were protected from general view by a hemmed piece of tarlatan that could be pulled across the shelf with a drawstring.

Every evening, as Ruiz checked to make sure that the contents of all of the jars and bins were in place, a cheerful, chubby mother of three limped in to sweep and scrub and polish and mop. Often Ruiz left her to lock up; since she was the sister of a friend of his, he knew he would find the store spotlessly clean when he opened the store the next morning.

"If you start the day with everything in order," he often told his assistant, "things stay in order throughout the day."

The assistant, of course, agreed. He was younger than Ruiz, though only by a year or two, a lean, fidgety vegetarian who once had wanted to be a poet and who felt martyred by his failure to achieve any sort of acclaim. He presided over the counter in front of the shelves of herbs and medicines and operated the cash register while Ruiz went back and forth from the main part of the pharmacy to a room that opened onto it through a hardwood door on which was carved the figure of a Spanish *conquistador*.

This side room was as important to Ruiz's business as the main part of the pharmacy itself. In it, around a table marked with the stains and polishings of many years of dignified usage, a tiny coterie of *queretanos* gathered to discuss their business and personal affairs. One of these daily visitors was a bank president; another was a lawyer and political organizer who had retired from a federal justiceship. The city's most respected physician often made an appearance, as did its most prominent architect, a newspaper editor and a former Army general.

Their laughter and the more boisterous of their comments, the smell of their cognac and whiffs of smoke from their Cuban cigars drifted into the pharmacy's main room, but neither customers nor casual visitors who entered it could see any of the side room's occupants. A separate street door, marked with the simple precaution NO ENTRADA - PRIVADO, provided egress and exit for the *farmacia*'s select guests.

While these distinguished personages talked, joked, laughed and smoked, Ruiz bustled back and forth, refilling a glass here, emptying an ash tray there, amending, adding to or correcting bits of gossip as he entered and left the room. He seemed to know everything that was happening in Queretaro and the surrounding area, for not only did he communicate with the dignitaries in the side room, but he made sure that he overheard all the bits of news that the pharmacy's customers told his assistant and he often inquired of maids and cabmen what and how their employers were doing.

He alone answered the telephone, a formidable wall instrument that rang with fire-alarm authority. He once told his assistant that he regarded all calls as important, for only the important people of Queretaro had telephones. His cheerful laughter crackled as he passed along orders for ozomulsion and agua de pionilla, semillas de linaza, boneset and Vapo-Rub, making sure that any and all instructions for pick up and delivery were confirmed, and he listened to complaints and chirped instructions about everything from how long to boil certain herbs to how to prepare epazotle to relieve menstrual pains.

Some of the calls required trips back and forth to the side room, for the banker and architect, physician and editor each had assistants or confidants who knew that they could interrupt if the business at hand really was important. Often, after Ruiz had passed along instructions or excuses and hung up the telephone, visitors to the main part of the pharmacy itself could hear bursts of coughed laughter or briefly intense baritone discussions. Or they would hear the door marked PRIVADO quickly open and close and the hum of voices, in volume one fewer than before, dwindle into quiet oscitancy.

As the source and disseminator of news and gossip, Ruiz naturally was party to many financial negotiations, particularly those that involved major bullfights, horse races and football games. He took care not to let the results of any of these transactions be known to anyone outside the intimate circle, particularly the seldom-seen wife that he seemed to fear.

It was not his wife but another's who disrupted the pharmacy's busy tranquility the day after Queretaro's most feared and famous fighting cock was defeated at a *palenque* on the outskirts of town, however. She strode through the doorway, umbrella in hand and a sister and two aunts behind her, announcing that she wanted to see her husband immediately and threatening to impale anyone who might get in her way.

"Of course! I will see if he's here!" Ruiz intercepted the armada. He caught the choleric wife's hand in his and manipulated a greeting kiss to her cheek.

Pirouetting to keep her from storming past him, he bowed to the sister and aunts, praising the cloth and cut, lace and jeweled adornments of their garments as he gestured to his assistant to arrange chairs so the women could sit down.

In no mood for honeyed demurrals, the irate wife thrust the umbrella at Ruiz, intending to forge past him, but he adroitly took the umbrella with one hand and her elbow with the other.

"*Mea culpa*," he flattered in his best church Latin, turning her like his partner in a formal dance as he slipped the corded loop of the umbrella handle over a nail beside one of the tables.

"You worse-than-a-worm destroyer-of-homes-and-everything-sacred!" one of the aunts burst, "you're worse than him, don't you try to protect him!"

"For shame!" expostulated the sister, "you know what he's done. Gambled away her stable. Her fine riding horses. Her wonderful mare!"

Thunderstruck, Pedro Arturo sank to his knees. "But no, surely, I cannot...!" Suddenly he stiffened. "And who said...oh no! I can't believe that he...! Please, sit down, please. You got this information from your husband?"

"The coward didn't tell her anything!" exclaimed the second aunt. "It wasn't until we went — "

"Please, oh! please, señoras!" Hands clasped imploringly, Pedro Arturo crossed himself, then announced, "I know who is responsible. I will kill...that is, I will see that this never happens again."

"What never happens again? Who is responsible? What are you talking about?" the second aunt demanded.

"I cannot...a practical joker, we know the guy, a poseur who...but never mind, never mind, I assure you, ladies, we will deal with him, this never will happen again." Stepping aside to let the flotilla pass, Pedro Arturo bowed his head, then followed the invaders as they swept past him and stormed into the side room.

Which, of course, was vacant. Had the women looked closely, they might have detected cigar smoke, might have noticed that the table top was moist from recently having been wiped clean, might have touched the chairs and found that the seats still were warm, but in the vibrancy of their emotions, they turned on the pharmacist instead.

"You've hidden him!" "You're defending him!" "You've let him get away!" they chorused. Pedro Arturo tried to calm them with offerings of pomades and jamaica, and with assurances that the irate wife's stable and horses had not, in fact, been gambled away, that it all was a malicious prank devised by an envious ne'er-do-well who himself had lost money and wanted to make trouble for others; but they seemed not to want to believe him. After all, he was a man and, in their separate and combined opinions, no man could be trusted — particularly one who was a friend and consort of the indicted husband.

Their departure occasioned even more placations and apologies from the beleaguered pharmacist but by afternoon life at the FARMACIA QUERETARO had returned to normal. Maids and *amas de casa* came in with their prescriptions, children popped in for honey- and cajeta-flavored jawbreakers, the phone rang, a teamster rushed in for balms for his mangled finger.

If there was any change, any unusual circumstance, it was the atypically animated discussion in the side room, where voices surged back and forth in complex debate that demanded the pouring of more cognac and produced more thickly billowing clouds of cigar smoke than such discussions usually entailed. However, like most such discussions, it peaked and resided into humorous boasts, garrulous stories and shared laughter, much of which seemed to focus on an imaginary tipster who had planted a rumor about gambled away horses and stables.

Pedro Arturo politely inquired about the stable and horses the next time one of the irate wife's servants came in for medication to treat her *amo's* acidic stomach. He learned (seemingly not to his surprise) that she had recovered from the dyspepsia brought on by mistakenly believing that her husband had lost her prized properties by betting on a cockfight.

He did not inquire if she had found out that that same husband had transferred the ownership of thousands of hectares of prime maguey plantings to one of his side-room associates shortly after she had appeared in Pedro Arturo's pharmacy. About that, he had no need to inquire, for that had not affected her well-being or health.

Besides, who could tell? By the time she found out, her husband might have regained that same land. Or have acquired businesses in Celaya. Or farms or cattle or opal mines, for there was always another cockfight, another horse race, another football game on which to place a small wager or two.

And other times to get together over cognac and cigars and laugh about the past, as he and his cohorts planned the future, indebted to and grateful for the inventiveness and perspicacity of their pharmacist, apologist and friend, Pedro Arturo Ruiz.

The Scar

For thousands of years gods have appeared on the hills surrounding Mexico City. Immersed as they were in the natural processes of planetary life — ocean and selva, earthquake and drought, eagle and ant — the ancient Toltecs worshipped Ixtaccihuatl and Popocatepetl, the Nevado de Toluca and Mount Zampoala as living beings, and they honored the hill of Tepeyac, which the Catholic Church later made holy to the Virgin of Guadalupe, as the shrine of their Earth Mother.

Even some of the Spanish conquerors, despite the strict duality they perceived between brain and soul, accorded a kind of mystic beauty to the environment that surrounded them. A sixteenth century monk claimed to have experienced the crucifixion — his body and Christ's having merged — while meditating in the hills south of Mexico City.

Almost every village in the states surrounding Mexico City — even those with less than a hundred permanent inhabitants — has a solid little church, built of stone or adobe. Loggers, hikers, hunters and construction workers frequently come across little *capillas* — some of them hundreds of years old — on hillsides, cliff tops and in caves. In fact, in 1934, a group of spelunkers discovered a filigreed altar while they were exploring a cave near Ajusco, southwest of Mexico City. Its stained glass backdrop, set against stalactites, contained finely worked obsidian and opals.

It is no coincidence, of course, that the imported Spanish Jesus quickly assimilated aspects of pre-Columbian culture. Aztec live sacrifice, condemned by the invaders, found re-representation on Mexican crucifixes, which even in the most wealthy and conservative churches depicted a tortured, struggling and often gory Christ. By the beginning of the 19th century, the two most celebrated manifestations of the Holy Story were Jesus' betrayal by Judas and His trip up Golgotha carrying the cross.

The carving of Judas masks dates to the late sixteenth century. Photographs taken in the late 19th century show elaborate expressions, many with Mephistophelian features, ornately fashioned to show elaborate detail — hair, eyebrows, even warts and pimples. The masks were sold and burned during all-night ceremonies that still are celebrated in many parts of Mexico.

Also celebrated are *cerritos de Golgota*, or *viacrucis* — reenactments of Christ's climb with the cross. Like pilgrimages to the shrine on Tepeyac on the

Day of the Virgin of Guadalupe, the *cerritos de Golgota* involve physical effort and physical pain. Some *cerritos* in the late 17th century so accurately duplicated the Biblical accounts that the soldiers actually drove nails through the Jesus' wrists.

The Christian overlay on Aztec customs even earlier in Mexican history led to crucifixions that resulted in the actor-Jesus' death. In some isolated towns of the Estado de Mexico, the road to the *viacrucis* borrowed from old Aztec custom by regaling the Jesus-to-be-sacrificed with special status for the year leading up to his crucifixion.

Those in charge of the ceremony chose the next Jesus before the current one was sacrificed. He spent the preparatory twelve months being waited upon hand and foot as he built up his strength to carry the cross and supposedly he prayed and meditated to become as much like Jesus as he possibly could. (Whether or not twelve-months of chastity also was required is debatable — the Jesus-to-be was supposed to enjoy the last year of his existence, and have every desire fulfilled.)

Many of the reenactments disappeared after the 1910-1917 revolution and the anti-clerical movement that followed it but they became popular again in the 1960s and early '70s. Since their reinstatement, Mexico City residents have poured into the mountainside suburbs before and during Semana Santa. As Mexico City journalist Angelica Enciso observed in the early '90s, these tourists complete the *cerritos'* cast of characters by becoming the curious, the festive, the vindictive, the appalled, as they rush to watch the Pilates and Herods, the centurions and the poor believers, and see Christ the King, humbled and sweating, hang from the cross.

Jesus Díaz knew about *viacrucis* — he had participated in one of them several Easters before I met him. Like many newer residents of the state of Mexico, Díaz grew up far away — in Nuevo Leon — and "was seduced, I think, by the richness of the merging cultures" that he found crowding together among Spanish arches, tiled roofs and cobble-stoned streets in and around Milpa Alta.

"The first year we were here wife and my son and I went to watch the *viacrucis,*" Díaz explained as our kindergarten-aged sons swapped Batman and Robin volleys at imaginary Jokers and Penguins in a yard so filled with shrubs, flowers, cactus, maguey and hedges that one barely could see the mortared stone walls that surrounded it. "It's the big event of the year. The participants rehearse for months. The Jesus — and the Gestas and the Dimas, the two thieves — build up their bodies so they can carry the crosses. You know, the one the Jesus carries weighs just under 100 kilos.

"And the costumes — all the preparations — I thought it was great. It was like, how can I describe it? an undercurrent, you know, connecting everybody. So the second year we were here in Milpa Alta I got caught up in it. Not, you know, so much emotionally as just socially — I thought it was a good way to meet people; I thought it might be fun for my little Jorge — and in a way it was. All the kids went along to the rehearsals — as one of the directors explained, there were kids in Jesus' time, too.

"The week before Semana Santa, tourists started to appear. Everything that anybody could rent was rented — garages, spare rooms, campsites, basketball courts. I was told — I don't know whether it was true or not — that the hospital sent patients home and rented the rooms they'd been in.

"And vendors — you never saw so many vendors in your life. Balloons. Balms. Painted eggs. Ice. Rosaries. Hot dogs. Styrofoam lizards on sticks. They came from all over the Federal District with carts and trays and tents and suitcases that folded down into counters. One guy even had scourges that he had made 'to whip the *chingaderos* carrying the crosses.' There were so many people you couldn't cross from one side of the street to the other.

"The pageant itself took about two hours. I was one of the Roman soldiers. It was a still day — almost no breeze; I don't think it was all that hot, but through our costumes it was stifling. As I marched along I could hear Carlos, the man who portrayed Christ, grunting each time he took a step — this was before he was supposed to fall the first time; we weren't even a third of the way up the hill.

" 'Are you all right?' I heard one of the centurions ask.

"Carlos grimaced — his eyes were bulging — and he whispered, 'For my father, I do this.'

"Of course, I thought he meant his biological father, but he grimaced again and muttered, 'And for my mother, I do this: Mary, Mary the Virgin my mother.'

"All of a sudden it didn't seem like play-acting anymore. People rushed in to touch Carlos' robe as we climbed. Mothers with little babies wrapped in shawls around their shoulders kissed the things Carlos was wearing. Cripples fell in front of him pleading that he make them well. People with deformities and diseases crawled up to him. One man — he was blind — staggered in front of me shouting, 'Where is He? Where is He?" Others threw themselves on the ground to kiss the footprints Carlos left in the dust.

"It took a long time to get the crosses up — and by now it felt really hot. People flung themselves in the dirt and cried — really cried — when, in a cracked voice, Carlos called out, 'God! God! Why have You forsaken me?'

"Then somebody, I don't know who, grabbed a lance away from one of the supposed-to-be soldiers and shoved it into Carlos' side. Blood gushed out. 'Water! Water! It's supposed to be water!' a woman behind me shouted. For a moment I was transfixed — I couldn't move, I couldn't believe that it was happening. Then, with many others, I rushed forward to get him down as quickly as we could.

"Would you believe? There were doctors there, watching, and some of them took care of him. At least one of them had a cellular phone and called an ambulance. It took forever for it to get through the crowd: We had to carry Carlos part way back down the hill to get to it.

"Bizarre, no? But even more bizarre, I tell you, is that Carlos enacted Christ again the next year. And even more people came. Many of them — many, many of them — begged to touch the scar that the wound from the lance had made.

"And the blind man — the blind man I'd seen the year before — claimed after touching it that he could see again."

Sacrificial Pigeons

Few neighbors, schoolmates or teachers in the *barrio* on the southern edge of Guadalajara where Ignacio Ruiz Olguin grew up would have guessed that he would become a federal policeman. An intense, nervous child, smaller than most youngsters his age, he made up for his lack of size with sporadically aggressive athleticism. He sniffed glue, broke windows, got in fights, shilled for shell games, peeping tommed prostitutes and curled into an angry ball when his sobbing mother clutched her beads and prayed for him in front of her plastic crucifix.

In spite of this delinquency (which was normal for his *barrio*), he finished *secundaria*, entered *prepa* then quit to join the Mexican army. His service career, like his childhood, was neither exemplary nor totally criminal. He was promoted, demoted, threatened with courts martial, caught several venereal diseases and developed a dependency on rum and tequila. Which of those assets most qualified him for acceptance into the judicial police is uncertain. But somehow he made it through PGR training and wound up being assigned to an anti-narcotics unit in the mountains north of Mexico City.

Ruiz Olguin apparently liked the work. The unit traveled in Suburbans and Jeeps, and the members carried Uzis and AK-47s. When they weren't traipsing through the high country between Queretaro and Morelia, south to Michoacan, they stayed in gaudy hotels, drank heavily and exercised their choice of call girls.

Now and then, following leads siphoned to them from Mexico City, they would bust some grower or trucker and confiscate whatever drugs they found. How much the *federales* set aside to distribute on their own is questionable, but apparently a side business provided easy-to-dispose-of extra income for both Ruiz Olguin and his immediate supervisor, an intemperate older *federale* nicknamed "Jequeton" ("Big Sheik").

Notified by a special radio code that a "sacrificial pigeon" would emerge from one of the barrancas[1] with several mule loads of freshly trimmed marijuana, the two arrived early one May evening for a stakeout in the ruggedly brushy country that twists alongside the Cerro de Aguila. Ruiz Olguin and Jequeton just had finished the last of the liter bottles of Modelo they'd packed into their ice chest when a pair of woodcutters emerged along a trail behind them. Fearing the pair might warn the pigeons, the two *federales* stopped them.

The woodcutters protested that they just had seen the *contrabandistas* emerge from a different barranca behind them with horses piled high with marijuana. Jequeton grabbed the younger of the two and threatened to make mush of his reproductive glands if he were lying. The poor *campesino* swore to gods, angels and the dust beneath him that he was telling the truth.

"We've got to intercept them before they get into open country!" Jequeton barked.

Leaving their vehicles behind, the two *federales* scrambled along the trail the two woodcutters had evacuated. Past a switchback and sudden descent along the side of an old landslide, they eased towards what seemed to be a clearing, their Uzis extended. A horse neighed, then another. Jequeton waved Ruiz Olguin to follow him and, pushing through the tangled vegetation, sent a warning burst of gunfire across the clearing.

A barrage of heavy caliber automatic weapon fire ripped the brush around them. Voices shouted orders as the gunfire continued, then stopped abruptly.

---

1. a gully or ravine.

"We've got the wrong — the wrong ones..." Jequeton gasped. He scrambled backwards, trying to find the trail they just had left. Ruiz Olguin stumbled after him just as a team of men in military-type fatigues charged through the brush. Jequeton lifted his weapon — perhaps to throw it aside, not shoot; before he could say a word or take a step, bullets tore into him. He pitched face forwards onto the bristly scrub. Ruiz Olguin dropped to his knees, aware that someone somewhere was shouting for the firing to stop.

He supposedly told bar acquaintances later that he only remembered that the hillside suddenly seemed to tip sideways and his shoulder felt like it was on fire. Whether or not, before he lost consciousness, he heard his executioners identify themselves as federal policeman never may be known for certain. Rumors have it that while Ruiz Olguin and Jequeton were chasing down and arresting a decoy, big-time drug traffickers protected by other members of the federal police were supposed to move a major shipment down from the mountains and into waiting trucks.

But the wandering woodcutters threw a monkey wrench into the works and the two good-timing *federales* may have walked into something they weren't supposed to know about. No one knows for sure. What is known for sure is that Ruiz Olguin awakened in a strange bed in a strange hospital a long way away from the gunfight. And, later, when he tried to collect a pension for being injured during the performance of his duty, the paperwork came back identifying him as "ineligible."

According to the "official" records that they cited, he had been rejected during PGR training as "undesirable" and never had become a member of the force. And when he tried to verify the events of that day, he only was able to learn that his friend and immediate supervisor, the gauche, self-aggrandizing Jequeton, according to the same "official records," had resigned from the PGR the day before that ambush and could not possibly have been on the trail leading down from Cerro de Aguila that bright afternoon in May.

Things Are Seldom What They Seem

In all the time that Bernabe Esquer taught school in Pachuca, he never looked like a schoolteacher. Nor did he act the way that one would expect a schoolteacher to act. In fact, he seldom was mistaken for a schoolteacher except by his students: They found him vital, exciting — even exhilarating.

Despite continuous attempts to keep himself well-groomed, he exuded a ruffianesque appearance. His beard, though short, bristled around his face as though trying to grow in a hundred different directions and his necktie continuously seemed to be trying to escape his collar. No one ever saw him with the pockets of his pants turned in without bulges, points, loose threads and papers sticking out of them.

"His clothes rumple the second he puts them on," his wife complained, "and no amount of gel keeps his hair in place." Not only that, she sighed, when he entered a room everything in it twitched and jumped and jiggled and moved, making it impossible to straighten things up while he was around.

It wasn't just his appearance that gusted and swirled. He would chase down students after school to add to or amend or rectify something that he'd said or done in class. He would scribble notes on book covers, matchbooks, even the tails of his half-tucked-in shirts. He would jump up from meals, or conversations — even from his sleep — to look something up or ask a question or sketch a diagram for someone he was trying to help to learn.

Everything he knew or discovered or, for that matter, invented, he shared with those around him. He loved birds, architecture, boats, caps and hamburgers, singly or together, and had a reedy but almost always on-key singing voice. He taught himself to play the recorder as well as various native flutes, to chart azimuthal equidistant projections and to blow eggs, fill them with confetti and paint delicate designs on their shells.

He was, said many parents after he left, a tireless dynamo, the kind of teacher they'd always wanted their children to have. (They said that, even though many of them had objected to some of his teaching methods while their students were in his classes.) Not only had he been what every good teacher should want to be, he had been an active participant in his own three children's lives and "a really good husband, though too often too busy," according to his wife.

Bernabe hadn't come to Pachuca as a teacher, however. Despite the fact that he had all the necessary credentials, he'd done others things with his life until hard times had forced him back into the classroom. What those other things were, few residents of Pachuca knew or remembered, although it was rumored that he'd been a house painter, an acrobat, a computer salesman and a movie photographer in his home state of Guanajuato. Others insisted that he had been the heir to a huge fortune that his brothers surreptitiously had gambled away.

Whatever his background, in his need for a new career he was no different from thousands of his countrymen, for massive layoffs and the closing of many small businesses had triggered a gigantic downward movement of Mexico's work force. Government workers, laid off when budget cuts eliminated their positions, became vendors. Lawyers became tour guides. Electricians became security guards. Assembly line foremen became ditch diggers. Bernabe, riding the downward spiral, left wherever he had been living and managed to convince a struggling private high school to hire him for half of what they had been paying the person he replaced.

The scant salary didn't diminish his enthusiasm. Nor did the fact that his students didn't want to study. Unable to competently explain the economics of work and pay, inflation and recession, hunger and migration, he showed up one morning with a handful of rags, a few wooden mop handles and some empty 12-liter buckets. The study assignment, he announced, was to renovate the classroom, a chipped and deteriorating uninsulated corner in a 19th century stone and stucco structure that the public education system had abandoned some twenty years before.

Of course the students had no idea where to begin. Or how. With water, soap, rags, dirt removers, Bernabe suggested. Within half an hour he was up to his elbows in scrubbing walls, scraping floors, sanding desk tops. Some of the 14- and 15-year-olds donated lunch money to buy paint and polish.

The next day others showed up with hammers, screwdrivers, paintbrushes and trowels they'd borrowed from their parents. When school authorities became alarmed that what they were doing was not "educative," Bernabe and his students shifted their work times to before school, after school and recesses.

Not only did they clean, they decorated. A mother who had a sideline cottage industry making *piñatas* spent two days teaching Bernabe's students to make papier-mâché. With her help they fashioned an eagle clenching a serpent to put over the blackboard and a griffin with obsidian eyes to put over the classroom doorway. They repaired desks, put in new shelving, baked pumpkin bread to earn what they needed for art supplies and cadged relatives, friends and strangers to donate window panes, textbook bindings and a VCR.

As they cleaned and painted and plastered and patched, Bernabe debated nutrition and *the tequila effect*, the disappearance of the prehistoric mammoths and changes to Article 17 of the Mexican constitution. The students measured angles and found square roots and converted meters to gallons and carpentered to the music of borrowed movie sound tracks.

Not only did they completely re-do their own classroom, they re-created a gymnasium from what had become a dank and putrid storeroom. Their energy — and accomplishments — triggered a series of building repairs by students' parents and prompted school administrators to suggest that other teachers try to emulate Bernabe.

He congratulated his students and gave each a favorable critique of the work, but when it came time to pass out grades on the regular bi-monthly report cards, he gave each of them a "6" (the equivalent of a D-). To vociferous claims, "That's not fair!" he pulled out sheets to show that none of them had completed their homework, regularly answered roll call nor turned in book reports.

Not only were they getting "6"s, he explained, they were going to have to repeat the work instead of going ahead to the next sections. He so adamantly refused to listen to any commonsense demands that a group of parents invaded his classroom.

How can you fail the entire class after all the work the students have done? the parents wanted to know.

Because I have the power to do so, he answered.

One mother called him a tyrant, another threatened to go to the archbishop. When a father suggested that he'd organize all the parents and picket the school, Bernabe asked what purpose that would serve.

"That would give us the power!" the father retorted.

"So what is your work worth?" Bernabe jumped onto a chair. As both his students and their parents gaped at him, he continued, "You see, there is not a fixed value here. If I have all the power, I give you nothing, then throw you away. If you have power, you force me to overpay and then what, will you work as hard at something again?"

Together, teacher, parents, students piled into the argument. That they never exactly came to a consensus was less important than that they learned the function of economics. Never in their lives would any of them have to ask questions about work and pay, inflation and recession, leadership and self worth, again.

Bernabe's school not only was one of the municipality's poorest private schools, it also had a reputation of being the most backward athletically and scholastically. The school hadn't won an inter-mural soccer game in almost a decade and had dropped out of most other sports.

"That will change! I guarantee within a year we will have our champions!" Bernabe impetuously responded to chiding during a teachers' union meeting.

At the time, he hadn't any idea how to achieve the guarantee, but he wasn't one to back down, even from an inopportune boast. He knew that sports programs at other schools, both public and private, were so well in place it would take years to catch up — unless it was in a new or previously under-participated-in sport. He paced, read sports pages, asked questions, bounced ideas here and there, and came up with a plan: girls' basketball.

He personally knew nothing about basketball, but a league, composed of both school and gymnasium teams, was being formed. He paid the school's entrance fees out of his own pocket, then hopped on a bus to Mexico City, where a struggling men's professional league was playing games.

Posting himself outside the players entranceway, he intercepted the first basketball player to approach — a nearly seven-feet tall African-American who spoke almost no Spanish. Undaunted, Bernabe managed to explain what he wanted: a quick course on how to coach. The ball player laughed, sighed, shook his head and drew a few diagrams.

That was enough for Bernabe. He got enough girls interested to form a team, put up a hoop and started coaching. His third practice session was just under way when a visitor showed up. He introduced himself as a friend of the basketball player Bernabe had collared in Mexico City and said he'd dropped by "to help out."

Help out he did. Bernabe wrangled room and board for him in an upscale Mexican family's home and the "helper-outer," whose name Pachucans remember only as "Bobby A.," took over the first few weeks of coaching.

The girls weren't great shots and barely could dribble, but they were the only team in the league that had any concept of blocking out to rebound or setting a screen, and they won nine straight games. By the time Bobby A. returned to the United States (to the dismay of a horde of amatory teen-aged girls) Bernabe and his players had learned enough to keep on winning. Nevertheless, when he was asked to give coaching clinics, Bernabe politely bowed out, citing "too much other work." Enthusiastic as he was, Bernabe knew limits, including his own.

These limits impeded other competitive programs. Bernabe's teenagers couldn't win science, mathematics or English prizes, but art, he felt, might be a different story. Art, he reasoned, is highly visible. In art one doesn't have to be traditional.

When local officials announced a *municipio*-wide mural contest, Bernabe found a short cut that he thought would be both startling and effective. Although his students weren't street kids prone to spray cans and graffiti, they jumped at his suggestion that they borrow ladders and start working on the school's walls.

The old building didn't lend itself to Diego Rivera-type images, and he knew his students didn't have the skills to do a Virgin of Guadalupe or ascending Christ, so he talked them into Day of the Dead evocations. Among the windows facing the street, they spray-painted an interlocking series of grimacing skulls and contorted skeletons.

While they were spraying the walls and each other, correcting expressions and coloring gaumed corners, Bernabe stumbled across some about-to-be-dumped cardboard boxes filled with old hospital X-rays. What he thought was a brilliant idea flashed through his imagination.

He and some students covered one window with the X-rays. Not only did the dark negatives cut the sunlight glare, they cast eerie images towards the street below. For days he and his students carefully edited and spliced until they had X-ray shades for every window on the side of the building containing the Day of the Dead mural.

In varying patterns of sun and darkness, this roentgenography showed sometimes glistening, sometimes wavering bones and skulls. Although the mural didn't win the contest, it attracted infinitely more attention than any of its competitors. Bernabe and his students completed their promise to school officials by repainting the entire building, including the murals (to the dismay of some students and townspeople).

These projects not only increased Bernabe's value as a teacher but provided some financial rewards as well. Several wealthier private schools and the best of the public high schools offered him teaching positions, but he decided to accept a modest raise to stay where he was. The local television station hired him for occasional commercials (even they were unable to subdue his ruffianesque appearance) and he spoke at various conventions and convocations. The school itself proudly promoted him for "teacher of the year."

Then he left. Suddenly. He simply didn't show up for class one May morning. Some of the older students ran across town to check on him at home. They found his house vacant: Bernabe and his family had moved out. School officials notified the police as students and their families darted around asking questions of anyone and everyone who might know something about his whereabouts.

Their answer came rather quickly. It did not, however, come from the police; it came from the state-run Institute of Basic Education. A broad-shouldered bland-faced apparatchik with a smile that seemed to be sucking sour lemons sidled into the school director's office with the notification that the credentials of Bernabe Esquer, *maestro*, were counterfeit.

"That can't be! There must be some mistake!" school officials insisted but the apparatchik had proof: Bernabe had purchased all of his degrees and certifications at a local discotheque.

He wasn't the only purchaser of false papers. The Institute, which functioned as the state department of education, pulled the plug on over 260 public school teachers in the state of Hidalgo alone. Someone apparently had warned Bernabe, or he had heard a rumor about the impending firings, probably because state officials cracked down first on the public schools, which were directly under their control.

Whoever Bernabe was — whatever his background had been — he may have had reason to pack up and leave rather than stick around while the Basic Education Institute turned their findings over to federal officials. Some of the people who had known him suspected that he'd owned a business somewhere and had gotten so far in over his head that he'd bailed out, leaving a bundle of unpaid bills behind.

But that scenario wasn't romantic enough for many former parents and friends. They preferred to imagine a Bernabe whose inventiveness, enthusiasms and charm had led him to become a heart surgeon, a psychiatrist, an airplane pilot, a stockbroker — all with false credentials, of course.

If he could pass himself off as a teacher and in two or three years become one of Pachuca's best, couldn't he as easily produce papers — and a past — that trained him in medicine, investment, psychotherapy? Couldn't he have gone on to another invented career and have become an anthropologist, a private investigator, a religious leader?

For years after he left, many of his former students and their parents looked for him every time they left Pachuca, expecting, perhaps, to see his face peer out from a limousine, or down from a trapeze. Some of his students even sketched pictures of what he might look like without a beard, just to make sure they would recognize his photograph in a newspaper or on a TV screen.

Whatever he was — and whatever he became — he left an unfilled gap behind. His students remember their first day in class without him. His replacement, fully credentialed and experienced, seated himself at the front desk, rasped "*Siéntense! Siéntense!*" and told the class, "You will turn in your workbooks to page 103. Read the passage and write down your answers to the questions. You have forty minutes to finish the work.

"And no talking, please."

PART II

ALL ROADS LEAD NORTH

North of Mexico's congested urban core, the landscape widens to form vast rolling plateaus bordered on each side by rugged mountain ranges. The Rockies, called the Sierra Madres in Mexico, split just south of the U.S.-Mexico border to create a huge trough, then merge again northwest of the capital city. West of these mountain ranges the arid Sonoran Desert stretches towards the Gulf of California; to the northeast, the farmlands of the state of Tamaulipas green the Gulf of Mexico coastlands.

For well over a century, the vast land area of northern and western Mexico has been tugged at by conflicting cultures. Even during colonial times, when Spain ruled Mexico, the northern states disregarded most of what was happening in Mexico City. Individual *hacenderos* ruled their huge estates with little or no interference from Mexico's changing governments. Mines provided ore for the federal treasury and ranches provided beef for city stomachs; otherwise the *hacenderos* did what they pleased.

Far to the north, on the fringes of what then was Mexican territory, Santa Fe and San Antonio became major trade centers. Most of what came into northern Mexico came from the United States. As the U.S. Midwest and West developed — and Texas and the Southwest became parts of the United States — the new border cities of El Paso (now Ciudad Juarez), Laredo and later Mexicali and Tijuana — began to assume more importance.

During the *porfirato* — the dictatorship of Porfirio Díaz in the late 19th and early 20th centuries — newly constructed railroads facilitated this flow of goods. U.S. and foreign investment prospered; the rich got richer and the poor got poorer until sixteen years of warfare (1910-1926) ripped the fabric apart and drove thousands of *campesinos* illegally into the United States.

Catholicism remained strong throughout the region, even after the Revolution officially abolished a state religion. That it primarily was a Catholicism of Sunday ceremonies and pious grandmothers rather than a theology of attaining perfectionism didn't diminish its importance as a stabilizing force. It gave definition to the culture, provided a tableau of shoulds and shouldn'ts for landowners and their serfs, and acted as a vehicle for social expression.

The Revolution wiped out many of the old *hacenderos* but new ones arose as the northern communities rebuilt. Industry and large scale agriculture — cotton, wheat, corn, alfalfa — absorbed much of the small-plot farming and the frontier cities, from Matamoros to Tijuana, swelled in importance, both as commercial and manufacturing centers and as sinful alternatives to Prohibition, military discipline, the Mann Act and, later, the use of drugs in the United States.

Despite these changes, northern Mexico has retained its conservative political and cultural outlook. Its great artists, sculptors, writers and theater directors leave in their youth and seldom return. Its richest ranchers, property owners and industrialists prefer Cessnas to opera and *carne asada* to sushi or crepes.

"I'm *norteño*," you'll hear one declare, not without a tinge of boastfulness. "I say what I think, do what I want and let the chips fall where they may."

CHAPTER 4. ELUSIVE DREAMS

"SOY CRISTIANO!"

Roberto Garcia's parents didn't intend to become tamarind growers. They merely were looking for business opportunities when they moved to Torreon from the eastern slopes of the Sierra Madres.

Garcia's father purchased the already planted orchards and, as the demand for his crops increased, he remodeled the solid stone house to provide more bedrooms, a storage shelter, a day room and a den. Roberto remembered an affluent boyhood spent among well-to-do peers, most of whom, like his parents, reflected creole prejudices[2] and most of whom, like them, were ardently Protestant in what was still, in the late '40s and early '50s, predominantly Catholic northern Mexico.

Nominally Protestant myself when I met him, my Spanish adequate for the girl-chasing, fair-going, football-playing friendships that mid-20-year-olds enjoy, I became, briefly, a sort of younger brother meeting Roberto's energetic need for socialization and admiration. He was only a year or two older than me, a strapping man with a sharp chin line, hawkish nose and broad shoulders; partly because my language skills were so faulty (and because he knew a little English)

---

2. In Mexico, *creoles* are/were Mexican-born persons of pure Spanish heritage. *Mestizo* refers to persons of mixed Spanish-Indian (and/or Negro, Filipino, etc.) heritage. (The word comes from the Spanish word "mezclar," to mix.)

he took it upon himself to introduce me to a Mexico City that he was just, himself, learning to appreciate.

Like me, he was older than most of his university classmates, more ambitious, and already entrenched in his values. He had left home after a year or two at a college in Torreon to work in a farming community in the northern part of the state.

Unlike many young men away from home for the first time, he hadn't succumbed to roistering male companionship but had stayed close to his roots, played music for a Protestant church and developed an appreciation for American ice cream and American autos. Limited by his lack of formal music education, he'd come to study in the capital, where we rented across-the-hall rooms in a boardinghouse in Colonia Polanco.

As unswervingly "Christian" as he was (he never used the term *protestante* but contrasted being *cristiano* to others being *católico*), Roberto was by no means an on-his-knees Bible-thumping proselytizer. The tinted sunglasses he wore, his arrogant pose and the swagger in his walk provoked covert glances and obsequious replies from shopkeepers and bystanders (as well fellow students and boardinghouse residents) who assumed he was the take-everything son of a well-heeled policeman or politician.

Roberto's Protestantism served him well socially. Unlike most students living in Mexico City boardinghouses, who grouped together in little clusters alienated from the overall flow of Mexican family life, Roberto, through his church, had infiltrated a society denied to the rest of us. I tagged along to private-home dinners and picnics at Las Truches, met young women and their parents, even played basketball in a Mexico City Baptist tournament.

The city *cristianos* represented a wider range of backgrounds and occupations than Roberto's Torreon *cachupines* and Roberto's musical skills put him at the center of most gatherings. He played the piano, the guitar, the organ, and several brass and reed instruments and knew all of the popular as well as religious songs. My status as Roberto's *amigo norteamericano* brought me confidences and compliments that I never would have developed otherwise.

But despite his extroversion, the demand for his presence socially (and the 18-year-old daughter of a Mexico City mechanic who fell in love with him), Roberto Garcia remained encased in his provincial creole shell. He corresponded with his childhood sweetheart in Torreon all the time that I knew him and she remained unattached until, the semester before he was to graduate, she and he formally announced their engagement to marry. (Like him, she was the daughter of well-to-do landowners two or three generations removed from northeastern Spain.) I never met her, but I saw several photographs: she appeared as he described her, remote but attractive, without any hint of imagination or a sense of humor, a vigorously virtuous and intelligent respecter of her parent's wishes — and, I presumed, Roberto's as well.

"If you have to trace their conversion to something, I think that something would be an individual identity," Roberto described the familial attachment to the evangelical Baptist Church. "They all came over at about the same time — my parents, my fiancée's parents, all of them — during the last years of Porfirio Díaz' reign. They weren't, as far as I know, particularly political, but they certainly weren't revolutionists, and they were by nature rather restrained — clannish, I think you could call them.

"They didn't blend right away with the Mexican culture. They spoke what sounded like a different language, and they acquired little chunks of land by purchasing it from the large *hacienda* owners. They put in orchards — an orchard could support a family — and started little businesses that hadn't existed before. Thus, you see, they found themselves wedged between the big landowners, who controlled most of the wealth and had most of the political power, and the *campesinos*, who had nothing and lived from hand to mouth with their goats and corn and beans.

"The Revolution turned everything topsy-turvy: armies stampeding this way and that way, confiscating, looting, forcing people into military service. These new arrivals, these *cachupines*, didn't have any reason to join the Revolution, nor did they have any reason to defend the *porfiristas*. They clung to what they had as best they could, trying to sort through the confusion.

"They would have been glad to annex to the United States if they could — in fact, some of them fled to Texas, then came back. They didn't belong to either side, and when things started to calm down, when they could go back to their orchards and stores and schools and marriages, they were ready to grab hold of anything that could make them feel secure.

"One of those things, for some of them like my grandparents, was the *cristiano* churches. They offered something immediate, not a God far away that one has to crawl to, throw oneself down in front of an altar decorated with the stolen wealth of the people and beg — bribe, I should say bribe — a whole army of priests and bishops and archbishops to get to, but a God who, through his Son, is right there, filling your heart, answering your prayers.

"And the churches, they were right there too — remember, the Revolution didn't forbid them, it only banned certain kinds of proselytizing; the churches were there and they offered rules that made sense — not like the Catholic Church, which seemed to say, 'Okay, you can go out and sin, do whatever you want, just come with your money and we'll act in place of God and — for a price — forgive you.'

"You see, we *cristianos* believe that God answers personal prayer — He helps you in this life, He brings you immediately into his Presence with His Spirit. That's exactly what these people, these immigrants I'm talking about, needed.

"They did not want to be part of the old regime, with its stratified class system, nor part of the Revolution, with its confiscations and patriotism and executions. So they — not all of them, obviously, many of them didn't break away, many of them stayed Catholics and their children and grandchildren too — but those like my grandparents became *cristianos* — good *cristianos*, healthy *cristianos*, with good values and they helped each other, they helped each other a lot.

"Strangely enough, after things calmed down, the Revolution created a need for the things that these immigrants and their children grew and the things that they made. After years of chaos, the new government had nothing — power, yes, but not typewriters, not milling wheels, not elastic for trousers, not tamarinds, not clocks. Both the agrarian reform and the nationalization of oil opened up situations for mechanics and store owners and managers and school teachers and people who could make bread and shoes and bricks.

"Yes, of course it's ironic. You have this revolution with all its Marxist overtones and it creates the very thing that Marxist revolutions are supposed to deplore: a conservative petite bourgeoisie. And this, of course, confirmed my family's belief that God had been watching out for them, that He personally cared about them.

"That's something that a *cristiano* has: The realization, 'I am important.' Oftentimes it is because people feel unimportant, unwanted, unloved, that they sin. It's hard to do something bad against someone who loves you — especially if others who love you are right there, watching.

"So that was part of it. Each of these immigrants who had become a *cristiano* felt important and they were bonded to others in a group that they felt was important, that gave them identity. What you will hear when someone suggests committing a sin to one of us, '*No, soy cristiano*' — that means more than, 'I cannot do it because I am afraid,' it means, 'I am this strong thing that realizes that I am strong and that I am loved.'

"That's the way my grandparents are. And my parents. Inside they are like rocks. They pray every night and every night they ask for help and the tamarinds on their trees get thicker and better and the money they have invested multiplies. And if something bad happens — a setback — they are strong and they surmount it. They don't ask for an easy life, they pray for strength to deal with it."

Roberto and I spent less time together after I moved from the rooming house to a little efficiency apartment on Calle Astronomos, just west of the Nuevo Leon intersection with Avenida Insurgentes. We still would get together in the afternoons, to talk, take walks, play ping-pong together, but the bus trips across the central part of the city were time consuming and I was emerging out of the penumbra as his *amigo norteamericano* to a life in, and knowledge of, the city on my own.

For a few weeks, as both his graduation and wedding dates loomed close, he and I re-bonded, primarily to sort through the temporary plunges of panic the incipient events sent him through. But he emerged from a moment of threatening to give up music as a career and to run away from his impending marriage with straightened shoulders and new resolve and he moved back to Torreon, where a job teaching music to high school-aged youth was waiting for him.

I visited him there once, while his wife was away on a vacation with her parents, and we sent letters back and forth after I got my degree and took a journalism job in Texas. A year or so after our last personal letters, he wrote to ask me to send him some possible plot scenarios for an atonal opera that he intended to compose, and added, almost apocryphally, that he missed the "variety" that our lives in Mexico City had offered.

The '*soy cristiano*' that I'd heard him declare a few years before no longer seemed either positive or strong.

Why Laws Mean Nothing

During the past fifty years, hundreds of thousands of immigrants have made their way along the two major thoroughfares from Saltillo through

Monclova to Piedras Negras and through Monterrey to Nuevo Laredo, and from Torreon through Chihuahua to Ciudad Juarez. Among them, would-be wage earners from Durango and Zacatecas, Jalisco, Michoacan and the surrounding states poured into Texas and from Texas sifted northward to Michigan and Wisconsin, Pennsylvania, Washington, D. C. and other points in the northern Midwest and Northeast.

Many of them returned: some by choice, others by necessity, still others because they were ejected by immigration officials on *The Other Side*. The migrant flux always has been connected to economic situations on both sides of the border: increasing when agricultural or industrial expansion creates an unfilled need for labor in the U.S., or when drought or land confiscation forces the unlanded and unemployed in Mexico to seek work wherever they can find it, and decreasing during U.S. recessions, when the need for cheap labor diminishes.

A great shift occurred early in this century when immigrants fleeing revolutionary conditions in northern and central Mexico surged into the United States to work in World War I-generated agriculture and construction projects. A generation later, over a million of them returned to Mexico during the "Great Depression" of the 1930s. World War II prompted a new flow of both legal and undocumented workers that subsided during the '50s (in part because of U.S. expulsions), increased during the boom years of the Vietnam War and crashed again in the mid-'80s when an increasingly isolationist U.S. Congress passed the Simpson-Rodino Immigration Act, which granted resident status to over a million *de facto* immigrants but tightened restrictions both on illegal immigration and the hiring of undocumented workers.

Blas Tamayo was one of those who returned. A painter and muralist, wildcat publisher and outspoken proponent of *indigena* customs and philosophy, Tamayo returned to Saltillo from the United States shortly after the Simpson-Rodino Act went into effect in January, 1987.

"I believed what I read in the United States newspapers," Tamayo admitted. Throughout Texas, where he had been living in San Antonio, misinformation and apprehension tangled Hispanic thinking.

Amnesty provisions of the Act stipulated that undocumented residents could obtain temporary legal status but to do so they would have to register with the Immigration and Naturalization Service, which many of them were afraid to do. A number of non-governmental agencies, particularly the Catholic Church, launched information and registration campaigns and the Mexican federal government invited a group of Chicano leaders to address both Mexico's Congress and Mexican President Miguel de la Madrid to discuss the problems that Mexican nationals in the United States were going to face.

Like many other *indocumentados*, Tamayo refused to register — not, he said, because he was afraid of being deported, but because he never intended to live permanently in the United States, only to work there because he couldn't find satisfactory employment in Mexico. Upset by the fear and consternation that passage of the Act generated, he began working for immigration rights groups, first in San Antonio, then in Piedras Negras and Saltillo.

Recent arrivals from Texas told Tamayo's group that duplicating documents needed for Amnesty registration had become big business in San Antonio, Houston, Dallas and El Paso. Entrepreneurs were generating green cards (temporary work permits), fabricating work histories that included the signatures of employers, even selling driver's licenses they'd obtained from the state department of motor vehicles by providing the birth certificates of children who'd died at childbirth. Unscrupulous lawyers charged hundreds — sometimes thousands — of dollars to provide what the *indocumentados* could have gotten for free, and Mexican customs officials tacked outrageous fees onto anything the displaced workers tried to bring back to Mexico.

One partly disabled former farm worker described being stopped by Border Patrol *migras* while driving outside of Del Rio; the agents not only confiscated his car, they held him at gunpoint while they burned his documents, then forced him to walk barefooted 30 miles to a remote part of the frontier, where they arrested him for trying to cross illegally and turned him over to Mexican authorities in Del Rio.

Incensed by that story, Tamayo rushed to file complaints both with the Mexican government and the U.S. consulate, then thought better of it and inquired around the Saltillo neighborhood in which the supposed farm worker had been living. Acquaintances and a relative confirmed that the "lying *pendejo*" had injured his back in a Saltillo car accident and hadn't been out of the city in years.

"I was blown away," Tamayo sighed. "There were so many stories going around — so many exaggerations and just plain lies — I began to doubt everything that I heard."

Nevertheless, he hooked up with a group of young activists who had ties to Chicano organizations in Texas. They worked out "what we thought was a comprehensive strategy" to reintegrate the returnees into life in Mexico. It proposed the establishment of micro-industries, appropriation of government-controlled land and establishment of cooperative housing and child-care ventures.

But few returnees seemed interested in their efforts. Border crossings from the U.S. back into Mexico increased dramatically during December, 1986, while the Simpson-Rodino Act was being hammered into shape by the U.S. Congress.

Amnesty enrollments had reached only a fraction of projections made in January, 1987, indicating that many *indocumentados* were going to stay in Mexico rather than try to legalize their status. When Christmas purchases dropped dramatically in cities like Saltillo, which derived a considerable portion of their incomes from emigrants sending money home to their families, Mexican officials warned that those providing that income were on their way back to Mexico en masse.

But none of those predications materialized. The "flood" of December and January returnees included thousands of *indocumentados* who were returning to Mexico only to spend Christmas with their families. Many of them had been laid off from agricultural jobs for the winter months; by mid-March they were back across the border, planting sugar beets and garlic and potatoes and cotton, or hammering nails and digging trenches for constructions crews that had gone back into operation after the winter storms.

Like other official and unofficial observers on both sides of the border, Tamayo and his young associates learned that "so few people in the business of running things knew anything about [the *indocumentados*]"

The picture of the furtive *indocumentado*, scurrying from place to place just ahead of the *migras* and collapsing once he was safely across the border just isn't true, Tamayo contended. Most of the returning emigrants arrived on buses, wearing new shoes and toting Mixmasters, curling irons and portable television sets.

Almost immediately they went to work building additions to their parents' houses, taking their grandmothers, aunts or cousins to specialists for medical treatment, and repairing washing machines and autos. Many single men came back to charivaris and weddings, and some to see children who'd been born while they were working in the United States.

But many married couples with young children did not return to Mexico, both for financial reasons and because they had non-seasonal jobs that they couldn't leave. By 1987 an increasing percentage of immigrants had moved into steady or semi-steady employment in legitimate as well as fly-by-night industries, in restaurants, in construction and as domestic workers. Even farm workers had begun to specialize in order to fulfill the needs of agricultural employers; many of them remained in the United States with their families even during the times when they were not working.

This situation, Tamayo explained, led to the creation of cohesive Mexican communities within cities and towns in the United States.

"In San Antonio, for instance, one hardly needed to speak English — just the few words like 'how much does it cost?' and 'where is the doctor?' that a tourist should know." Many immigrants with children accommodated to the culture and lost interest in ever returning to Mexico.

Tamayo downplayed the treatment that *indocumentados* suffered in the United States by suggesting that many Mexican citizens suffered equal or worse treatment while trying to find work and establish homes in cities in Mexico. The hundreds of laws and regulations put into effect by both countries, he contended, had little or no effect on the overall migration, which had a undercurrent and rhythm of its own, just as previous migrations, including the ancestors of the Aztecs surging southward, Europeans swarming into the New World, the United States suddenly pushing westward, grew out of the demanding needs of civilizations, not individuals.

The migration, he argued, will continue. And as it continues, it will create its own rules and adjustments, adding, subtracting and modifying as situations require. Out of it changed cultural and ethnic values may emerge. All that the laws — and those who design them — will do is temporarily abet or thwart the inevitable.

"And maybe warp what we, as individuals, want, perceive and need."

Highway Ants

The great highways that connect north to south carry more than people. Huge semis haul fruits and vegetables, cotton and kerosene, newly assembled automobiles and straw-packed clay pots towards markets in the United States.

Others like them roar southward towards the cities in Mexico's heartlands carrying televisions, cookware, canned goods, appliances and hundreds of other kinds of manufactured and processed goods. They honk as they pass each other — and as they pass the thousands of trucks, trailers, pickups and vans that, like them, haul everything from over-ripe melons and tanned hides to T-shirts and pocket calculators to be distributed to street vendors and *tanguis* throughout central Mexico.

"The *chilangos* call us *hormigas* [ants] for good reason," Fanny Manriquez confided to me. "Back and forth we go, thousands of us, carrying things that can be bought cheaply in the United States to be sold cheaply in Mexico."

Hormiga, she explained, was a term she preferred to *contrabandista* [smuggler]. A slender woman with large, luminous eyes and a tense set to fragile, high-cheek-boned features, Manriquez forced a barely audible laugh and glanced around the cluttered living room as her children, my children and the neighbor's boy, Memo, darted in and out of the front door.

Periodically she and her two youngsters stayed with her sister-in-law, who lived across the street from me and my family in a little neighborhood of 1930s houses tucked among hills south of Town Lake in Austin, Texas. Her husband, a determined and assertive former airport employee, scoured central Texas for cheap clothing, sports equipment, electronic gadgets, games and tires that they crammed onto a high-sided farm truck and, evading Mexican customs guards, hauled to Torreon.

"It is not as dangerous as you might think — only when the [Mexican] army sends out special patrols along the highways. Even then, they do not care about us — they are looking for drugs and guns. And, well, you can understand, we do not carry anything that is illegal to sell, it is just that no taxes are being paid on what we take across the border.

"We have carried everything. Clothes. A man here, a *judeo* down on East Sixth Street, he set us up with people who sold, very cheaply, what do you call them? 'seconds?' — new jeans that weren't perfect, no? Huge boxes filled with them.

"And when we first started doing this, we worked with a man, a *chicano*, who had a business cleaning up after, what do you call them? garbage sales? no, no, I mean, what? yard sales, *garage* sales — almost the same, no? He would take everything that people didn't sell, here and in San Antonio, and he and his wife would sort it and stack it and once a month or so we would pack it all in our truck and take it to Torreon and sell it to the *ambulantes* there.

"Tires. You call them 'recaps,' no? They are a very good business. In Torreon we have a place that sells them — it is owned by a cousin of my husband's. At first he would give us a percentage each time he sold one of the tires that we brought him but now he pays us cash for as many as we can bring him.

"Televisions, of course, they are the best. Here and in San Antonio, my husband, he buys...what do you say? 'Trade-ins,' yes, from the big stores. The same with air conditioners. And always we look for stores that are going out of business, and restaurants. My husband will buy all of a restaurant's equipment — grills, steamers, all those kinds of things — I mean, if he has the money at hand, that's always a chance we take, we have to sell what we carry across in order to buy more things, isn't that the way it goes?

"But it is a good life, even though we go back and forth a lot. The children, when school is in session, they stay with their grandparents in Torreon. We always have enough to buy them things, their school supplies and clothes and toys for Christmas and they get to spend a lot of time with us. Certainly it is better than working in a factory, being shouted at by a boss and never knowing when is going to go on strike or get laid off."

The Hunger March

Until the hunger march, no one in San Pedro de las Colonias took much notice of Jose Luis Díaz. He had the kind of face one could look at, then fail to remember, it was so like the faces of thousands of other northern Mexico farmers: small cheekbones guarding eyes whose resilience seemed to be on the verge of bursting into emotion, but never quite doing so; crooked teeth, resistant lips. While listening, or watching those around him, he stood with his legs bowed slightly, as though he were just about to lift some huge weight.

Although he only was in his early thirties, his skin was so hard and weathered its wrinkles seemed etched into permanent ridges. His straw hat, with its grizzled red band, seemed to be a natural extension of his physique — one scarcely could imagine him bareheaded — and his boot heels were so worn he walked with a kind of rolling gait that caused his shoulders to rock from side to side.

Díaz didn't start the hunger march — he only joined it, he said later, because his brother and cousins and in-laws insisted that he make the 148-mile hegira to Saltillo, the state capital, with them. Like him, they all raised cotton on tediously tilled and irrigated fringes of the Desierto de Mayran outside of San Pedro de las Colonias.

Because they were small landholders, each with his own separate acreage, they worked cooperatively and, from year to year, earned enough to provide for their families but never to amass any savings. The year of the hunger march, the government-subsidized Banco Nacional de Credito (Banrural) changed its policies; its administrators told the farmers that the bank no longer would give them direct credit to buy seed and fertilizer, as it had done in the past, then collect from them when they harvested their crops. Instead, the bank merely would process and pass along loans from private sources.

Jose Luis Díaz may not have known much about banking, but he had learned almost everything that a man could learn about cotton. One of the things he had learned was that the seed for the spring-summer cycle had to be in the ground by the middle of February.

He and his companions also knew, from their experiences and the experiences of their fathers and grandfathers, that private investors could not be trusted the way the government could. To get the private loans, they would have to put their property up as security, thus risking losing it as hundreds of thousands of small farmers throughout northern Mexico already had done. So instead of conforming, they decided to march, but not with guns and machetes and drums. They would march peacefully — hundreds of them — and while they marched they would not eat they only would drink a little water.

Their families, supporters, and two mariachi bands cheered the speeches that marked their send-off from San Pedro de las Colonias. Police contingents patrolled the highway in front of and behind them, with bullhorns instructing the marchers to keep one lane free for traffic to pass. Hand-lettered banners, some of them eight and ten feet across, proclaimed *CARAVANA DE HAMBRE*, denounced the new government bank policies and linked the march with patriotic peregrinations in the past.

Jose Luis Díaz, inexpressive and conforming, trudged beside his brother in the center of the pack. With him he carried only blankets and seedling agaves, one of which he planned to plant at each place the caravan stopped for the night.

By the end of the second day of the march, some of the participants had begun to drop out. Others rode for brief (or long) periods of time in the trucks that accompanied the demonstrators. And by then some of the marchers were taking some food with their water. But not the march organizers. Nor Jose Luis Díaz.

Without any intent that anyone could detect, he had moved to the front rank of the marchers by the third day. Still he took no food, and though he seldom spoke, he answered questions intelligently and clearly.

Without seed, he explained to reporters, to TV cameramen, to political organizers from the opposition to the party in power, without fertilizer, without the help of machines, the cotton could not be planted. It was not fair that each of the more than 200 farmers who'd begun the march should have to risk losing their property just to get those simple things that they needed.

Every one of the more than 200 had paid off what he'd borrowed in the past. Did the government want them to starve? Did the government want the people they hired to work for them to starve? Or the store people in San Pedro de las Colonias from whom they bought their vegetables and firewood and beans to starve?

His face grew leaner, and his walk a little wobbly as the caravan approached Saltillo, but Díaz continued to refuse to ingest more than a few drops of water now and then. Many of those who'd dropped out earlier, or who had started to eat and drink, renewed their fasts, inspired by his example. One by one, even the march organizers deferred to his presence. Without an election, or even consulting each other, they acknowledged his quiet, determined leadership.

As the caravan passed through the little pueblo of La Rosa, thirty miles west of Saltillo, children left school to stand along the roadside and cheer as the cotton farmers marched past. Buses from the city brought scores of supporters, including representatives from dozens of farm and peasant organizations throughout northern Mexico, anti-government activists and a couple of local TV singing stars.

The caravan, which had numbered over 200 when it started, then dwindled by half by the third day, now swelled to over 3000 as it entered the city limits of Saltillo. Representatives from both Banrural and the federal Department of Agriculture, Livestock and Rural Development greeted the marchers in front of the government palace, congratulated their resolve and promised to do everything in their power to help them.

These assurances were enough for some members of the caravan, but not for Jose Luis Díaz. Groups of his supporters gathered around him; he spread his blanket at the foot of the palace steps and quietly told the officials that he would leave when the seeds and fertilizers that he and his companions needed were on trucks heading for San Pedro de las Colonias.

And, he added, not a single one of them would sign anything that would permit any foreign investors to take their land away from them.

The five days without food — five days of walking over thirty miles a day — had brought an almost translucent sheen to Díaz's features. Those who participated in the hunger strike with him said his presence exuded a radiant energy that affected everyone who came into contact with him. Without consciously intending to do so, his followers formed a series of concentric circles around him, with those belonging to the innermost circle committed — like him — to total fasting.

Someone within the governor's palace dispatched medical personnel to examine and attend to the fasters, but the circle around Díaz prevented the doctors or nurses from coming close to him. They did allow a Saltillo television interviewer to question him and Díaz peered directly into the camera and stated, simply, that he was a farmer who needed to plant his cotton crop and, prevented from doing that, he would sit where he was until he starved to death.

On radio and television throughout the region, talk show callers berated the authorities for everything from calculated murder to organized fraud. Newspaper and television shots showed his increasingly emaciated face and figure beneath *VICTIMA DE REPRESIÓN* captions. Farmers, laborers, students, housewives and school children brought flowers and bags of fruit and other gifts.

Pilgrimages organized in other parts of the state began to filter towards Saltillo, each adding its own list of demands to *APOYA DE ALGODONEROS DE SAN PEDRO DE LAS COLONIAS* banners. Díaz stood — or rather sat — his ground, refusing to move except to help chip holes in the palace courtyard to plant a new agave for each day of his fast.

Finally, five agaves after the caravan arrived in Saltillo, the federal government informed the press (and through them the demonstrators and the public) that a review of the previous year's Banrural funding had turned up an unused sum of credit that Díaz and his fellow cotton growers could use to purchase seed and fertilizer without putting up their land as security.

Celebrations broke out among the demonstrators who'd been camping in front of the *palacio*. Television and newspaper cameras showed Díaz, surrounded by supporters, waiting to inspect the seed as two trucks, led by an escort of three federal police vehicles, wound through the streets of Saltillo.

To the question, "What will you do now?" he answered, simply, "Plant, of course," and to other questions involving his thoughts and feelings, "I have to get back to my farm; it's late."

After sipping juice and liquid vitamins that some medical personnel had given him, he let some fellow demonstrators help him into a farm truck. He did not wave towards the cameras as the vehicle pulled away from the square in front of the *palacio*, but merely gestured to his driver to follow the trucks carrying the seed and fertilizer. The cameras had to content themselves with closing shots of the seven seedling agaves.

Despite his weakened condition, Jose Luis Díaz was in his field the next day, planting his cotton.

"It is good seed," he is supposed to have told one of the other farmers. "If we work hard, we will have a good crop."

Past that, he would say nothing about his march, or the hunger strike, even in the *cantina* where, some Saturday nights, he stopped to share a drink of two with some of his farmer friends.

THE CURE

To reach the lobby of the Hotel Tres Dolores in the stark, diesel-smelling, dusty frontier town of Cuatrocienegas one passed through a grillwork archway barely visible from the street. Tiny rooms opened onto a slanted courtyard crowded with huge, cracked *ollas* crammed with shrubs whose branches bore more dead twigs than green leaves. The proprietor, a quivering little toad who seemed to have shrunk to half the size of the clothes that he was wearing, casually waved towards one of the rooms from his bench beside a battered concrete fountain when I entered and asked for accommodations.

A few minutes later, when I emerged to request a wash basin, glass, and pillow, he wheezed a coughed signal to someone inside the room closest to the archway. A plumpish woman backed slowly out of the nook, her attention riveted on the grainy *telenovela* she was watching on an old black-and-white TV, to reluctantly perform the requested chores.

True to the promise he'd made over the telephone, Antonio Hintze Organista limped into the Restaurant Super Burro within an hour of the time set for our meeting. A slack, pained man whose face twisted inward, accentuating his slumped shouldered squint, Hintze Organista shifted from beer to brandy after our second order of hotly spiced goat meat tacos.

He promised to meet me the next morning to start our drive towards the cave paintings and fossil diggings he had discovered some years before while installing telephone lines across the desert. I strolled slowly back to the Tres Dolores and, tired from the day's long bus trip, slipped into my narrow, lumpy bed.

I awakened suddenly, realizing that I was not alone in the little room. A figure darkened the open doorway.

"*Qui-Quién...?*" I gasped, unable to distinguish more than an aggressive pose in the dim and diffused moonlight. *You have the wrong room....* I tried to formulate the words in Spanish but my brain couldn't get the signals through to my tongue. The intruder's hand moved towards his hip and the pistol visible there.

"Who are you?" he growled in Spanish.

"Roberto," I replied. "A stranger. My first time here."

"I should kill you." His hand settled onto the weapon.

I have done nothing! I tried to force the words through my tightening chest. As he leaned towards me, I could smell his harsh, fetid breath.

He coughed and spat, "You are lucky, stranger. I should kill you, but I will not." As quickly as he had come, he disappeared.

My surge of relief was so great that several minutes passed before I could push myself erect and turn on the light. Only then did I realize that the door was closed — whoever he was, I thought, he must have pulled it shut behind him when he left.

I pulled a corner of the room's heavy muslin curtain aside and peeked into the courtyard. The potted plants' long shadows etched dark figures across the stone floor. I held my breath. Three or four sharp metallic clicks reverberated against the walls — my first impression was jangling spurs; I dropped the curtain and stood, silently, waiting.

But nothing more happened. A whisk of breeze rubbed the dry twigs. My breathing returned more or less to normal and, the light still on, I lay back down on the narrow bed. I did not sleep well — every crackle, every murmuring in the courtyard awakened me — but I did sleep, between awakenings rehearsing the story I would tell Antonio Hintze Organista the following day.

"What 'figure'? What did he look like?" Hintze Organista slammed his ten-year-old pickup to an abrupt stop after I'd described the encounter. The face muscles on one cheek vibrated as though something just under the skin was trying to get out.

Surprised by his fervor, I stammered a description, glancing past him at hills sloping gently through chaparral towards a chalky, treeless mesa. Hintze Organista nodded, sighed, and eased the big vehicle back into motion (he pronounced his surname "Een-say," explaining that one of his ancestors was a "German from Monterrey" who'd come to Mexico late in the 19th century).

"That is not so bad," he muttered, as though talking to the windshield in front of him, not to me. "I, too, have seen him. His name is Rodrigo. He talks more than he kills. Perhaps he means no real harm."

"Seen him? Dreamed, you mean?"

"Dreamed, seen — it is the same."

"What do you mean, 'no real harm?'" I persisted. "What are you talking about?"

Cursing the rough roadway, Hintze Organista squinted through the dust churned up by a truck that passed us going in the opposite direction. From a cardboard box wedged between us on the floor of the pickup, he extracted a bottle of tequila. "*Chinga tu!*" he choked as the first swig he took hit his stomach. Calming it with another draught, he passed the bottle to me.

"Not yet — too early," I demurred.

He nodded. Years ago, during the Revolution, he explained, Mexico's famous revolutionary leader (adventurer, bandit and notorious womanizer) Pancho Villa had buried an immense treasure near Cuatrocienegas (gold, coins, jeweled antiques ripped from *haciendas capuchines*). Not only that, one of his most trusted lieutenants, Gonzalez, had tucked tens of thousands in robbed gold bullion into a cave protected, legend says, by the spirits of the men executed for the theft that Gonzalez himself had committed.

One of those men — the one I thought I'd seen in my room — was named Rodrigo. Now and then a body would turn up, Hintze Organista grunted, a body whose mortal wound had been caused by a hand-cast bullet from an ancient .45. Or someone would disappear and never be found.

Pedro Domingo Alzugaray, the former regional director of the federal police who sold out to the Columbian *cartel del Golfo* was one of the missing, my companion told me. Throughout the 1980s, the profits from the cartel's extensive cocaine-smuggling operations had enriched every rancher, trucker and store owner in Cuatrocienegas. Every week, airplanes had landed on flat stretches of the Coahuilan Desert, and trucks and smaller planes had headed northward, into the United States.

"They [the *cartel de Golfo*] were the rulers of the desert," my companion again reached for the bottle of tequila. "You either worked for them or..." he shrugged, then described the morning the dead bodies of five local citizens had been found hanging in the courtyard of the Tres Dolores Hotel.

"The Tres Dolores? That's where I — !"

The pickup, slamming into a hidden rut, truncated Hintze Organista's burst of brusque laughter. The pickup lurched sideways, flinging him against me so violently he lost control of both the steering wheel and the bottle of tequila. It crashed against the window beside me, spilling its contents over both of us. As we hopped out of the pickup to inspect the roadway and our camping equipment tied to the bed, he told me not to worry, we would have enough to drink. He had packed plenty of bottles among our supplies.

After getting the pickup back on the road, Hintze Organista told me that Alzugaray and the Colombians somehow had angered the ghosts of the Villistas — or gotten too close to their treasures. In fact, one of them had ambushed Alzugaray in Ciudad Frontera, knocked him unconscious and left him for the federal police with Columbian drugs and American dollars in his possession.

The Colombians had moved their operations to another part of Mexico "but nevertheless," he warned me, "you don't say much about what you see out on the desert. Whether it is alive, or whether it is dead, you don't say much."

A herd of cattle interrupted our progress towards the little community of La Mora. Hintze Organista opened a new bottle of tequila as we leaned against the fender to watch them bawl and shove each other along the road. They were humped, ugly beasts — part Brahma and part Hereford — all leather and no meat.

Hintze Organista whistled and waved to the cow herd and he rode up to us. He couldn't have been over fifteen years old, a bright-faced cheerful lad with just the hint of a mustache across his upper lip. Slung across his shoulder was an AK-47; another like it protruded from the pack behind his saddle.

As he rode off, I asked Hintze Organista about the weapons. The former telephone lineman shrugged and explained that everyone had them, the *cartel* had brought so many with them they couldn't haul them away when they left.

"The ranchers around here have everything — pistols, shotguns, grenade launchers, jeeps, radios, everything. In Cuatrocienegas there is a *viejo* who loans money and takes the weapons and *aparatos* as a guarantee the money will be paid back. One time the state police arrested him and opened his cache: They thought he was going to start a revolution!"

An hour or two later, after we'd bounced through the tiny village of La Mora, Hintze Organista wedged the pickup off a steep incline, set the brake and beckoned me to follow him. He tucked the just-opened bottle of tequila in his hip pocket and, after some bumbling around to find a trail, he led me along a narrow ridge to a half-caved-in mineshaft. Another small trail led past it to the top of the hill.

"Wait, soon it will be time." He gestured behind us towards two massive timbers over which pulleys once pulled ore cars in and out of the mine.

I took a swig from the bottle he offered, passed it back and peered where he pointed at afternoon shadows moving across the chaparral-crusted slope opposite us. With the sun behind them, the timbers of the old pulley system gradually extended the shadows of their structure past us.

Hintze Organista lifted his forefinger, as though he were keeping time to some inaudible music, as the shadows of the two upright timbers merged into one and the shadows of the separate crosspieces extended outward to form a cross. Entwined along it, the shadows of the rope and pulleys twisted into what one could have perceived were the head and body of a crucified Jesus.

"Amazing! It's amazing!" I gasped.

A sliver of sunlight penetrating the space between the pulley and the timbers shivered across the shadows just as the breeze moved the old ropes. The shadow on the cross seemed to move and the timbers to groan. A sudden glowing seemed to splay its face — caused by a shifting cloud, perhaps. "I've never seen anything...!"

Hintze Organista's pained groan cut me short. He tottered forward, the tequila bottle in one hand, his other drawing signs in the air. Suddenly the bottle flew out of his grasp. For a second — a few seconds — it seemed to hover in the air in front of us, then descend, end over end, until it crashed hundreds of feet below us.

I don't know how long we stood there — a few seconds, a few minutes perhaps — staring at each other. Then Hintze Organista peered down at his hand — the empty hand that moments before had been holding the bottle of tequila. Suddenly he whirled, tripping and coughing as he clambered over the slope and back along the trail past the mine. When I caught up to him he was leaning against the open door of the pickup surrounded by smashed tequila bottles.

"Hey, *amigo*, are you all right?"

His left cheek quivering erratically, he gaped at me, then at the wasteland of glass surrounding him.

"It's the desert," he muttered, the words barely perceptible. "It makes a man do strange things."

"Yes," I confirmed.

He pawed at his cheek, trying to get the twitching to stop. His eyes, focusing on mine, were space ships from an alien planet.

"I don't need it," he coughed. "Get in. What the hell. The fresh air will be good for us."

We camped in an abandoned adobe shell that Hintze Organista said once had been a mission and later a fort to protect miners from raiding Indians. He stumbled restlessly around the small enclosure before curling up in a corner with a folded-up jacket for a pillow.

By that time I already had crawled into my sleeping bag, but I remember thinking that I wouldn't have minded having, for a nightcap, a little of the tequila that he had dumped on the ground. Finally I drifted into an uncomfortable, coyote-haunted sleep. Their howling grew louder, closer. I flung myself awake. Hintze Organista was braced against the crumbled remains of what once had been a window, pleading for mercy. Seeing me, he sagged backwards.

"They were going to cut my balls off." His voice trembled so badly I barely could understand him. "Cut my balls off and make me eat them."

Throughout the night he moaned and shouted and shivered and coughed. Not only did he keep me awake, his ghosts brought ghosts to my dreams: Pancho Villa figures on huge horses with foaming nostrils, suave *narcotraficantes* demanding money, half-man, half-wolf figures snarling from every bush.

And of course the intruder that I had seen in the Tres Dolores Hotel reappeared, squinting as he reached for the weapon on his belt and muttering that he should kill me — this time, for sure, he should kill me. By the time Hintze Organista and I got up, we both were exhausted. Even the coffee that we boiled in a metal pot did little to wake us.

Despite attacks of severe trembling that were transmitted from my companion throughout the pickup, Hintze Organista managed to drive to the opening of the canyon that he said would lead us to the cave paintings. I made another fire and we boiled coffee and ate tortillas and bread and Machego cheese, then started our ascent. But my guide and companion had to stop every forty or fifty feet.

"I'm all right, it will pass, I've been this way before, I'm all right, this will pass," he mumbled, but his quavering voice did little to reassure me.

Worse than that, he kept losing the way and became unsure of the landmarks. Then he started to weep. Tears splattered from his twitching left cheek across the front of his shirt. I put my arm around his shoulders to try to calm him. He gaped up at me as though never having seen me before.

"We can't go on," I whispered to myself. "Time to turn back."

It was mid-day before we found our way back to the pickup. Fortunately, Hintze Organista recovered enough sense of who and where he was to get a read on the landscape, or it might have taken even longer. I tried to get him to eat, but even coffee made him sick. Periodically he would berate himself for breaking all of the tequila bottles, then he would insist that it would be over soon, he would be all right, and he never would drink again.

He let me drive us back to the remains of the old fort. Our second night there turned out to be no better than the first. If anything, his dreams were more vivid and more frightening than they had been the first time. In one of them, his mother was crying out to him from beneath the body of a bear-like man who was making love to her. In another, long-nailed women were peeling his skin from his flesh.

Come morning, Hintze Organista's voice was so strained he couldn't speak above a whisper. He was so thirsty he was gulping water a liter at a time. It was flowing through him so fast he had to stop to urinate every few hundred feet as we tried, again, to make it to the cave paintings. We did make it further along the canyon — and without continually losing our way — but we both were so tired that the prospect of two hours of more strenuous climbing forced us, again, to return to the pickup.

Hintze Organista seemed to get a little stronger that afternoon, but the shakes and vomiting returned full force by nightfall. He tried to sleep but, he now admitted, he couldn't think about anything but getting something alcoholic to drink.

"Maybe somebody will come by, maybe there's a little *tienda* on some *ejido*, maybe..."

I urged him to try to rest, but as soon as he would drift off the ghosts would return.

"They want me to drink with them," he whimpered. "They have a lot to drink and they laugh at me because I have none."

I was too tired either to humor him or empathize with him. I pulled the flap of my sleeping bag over my head and lurched into troubled, dream-filled sleep. How or when I got out of my sleeping bag, I don't know, but I awoke facing the armed intruder who'd given me such a scare four nights earlier in Cuatrocienegas. This time there was no mistaking his intent.

"I should have killed you that first time," he growled. "You are a worm, a cockroach." Slowly he lifted his huge pistol.

"*Por fa-favor...*" I whimpered, as he lowered the pistol and shoved it back into its holster.

"No, I'll do it with my hands!" he hissed, his grin wide and malevolent, like a savage animal's.

"Stop!" I cried out as his huge fingers tightened around my throat. Vainly I struck out, trying to ward him off. "Stop! Please! In the name of the Virgin...!"

My body thrashed back and forth in his grasp. I felt my head bang against something hard and I seemed to lose consciousness as his voice screamed at me from far away. Then I realized that the shouts were coming from outside the dream, and the hands shaking me were not the intruder's but Hintze Organista's. Limply I peered up at him.

"*Despiértate*," he was saying, "Wake up. Wake up."

"The..." *ghost* I was going to say, but saw in his eyes that he needed no explanation.

"We have to go," he murmured. "We have to go, or leave our bodies here on the desert forever."

Despite daylight, the jolting pickup and the prospects of seeing more civilized faces, hearing more civilized voices, the feelings that the intruder had induced wouldn't leave me. To my surprise, Hintze Organista seemed both calmer and stronger. His hands weren't trembling and the muscles along his neck and shoulders seemed to have relaxed.

"It was Rodrigo," he interrupted my rehashing the violent dream. "The one who they say guards the treasure stolen from Gonzalez, the lieutenant of Villa."

"I was not after his treasure," I sighed.

"Perhaps he guards other things, too," my companion suggested. "Perhaps..." His voice trailed off; for several minutes he said nothing more. Then he told me, "I have seen him. Many times I have seen him. It was he..." He jerked at the steering wheel to negotiate through deeply rutted crevices in the unpaved road "Remember when we saw the cross? He was there when I got back to the car.

"It was he who broke the bottles. Not me."

In La Mora we stopped to buy thirty liters of gasoline from a farm owner. While we talked, his wife brought us warm *quesadillas* and hot coffee. To my surprise, Hintze Organista neither asked for tequila nor stopped at either of the little stores to try to buy a bottle. He looked tired, but seemed to be in control of both his body and his emotions.

I listened to him describe another encounter he'd had on the desert, but my own experiences involving the malevolent Rodrigo — which I did not want to believe had happened except as nightmares/dreams — continued to intrude. To evade them, I closed my eyes and drifted into a fitful, uncomfortable sleep that I really didn't awaken from until we were pulling into Cuatrocienegas.

Instead of returning to the Tres Dolores, I hunched in the cramped Cuatrocienegas bus station until the express to Monclova rattled through the former *town of the cartel*. To my great relief, Rodrigo did not follow me, and I spent — if not a peaceful night, a quiet one — in a hotel in the center of town.

I never did get to see the cave paintings, but three years later an acquaintance I sent to Hintze Organista went to see them. They were not spectacular, he said, but vital and interesting.

Not only did he show me photographs of them, he brought a note from my former guide. The handwriting on the back of what once had been a mimeographed government document of some kind was difficult to read, but I finally deciphered and translated:

Amigo Roberto,

In my mind you are most esteemed. Only once have I had tequila since you and Rodrigo cured me, and then it made me sick.

He still tries to frighten strangers, but has killed no one except one *narcotraficante*. That, *amigo*, was a job well done.

Thank you for sending your friend.

Most exceedingly respectfully,

Antonio Hintze Organista

Chapter 5. Nowhere-Land

"Mojado" No More!

"See this, señor? A tamale like this you cannot buy on the Other Side. For seventeen years my mouth has not touched a *buenissimo* tamale like these that my sisters make!

"You cannot guess, señor, how good it is to sit with my darling sisters, and watch for the sun to go down over the fields of Sonora. Everything is ready for the *posadas*.

"Can you believe it? Nine great-grandchildren they have, living here in Yaqui alone; these little ones will swing at the *piñatas* — so many *piñatas*, all made by my sisters with their own beautiful hands — you should stay and see how well made these *piñatas* are! Oh! It will take a lot of batting to tear them apart! And the great-grandchildren — you should stay and watch them dive for the candies, and wrestle and laugh — oh, yes! They will laugh! It is a beautiful place here to spend Christmas, no one is a stranger here — they will invite you to all of the parties.

"Here it is not like it is on the Other Side. Since I was a young man I have been going to the Other Side. Would you believe it? This is my first time back to see my sisters in seventeen years! Look! Look! You see, I have my papers! I strode across the border, to the *migras* I said, 'Here, señores, my documents, you may stamp them, please!' with my suitcases, my packages in my hands — and when I go back it will be the same, no more *mojado*! No more paying a *coyote* to take me across.

"When I was a young man, forty, fifty years ago, it was not so difficult to cross. I went back and forth many times. All the young men from here did — and even some of the older ones. There was no work here, and it was not so hard to cross. We would go back and forth — to work from early in the spring until after all of the harvests, then come back bringing some money with us. For many years when I was younger, I spent my Christmases here, visiting my darling sisters.

"But things changed. When I became older, I stopped coming back to Mexico for the holidays because I was afraid to cross back into the United States. People that I knew were robbed when they stepped off the bus in Mexicali. The *coyotes* would rob you, or turn you over to the *migras*. This man that I knew, who had planned to come across shortly after I did, his skeleton was found with a bullet in its head out on the desert and of course all of his money was gone — the *coyote* didn't even get him close to the border. That was twenty years ago, and it got worse after that.

"At the same time, the *migras* on the American side, they too got very vicious. The last time I went back across, I was 54 years old. The coyote I had was very trustworthy, but it was a difficult trip — we almost got caught twice. That was not at Christmas-time, that was a month or so afterwards. I had my wife and my children in California; during that trip I thought to myself, 'I can't do this again. If I get caught what will my wife and children do? I may never see them again!'

"So for all these many years, I stayed in California, until the 'Amnesty' came and I was able to get my papers. I did not see my darling sisters here for so long they almost didn't recognize me when I arrived with my suitcases filled with gifts.

"Now that I no longer am *mojado*, I am like you, señor, I can cross whenever I choose. I will not have to wait seventeen years for my next tamales — here, here señor, if you must go, do us the honor to take some tamales with you, it is a long bus ride to wherever it is that you are going.

"But really, you should stay for at least one of our *posadas*. Then you'd see! You wouldn't feel like a stranger!

"No one is a stranger in my darling sisters' house!"

No Way Forward, No Way Back

Nobel Prize winner Octavio Paz compared Mexico's accelerated and difficult surge from a society of subsistence farmers to an industrial national focused on large scale production with the European experience of rapid industrialization in the 19th century. The trauma of these abrupt changes not only disrupts the pattern of how people live (and how they earn a living), it destroys traditional culture. Mention Nogales (or Mexicali or Ciudad Juarez) anywhere in Mexico and you'll hear, "Oh, Nogales isn't Mexico!" (What they mean, of course, is that "Nogales isn't the 'Mexico' I think of when I use the term 'Mexico.'")

Like thousands of border city residents, Maribel Reyes Tranvina felt trapped by circumstances that neither would allow her to return to Durango, where she was born, or prosper in Nogales. Twenty-eight years old, married and the mother of two when she came with her husband to the frontier, Reyes found *maquiladora* work within three weeks of her arrival.

For three years she worked 40-50 hours a week, first assembling electric switches for garage door openers, then blank audio cassettes. Besides a small regular income, her employment provided Social Security medical benefits; with it and her husband's salary from a chemical processing firm, the couple was able to buy a plot of land on which to build a house.

Maribel Reyes Tranvina took only a month off for the birth of her third child, but she left the *maquiladora* several months later because she could not find anyone to take care of her children while she was at work. In Durango, she said, that wouldn't have been a problem: She had relatives and close friends, the streets were safe and there were many things for children to do. Nogales, however, was not Durango. The little plot Maribel Reyes and her husband had purchased was boxed between dusty, heavily trafficked streets on which fights and knifings were common.

The move left the family strapped financially — a position that many such families share. Over 75 percent of the 400,000 workers in the frontier's *maquiladoras* are women; the plants in which Reyes Tranvina worked hired primarily single women under the age of 18 who, she said, "needed only to spend their money on clothes, to look pretty until they found husbands." Three years after leaving the cassette assembly plant, Reyes Tranvina returned to work: "A matter of money," she said simply.

A Durango relative came to live in a tiny addition Reyes Tranvina's husband was able to add to their house; while the relative took care of the children and cooked, Maribel commuted back and forth to a job that she found both aggravating and so tedious she would "literally run" half a mile to her bus stop just to release the tension that built up in her nerves.

"No way forward, no way back." Reyes Tranvina echoes an oft-seen bit of frontier graffiti. No matter how hard — or how long — they work, she and her husband know that they have reached a maximum of accomplishment — marginal housing, jobs that offer little possibility of promotion, and a three-year-old television set.

They have no plans to leave Nogales. ("Where would we go? *The Other Side*? Things are worse there. Durango, where there is no work at all? And no way to get land?") Their one hope — a hope shared by hundreds of thousands of border laborers — is the same that drove hundred of thousands of 19th-century European immigrants to the United States: To make things better for their children.

They are not at all sure that they will succeed.

What Are They Talking About?

"*Compa! Áyudame pushear esta* f—ing *carumfla!*"

Everyone except me on the crowded street corner near downtown Ciudad Juarez seemed to understand the shouted request. A swarthy young man swiped at his face with his chambray shirtsleeve and charged through a cluster of men kneeling in front of rusted car radiator, his white teeth flashing through his bristly black beard as he cursed, "*Chinga tú* mother, *tecato. Por que no robas* a *pinche* battery *que trabaja*?" With the help of several additional sets of shoulders, the two young men got an old car that the first speaker had been trying to start spluttering down the rutted, once-paved street.

"F—ing *pendejo*!" the bearded Samaritan swiped at his sweaty face as he jogged back towards the group around the rusted radiator. "*Pinche* son-of-a-bitch *no entiende nada de los* Chevies."

Spanish is not the only language spoken on the U.S.-Mexico frontier. (Visitors from other parts of Mexico often argue that Spanish isn't spoken there at all.) The frontier's history as a source of vice and lawlessness have given it a language that fits its personality: a chaotic clashing of sounds and rhythms, vulgar, opportunistic and original.

A Nogales taxi driver, a "*pirata*" (unregistered and hence technically illegal *transportista*), told me that he could identify how long someone had lived on the border by the percentage of *groserías* he or she used in the space of one sentence. To prove his point, he leaned out the window of his fifteen-year-old station wagon and shouted at two young women stepping towards the intersection. Their immediate retaliation, of which I only caught one word, sent him into a spasm of laughter that almost catapulted us against the side of a parked delivery truck.

"What did I tell you?" he pounded the steering wheel. "'You see what I mean!"

This "Spanglish" (or "*espangles*" or "Tex-Mex") is more than an overlapping of expressions from two different cultures. It is a pounding of classic Spanish word-flow into direct, violent language.

Reflexive verbs, like the Spanish "*se me olvidó*" (something like "it got itself forgotten to me") or "*a mí me gustan*" ("those things are like-ing to me"), give way to cause and effect imitation of English grammar, with the English direct action verb sometimes substituted for the reflexive Spanish impersonal, as in, "I like *tacos con mucha carne, que pica, pica...*" or "*Yo* f— *todas las pinches gueras que veo in la calle...*" In similar fashion, possession often hardens into the American form of identity, with an implied apostrophe instead of the classical Spanish *de*: "*Traigo* Mario's *pistola...*"; "*Comí* Maria Isabel's *hambourguer...*"

Because it is argot, a hybrid, border Spanish varies from one speaker to another (or even from one occasion to another with the same speaker). For years, vendors have hawked their wares in some form of English ("Very good the sandals"; "Warsh you *carro*, no?"; "You want fock pretty girl?") but a new language began to emerge as emigration to American cities increased and the emigrants, many of them young, began to communicate in distinctly original terms.

Many Mexicans who grew up speaking Spanish at home were thrust into English-only classrooms when they started school in the United States. The new language squashed both their accepted means of communication and their sensibilities. Some of these young students adeptly learned both English and Spanish — and "Spanglish," the dialect, as well — but most of them acquired and used only the vulgar hybrid.

Several generations of use have given this form of "Spanglish" — the "Chicano dialect," as some educators prefer to call it, undefined and unregulated as it is — a kind of status that non-Chicanos on the Mexican side of the border find worth imitating. To speak "Chicano" in Mexicali, Ciudad Juarez or Nogales is to be hip, sharp, savvy, on the make.

It conveys, "Hey, I'm a local, I know what's happening, man!" It also implies, "I know all about the scene up there [in L.A. or San Antonio]; I've got the rap down, the language." Having that language, with its mix of Spanish, English and jive, gives a border resident a sense of power, of superiority, over those who merely speak Spanish.

That power often disappears when the "Spanglish" speaker confronts someone from the interior. Mexican philosopher Ramon Xirau, in classes at Mexico City College, described what he called "the use of language to determine and maintain class structure." Non-*mestizo* Spaniards refused to fall into Mexican dialects in order to maintain their creole superiority, just as educated Mexicans today look down upon those who use argot.

With few exceptions, the Spanish taught in Mexican schools on the border closely resembles what is being taught in Guanajuato, Saltillo, Mexico City and the rest of the country. (Mexico's centralized education system requires that children throughout the country complete specific phases from standardized texts each year.)

Thus border youngsters who grow up speaking argot now undergo something similar to what Spanish-speaking Chicanos experience in the United States. Some of them respond by learning and using the "school language" in formal settings and reverting to argot socially. Others merely mingle the two, letting most of what they learned in school slide towards the more popular *espanglés*.

Virtually everyone on the border speaks, reads or understands some English. English nouns pop up in everyday speech, even among newcomers to the area. So many solid, identifiable things — cars and TVs and mixers and refrigerators and fishing reels and guns — come from the United States that it is only natural that the words that describe them should come with them across the border.

Some of these English nouns are difficult for the Spanish-trained tongue and have to be modified: "Wheels" becomes "*huilas,*" instead of the Spanish *ruedas*; "truck" becomes "*troque*" and the Sunday comic strips become the "*fonis*" (funnies) instead of *cariacaturas*.

Virtually everybody who lives in Mexico's frontier cities has come from somewhere else — or their parents did — bringing with them different accents, rhythms, *modismos* and ways of speaking. In addition, recent migrations brought groups for whom Spanish is a second, not a primary, language. Each of these groups thrust words and concepts of their own into the push-pull of expression spoken on the frontier. In addition, lifestyle — as well as immigration — affects both what is said and how it is said.

The border cities' reputation (not entirely unearned) as a center of crime and vice has colored their perceptions of what daily living is all about. *Espanglés* slang is filled with profanity, sexual references and a matter-of-fact acceptance of guns, drugs, smuggling and prostitution. Outsiders find it coarse and shocking. Border residents consider it frank, open and highly descriptive.

If language expresses environment and like a living organism revises and keeps reinventing itself in order accurately to express that environment, as Xirau maintained, then the "Spanglish" of the Mexico-U.S. border can be understood as an accurate reflection of the lives of the people who speak it. Thus defined, it becomes "right" as a language, rather than "bad Spanish" or a corrupt combination of two languages.

As a language, it has power — the power of the environment that it represents, an environment that is constantly shifting, constantly struggling, constantly being pushed by outside forces. It is vital and alive; forms of it are spoken by over 30 million border residents and over half that many American residents of Mexican descent.

"*Con toda mi corazón yo amo* the little bitch! *Cuándo cogemos*, it's Disneyland, *chinga! Qué* grand!" I heard a young Nogales printshop apprentice exclaim when a fellow apprentice asked him about his latest flame. The vigor of his way of speech matched the intensity of his statement. In equally clear and dynamic terms, a private security guard told me about a *pandillero*'s attempt to mug him:

"*Ese pinche pendejo*, zsst! Switchblade, *aquí en la cara*, you know?" Forefinger at his Adam's apple, indicating the mugger's knife, he slid his other hand towards his belt and extracted a make-believe pistol. His thick, neatly trimmed mustache twitched as he leaned towards me, his trigger finger testing the non-existent gun.

"*Oye!*" he grinned, obviously enjoying the reliving of the moment, "'Make my day!' *lo dije.* '*Ay, hombre!*' *le dije.* 'Make my day!'"

MEDICINE WITHOUT A LICENSE

It appeared suddenly, as all little mountain villages do, a thousand square meters of graveled stumps, a corrugated metal lean-to, a thick rock wall half caved in, a couple of paths disappearing into pine forests.

Reynaldo Lucero cranked his seven-year-old government pickup across the road's deepest ruts and braked to a stop in front of an ancient adobe that, from its appearance, could have been a pre-historic cave dwelling.

"Mata," he thrust both elbows against the steering wheel, shook his head and mumbled under his breath, "Greater downtown Mata, the *chaboches* call it. The *indigenas* call it something else."

Stiff-legged, thirsty, our backs sore and kidneys jolted by two hours of roads that hardly were more than mountain trails, we slid out of the pickup. (The only vehicle we'd passed going either way had been a steaming International four-ton without doors, windshields or hood, its rattling welded-together bin loaded with logging slag.)

Lucero squinted at his watch, wiped his mouth and chin with the back of his hand and turned towards the tarpaulin-covered boxes in the bed behind the cab, as a few figures took shape among the disintegrating buildings. Gray, slow-moving, watchful, they seemed to have been created by the dust that the pickup had stirred up when we'd swung into the clearing.

His hands working at the ropes he'd tied to hold the containers in place, Lucero ignored all but one of them moving towards us from the adobe. All that I could see was a muffled pile of sweaters and scarves topped by a huge knit cap. The voice emerging from this bundle was surprisingly high and squeaky for its bearer's broad-shouldered, bull-necked bulk.

Lucero pulled a can of cold Modelo from the big ice chest he'd refilled in Ocampo, held one out to me and slid a third one across the top of the cab for the figure inside the sweaters, who caught it and tossed it back.

"*Gracias,*" a dark, porcine face emerged from the bundling, "but it doesn't sit well with me in the afternoon."

Lucero introduced the pile of sweaters as "Fierro, Mata's only truly permanent resident." An *indigena*, but not a Tarahumara — a Mayo from closer to Ciudad Obregon — Fierro had come to the mining camps years before, when drillers and burros still were pulling copper out of the mountains, and had stayed to become the storekeeper and mechanic, sheriff and road repairer, living off game he hunted and tortillas that occasional passers-through brought him. He rubbed his thick, liver-colored tongue across yellow teeth between phrases as he talked about the Taras who lived in and around the once bustling camp and about the "*maestro*" who'd arrived earlier that morning and had gone down the steep slope across the road to a Tara rancho in the valley below.

"He knows you're coming; he'll be up soon."

Lucero nodded and lifted his cold Modelo. "It's not like we have any place better to go," he sighed.

Forty minutes later the maestro appeared, a grimacing robot whose chin and neck were encased in a plaster cast, the outcome, he explained with self-effacing annoyance, of a fall off a mule he'd tried to ride into an old mining camp across the Divide.

"Salvador Geraldo, *a sus ordenes*," he answered my handshake with a touch of his fingers, the grimace widening into an apology that handshakes, among other physical activities, caused him sharp jerks of pain. He was, as Lucero and Fierro had related while we were waiting, neither a teacher nor a doctor, but served the indigenas in both of those capacities and as an ombudsman, courier and caretaker as well.

A dozen or more indigenas, most of whom had followed the maestro from their little vegetable patches and cave homes down the slope, gathered around the pickup. Forced by his cast and neck and shoulder braces to move mechanically, like a block figure on a pivot, the maestro pushed himself to a perch on the tailgate and extended his arms to a woman he obviously had treated on previous occasions.

She approached slowly, the child she carried in a coarse serape sling swaying back and forth as she moved. A short deep crease scarred one cheek, tying her mouth against a lower incisor when she spoke, her voice a mere whisper that the maestro craned forward to try to understand.

"Ask her about the diarrhea," he grimaced to Fierro through gritted teeth.

Face still muffled beneath collars, knit cap and mufflers, Fierro hulked over to him, a disagreeable cast to his seemingly uncooperative expression. But his high voice — almost soprano — had a pleasant, conciliatory cadence as he spoke to her.

The woman nodded, small delicate fingers lifting to brush something from her cheek. Momentarily in bright sunlight as clouds shifted over the dense, rustling pines above us, her features softened into childlike, fearful veneration, and I realized that she was much younger than I'd thought at first.

Geraldo called to Lucero for some kind of medicine. I pulled myself into the pickup to pass a carton forward. Geraldo fumbled through his ski jacket pockets for a bent pair of bifocals, one stem of which had been replaced by a piece of coat hanger, put them on and inspected the ampules and ointments I handed him. (I noticed that a number of the cardboard containers bore labels in English: *Doctors' Samples/Not for Sale.*)

Because of the cast, Geraldo had to hold the carton at arms' length to read the writing. His voice and Lucero's reverberated off the rock wall behind the adobe as they argued the relative dangers of giving the child adult dosages. The maestro winced with pain every time he tried to turn his injured neck, but he counted out the boxes of vials of prescription medicine, repeating and re-repeating to the woman instructions for its use.

While the maestro portioned out more 10-day cycles of the intestinal medicine to shy, shadowy Tarahumaras who'd edged closer to the pickup, he remarked over his shoulder that he and Lucero really had no way of knowing whether the handouts would forestall an epidemic; "but it does something, maybe it gives them a chance."

Passing out penicillin he was more casual, although he admitted that he never could get his patients to take it consistently enough to actually cure the tuberculosis that many of them had contacted.

"But it retards it, it gives their bodies something to fight with," he muttered as Lucero and I dug through boxes on the back of the pickup to hand him supplies. In voices that lacked real humor he and Lucero joked that someday, sure as Hell, the *federales* would bust the two of them for trafficking in illegal drugs.

Before the Tarahumaras could melt back into the forest, Lucero pulled some hooded sweatshirts adorned with *USC Trojans* logos out of a pasteboard container and tossed them to Fierro to distribute. From another corner of the pickup bed he extracted a crate of half-liter packages of condensed orange juice. Fierro ripped the lids off several of the containers and passed them around, gesturing and ordering, in Tarahumara, that they drink some now and save the rest until later.

That night, bundled beneath coarse Indian serapes but comfortable on foam mattresses tugged from boxes in Lucero's traveling storehouse, the three of us talked about the mountains and about our families and about various things that we'd done and seen. Geraldo told me that, though a *chaboche*, he was a native Chihuahuan and was not by trade a teacher but a mason.

He first had come to the Sierras to "relax, forget the mess I'd made of my marriage, contemplate the beauty of the mountains"; had built a rock house "overlooking a beautiful valley" and gradually, affected by friendships he had formed with some of the indigenas, had accepted a provisional license to teach at a rural school. The district still listed him as an in-school teacher, and paid him a small salary, but his teaching had evolved into "my henchmanship with my friend here, practicing medicine without a license."

Lucero drew his salary as a health inspector from an office in Chihuahua City but had badgered several agencies, including the World Health Organization, a couple of Lions' Clubs in California and the International Red Cross, into contributing money, medicines and goods for the isolated villages. He missed being with his sons and daughter, he said, and bragged about their athletic accomplishments. ("The boys, they are good — first-string in every sport they try — but the youngest, my daughter, she is superlative! She could turn out to be a professional!"). Each said he would not — could not — continue this lifestyle forever, but each admitted that he felt a kind of addiction to do what he was doing, knowing that there was a need; and neither would feel comfortable just sitting in an office or teaching in a learn-by-rote primary school.

Just before I went to sleep, I remembered Reynaldo Lucero sighing, "it's not like we have any place better to go..." and I smiled, thinking that in fact, Mata, right now, really was the best place that we possibly could be.

CHAPTER 6. THE BAJA ABERRATION

TOO CLOSE TO HELL

Anchoring Baja California's northern passage to the United States is a shantytown-surrounded melee of nearly four million men, women and children, few of them permanent, many of them desperate and most of them poor. Paraphrasing the old saw, "Mexico is too far from God and too close to the United States," importer Mario Cota asserts that Tijuana, by contrast, "is too far from Mexico and too close to Hell!"

It wasn't always that way. An Ellison-White Chautauqua lecturer began his description of a visit to pre-World War I Tijuana:

> Two or three bands were playing simultaneously discordant energetic tunes. The main street, a wide cavern from which and into which various dusty figures emerged and disappeared, sported dozens of sturdy false-fronted stores, a stage station, a livery, a bull ring and hundreds of raucous little stalls, all of which seemed simultaneously to be selling hot peppers, steaming bits of steer heads and vile drinks sold variously as *'veza*, *'kila* and *pulchay*.

Countering a claim made by a San Diego newspaper's 1980s historical review, "Tijuana didn't amount to much" before the 1920s, Tijuana civil rights activist Juan Ruiz Lopez laughed and told me that "before 1920, neither did San Diego!" Each city had its missions, its beaches and its little orange and lemon groves (and San Diego had a harbor and naval base) but each was surrounded by farm country; crossing the border was a civility that involved waving to the customs' official and commenting on the weather. Some Mexican maps published before 1900 put Tijuana on the U.S. side of the border; others spelled the city's name "Tia Juana" or "Tia Juana del Pacifico."

The coups d'états, insurrections, forced migrations and nationalizations that altered the political and social structures of the rest of Mexico throughout the 19th and early 20th centuries scarcely affected Tijuana. Like Bisbee, Cananea, Tombstone and Yuma, it was a territorial frontier town run as much by whim and six-gun as it was by merchants or politicians. *Out West* magazine in 1902 described it as "a sunny little *pueblo* filled with curio shops whose proprietors seemed more inclined to talk about each other than to sell their colorful hand-made products."

Most of Tijuana's permanent Mexican population had come from other parts of the republic: miners pushed northwestward from Michoacan and Sonora, teamsters, horse traders and cowboys, farmers attracted to the thin strips of arable land bordering the Pacific, lumberjacks, field hands returning to Mexico from the United States, crabbers, shrimpers and professional fishermen. The hills surrounding the town hosted runaway Apaches from the San Carlos Reservation in Arizona and refugee Yaquis from Porfirio Díaz's purge of their northern Sonora homelands.

A majority of the mercantile stores were run by Jewish peddlers who'd set up shop on the main streets; many of the restaurants, laundries and groceries bore names like Yee, Yuen and Chang. Stores sold American as well as Mexican products and many of the larger and more expensive homes belonged to English investors who were trying to develop the mining and range lands of north-central Baja.

The shantytowns that crept down the slopes leading away from the central business district alternately burned up or were washed away in rainstorms swept northward by the Santa Ana winds. These shantytowns housed a polyglot of poor workmen, runaway sailors, half-blood American Indians, fugitive gunmen and petty criminals, opium addicts, derelicts, drifters and prostitutes. The *federales* swept through now and then to restore order but the town government (like that of most Western towns in the United States) derived from the permanent middle class who hired Wyatt Earp types to protect their investments.

The main artery leading to Tijuana from Sonora and Chihuahua ran through the United States, and it is from the United States that Tijuana has drawn many aspects of its personality. Jose Ruiz Lopez has studied the city's history as well as its crises as a border city separating distinct and often antagonistic cultures.

He contends that Tijuana has provided California with an alter ego — a dangerous dark side replete with all that conservative California wants and needs but would rather keep out of its own fenced yard. From shelves and boxes and bookcases in his cramped, document-stuffed housing development casita, where he lives alone beside his television, a telephone that rings constantly, an old electric typewriter and snapshots of his children, Jose Ruiz Lopez insists that Tijuana is a testimony to free market responsiveness in action.

Tijuana was California's first Las Vegas, Ruiz Lopez contends. Its distance from Mexico City "protected it" from Mexican authority and law. By the same token, the fact that it was part of Mexico gave Tijuana immunity from U.S. regulations.

As laws in the United States became more restrictive, the frontier — particularly Tijuana, given its proximity to the rapidly expanding southern California population — offered alternatives, both in commerce and lifestyle. Tijuana reacted to the U.S. Food and Drug Act of 1907, the Mann Act restricting prostitution, and California laws aimed at gambling by providing the proscribed services on its side of the border.

"Then came Prohibition!" Ruiz Lopez chuckled the last time that I visited his casita. Dark and angular, his taut skin encasing strong cheekbones that show few wrinkles despite the years that have grayed his thinning hairline and put a slight limp in his walk, Ruiz Lopez spread newspaper clippings from the 1920s across his lap.

The little cantinas, he continued, became lavish night clubs. Smugglers not only shipped thousands of cases of tequila, beer and rum across the border but imported intoxicants like Scotch and bourbon and transported them by car, boat, burro and train.

What drug smugglers would be doing 50 years later, booze smugglers were doing in the '20s. Yellowed newspaper clippings describe speed boat races that were fronts for smuggling operations, truck convoys burying their cargoes of booze in the desert, *gasolineras* that pumped pure whiskey instead of kerosene. Everything that southern California wanted — and couldn't have — Tijuana provided. And it continued to provide it throughout the Second World War and the post-War boom that followed.

A few people got rich — exceedingly rich — during these years of Free Market responsiveness. Millions of others lived in dire poverty. (Tijuana's "official" population in 1997 was 2.2 million residents, but Jose Lucero E. of Tijuana's University of Baja California Norte places the actual count, including transient residents of the shantytowns that cling to the city's outskirts, at 3-3.75 million.) One of Tijuana's biggest businesses during the last two decades has been in human beings. It has been the pipeline for Mexico's displaced poor to reach jobs in the United States.

"Of every ten persons who comes through Tijuana, hoping to work on The Other Side, only one reaches that goal without being robbed, beaten, raped, tortured or killed." Lucero E. cites figures gathered by government and university investigative agencies. A quiet, reticently outgoing scholar whose straight black hair perpetually flaps across his broad, strong-boned forehead, Lucero E. listed five distinctive forces converging on the city that have compressed the "sunny little pueblo filled with curio shops" of a hundred years ago into a hectic tangle of rich and poor, immigrant, minimum-wage worker and tourist:

- The northward thrust, estimated at 1,000 persons a day, of rural farm workers forced to seek work away from their native pueblos in order to survive;
- The southward thrust of returning *indocumentados* either deported by the United States or victimized by their experiences there;
- A high birth rate among the city's poorer residents that has created a generation caught between their parents' rural values and the actualities of city life;
- An accelerated expansion of low-level industrial jobs in Tijuana itself, many of which hire only young, untrained workers for short periods of time; and
- Increased mechanization in both the U.S. and Mexico that has decreased the need for *mano de obra* but increased the costs of housing, food and transportation.

The compacting of these forces on nearly four million people has created "an ungovernable city of tremendous vitality," Lucero E. notes. It is a city "vibrating with aggression" as well, a city manipulated by politicians who have broken away from Mexico's mainstream PRI organization and oligarchs whose private jets whisk them across continents and whose bougainvillea-draped mansions are protected by highly paid, well-armed security guards. At the same time, Ruiz Lopez told me, Tijuana is a city in which hundreds of thousands of people daily jam against each other, "inventing ways to survive.

"It's like three million flies have descended upon one carcass and are feeding on each other!

"If you don't believe me, just look around you when you leave my house. People will jump on your car windshields to clean them. They'll trip you to shine your shoes. They'll splash mud on you and beg a few centavos to wipe it off. They'll find you a place to park, they'll fling themselves in the gutter and let you cross through the offal by walking on their backs. They'll sell you anything from their 12-year-old sister to a wristwatch they've stolen from the guy who just crossed the street in front of you!"

They'll also tell stories, Ruiz Lopez continued, about beatings and shakedowns and lies. If there is any constant to life in Tijuana, it is fear of the police. In the eyes of the police, Ruiz Lopez says, every Tijuanan is a criminal. By definition, an immigrant without papers becomes a criminal the minute he or she steps across the border into U.S. territory. From among notes typed and paper-clipped together with handwritten testimony and newspaper clippings, Ruiz Lopez extracted what he told me was a typical story:

Jose Frausto Ramos, 26, and his wife, Maria del Carmen, 24, coming from Mexico City, left two children there with Maria del Carmen's relatives. Paid a *pollero* $250 each to take them across the frontier. Destination: San Francisco, California. Apprehended with six others. Jose accused of resisting arrest; hand- and leg-cuffed; left for 10-12 hours without food or water in detention cell. Maria del Carmen delivered to Mexican authorities at border. Forced to submit to strip search; threatened with incarceration unless she paid $40 U.S. for her release. Paid $32 (all she had in her possession). Solicited by brothel keeper; angrily declined offer. Jose turned over to Mexican authorities 16 hours later. Paid $50 for his release. Finally reunited with Maria del Carmen 11 days later. Shoulder so sore from handcuffing he could not lift his left arm higher than his waist. Finally found employment in a *maquila* making pirated music tapes, Maria del Carmen as sub-minimum wage employee in a plant stamping out plastic washbowls. Both still planning to attempt more border crossings.

Ruiz Lopez said he could document hundreds of similar cases involving the U.S. border patrol and hundreds of others involving California and Arizona sheriff's and police departments. Almost without exception, he claimed, the victims were indocumentados like the Fraustos — poor people who'd invested everything they had in attempts to better themselves economically, none of whom were criminals until they were forced into illegal work by U.S. immigration laws.

His files also show that, shortly after the passage of the Simpson-Rodino Immigration Act by the U.S. Congress in December 1986, Mexican labor unions petitioned the United Nations to investigate abuses against indocumentados. Mexican university investigator Juventino Wins labeled the pogroms initiated by Simpson-Rodino "an active aggression" on the part of U.S. law enforcement officials and Mexican Foreign Secretary Bernardo Sepulveda publicly denounced the ways that Mexican citizens were being treated by U.S. immigration officials.

Ruiz Lopez's files reveal that would-be immigrants were no safer on the Mexican side of the border. By 1987 the extortions and assaults on indocumentados being deported into Tijuana had gotten so bad that the new director of Immigration Services, Alfredo Alvarez, brought criminal charges against an handful of the agents who'd been working in his department. And Jorge Bustamante, president of the Colegio de la Frontera Norte in Tijuana, stated on national television that he doubted that anyone could find a Tijuana police commander who hadn't gouged undocumented workers for payoffs or bribes at one time or another.

"You have a river of people that is getting deeper by the hour pouring into Tijuana," Ruiz Lopez affirms. "They are drowning; but they are beaten when they try to flow over the banks to one side or the other.

"What are they to do? Work, steal, beg, sell themselves or something else. There is not room for them all so they clamber on top of each other to get out. Of course they will try to cross to *The Other Side.* No matter how bad it is, they tell themselves, it can't be worse than the river they're in.

"Can it?"

Igniting Everything

Rafael Duarte was in a hurry. Which was not surprising. Rafael Duarte always was in a hurry, even when he had no place to go. He grabbed my sleeve to yank me past an overturned bucket of half-dried concrete, sidestepped an oncoming bicyclist, and waved towards a pair of dirty beach umbrellas propped awkwardly above open baskets of tomatoes, chilis and haba and algarroba pods half a block down the narrow street.

"You think these streets, they're dangerous? *Chíngale, mano!* These streets in Mexico City, here in this *barrio,* where no tourists come, where sons of *putas, chingale!* lurk everywhere, ready to slit our throats for a few *pesos*, for our shoes, *chinga!* for entertainment! Here it is dangerous?

"No, '*migo*, I tell you, no, here it is nothing. No matter how vicious the *pandilleros*, how ugly the whores, where I spent my boyhood was worse, ten times worse, twenty times worse — a hundred times worse! The sewer of the world! Here, *oyeme!* This? Nothing! A playground, ha!

"I tell you, *mano*, I know!

"I come from Tijuana!"

I'd met Duarte because of my bad Spanish. He'd overheard me talking to a taxi driver and intervened. At the same time that he was telling me that I spoke well, he half-gargled, half-shouted a *modismo*-laced Spanish that the taxi driver answered in kind.

One of eight children born into a family of laborers who'd migrated from Guadalajara to the border in the late 1960s, Duarte claimed that he'd had the run of Tijuana by the time he was twelve. One of his earliest discoveries, he said, was the Agua Caliente race track, where he hustled drunken tourists who didn't know that "a five-dollar tip equaled a [Tijuana] construction worker's daily pay."

He pawed through the fruit beneath the umbrellas as his expostulations continued. The proprietress, a youngish woman whose tiredness made her seem old, gestured as though to warn me, "Pay him no mind"; but he waved her gesture aside.

In the '70s, when he was growing up, he said, Tijuana was a boomtown. There were tourists everywhere. Whatever class consciousness other might have felt, Duarte lacked. He had friends among immigrant Mixtecos, money-squandering gringos and itinerant street hustlers. His "territory" was the downtown north to the red light district.

"To the 'Devil's Bar,' *sí!* Tourists, there I'd take them! Flaming torches outside, *fígate!* Inside everything red — bar, lights, the tables. *Ay!* And this *pendejo!* Big! *Pinche monstruo!* Painted red, *sí!* He was! Hair to toe! Wearing a little, you know, jock strap, nothing more! Dancing, pinching the women, *ay!* The blondes, the *guera* tourists! Young! Knockouts! Giggling, laughing, drunk, dancing! Oh! *Pinches* dreams I had about them! *Ay, cabrón!*"

Duarte's one possession, he said, was the guitar that a race track tout gave him.

"I played. I sang. *Chinga!* I went everywhere. I knew everything! The streets, the bars, hey! I was young. Everybody liked me — everybody! *Cholos!* It would scare you to look at them — tattooed, their bodies, faces! *Chinga!* Junkies — yes! Smoking their sh—, hanging out. They would give me errands, they could trust me, see? Ha! Nothing so bad like that in Mexico [City], nothing!"

Though tourists — sailors, construction workers, college students — occasionally paid Duarte to play for them, it was from prostitutes that he earned most of his performance money. Most of them were young and naive, girls from ranchos, from poor families; they "dreamed *telenovelas*, babies, tract homes on *The Other Side*."

They would want to hear sentimental songs, love songs; Duarte remembered, "I was little brother, *sí*, to all of them."

Until he was fourteen or fifteen, he said he didn't see Tijuana as good or bad: It was what it was. But he did see people as good or bad for what they did, and gradually it was the bad that overwhelmed his awareness and it was the bad that he fantasized destroying.

"*Sí!* Running down Calle Primera I would pretend my guitar was a flame thrower. Out from it, fire! A huge jet! Igniting everything! Shuush! Up would go *polleros*! In flames, the police! Shrieking! Burning to a crisp! Bullets from the *pistolas* in their belts exploding!

"Yes, I would run, pointing, firing! An inferno, the Jai Alai palace! Tourists bursting into flames, bits of ashes, their money — all of it! And the night clubs! Erupting! The Molino Rojo a tower of fire! The Manhattan! The Scorpio Negro! Exploding! Burning! Until everything, everything was gone!"

His fantasy ended, Duarte grunted, not with flames, but with water. Floods gushing down the hillside above the Duartes' home ripped the walls apart and grooved a gully through what had been their *terreno*.

Convinced he could fashion a better life as an artisan-musician in Mexico City, Duarte left Tijuana, and returned only briefly "to, *digo*, be surprised, *mano*, that the buildings are not rubble and ashes. Just to see them, *ay! chingada!* I feel again the dreams, imagine the flame thrower, shuush! the rich houses of the *capos*, the maquiladoras, everything, burning! Pinnacles of fire, high in the sky..!"

I ducked as his gyrating arms almost struck me. He laughed and grasped my shoulder. For a moment, serious, he nodded his head, then shrugged.

"If you could do it, it would be good. It would be the only way to make this city fit for people to live in again."

Nothing Is Simple

"Hell, yes, I was there — everybody in Tijuana was in Lomas Taurinas the day that Colosio got shot, not only everybody who lived there but everybody who saw the clips on television, everybody who read about the assassination in the newspapers. I've talked to hundreds of people who said they were there, people who couldn't find Lomas Taurinas on a map, much less find their way there in a car. They say they heard the shots, they say they saw the blood spurt from Colosio's head or neck or shoulders; they say they were only a few feet away from him when he fell, they say they just had shaken his hand, or just had spoken to him; they say they were right beside him, and saw that he recognized the man who shot him — even pronounced his name — but they insist that the *politicos* edited that off the television clips.

"They say a man beside him held him, pulled him backwards so that he could be shot. Even things that they invented — things they knew weren't true — they began to believe after a while. It was like that day in your county, that day that your President Kennedy was shot.

"What did I see? You want Quintin Medina's eye-witness account? The impeccably honest Quintin Medina, former newspaper reporter, failed farmer, private investigator Quintin Medina? You want the truth because you know I'm a loquacious radical: I quit all my writing jobs because I wouldn't put up with the sh— I got from editors?

"No, okay, I apologize, I don't need to drip acid. These are nice people here, this is a nice little rancho, you wouldn't know it was so close to Ensenada. Grab a couple more beers from the porch, we'll stand by the fire, eh? Like in the movies — men around a big open fire, kicking the chaparral roots to make them burn.

"Now, about Colosio — I'll tell you the truth: I saw what most of the ten thousand people who there at Lomas Taurinas saw: Nothing. I saw nothing. *Nada.*

"Listen, I went there because I was curious, and I had subpoenas to serve not too far away. It was hot, and traffic police already were blocking off the streets. Colosio's campaign people knew what they were doing: There were PRI banners everywhere, and people were waving and shouting like they were at a soccer game.

"God! The radios! Everybody seemed to keep turning the volume up to hear their own station and drown out those around them. All the little stores and stands were selling Pepsis and hot dogs and people were crowding onto rooftops, waving flags and banners and shooting off firecrackers and drinking beer.

"I wedged my way through to a window sill that I could stand on to see the parade route. I had a couple of bags of peanuts with me and I ate those while I was waiting. '*Ya vienen! Ya vienen!*' I heard time after time, but it was always just more PRI officials and police cars.

"Finally Colosio came. I had a good view of the street beneath me; even so, I couldn't actually see him. He was in a car — a big car, one of those Suburbans the officials around here always drive. Once I saw a white-sleeved arm reach out the window and wave, but I don't know for certain that it was him.

"The police were pushing at the crowd — remember, there were hundreds of police, *uniformados* and plain clothes — to clear a path for him and his campaign people. The streets, now, were packed with people; every time the police pushed one way, the crowd would push back in from the other. It went on that way even when Colosio got out of the car — police had to shove people away to get the door open and to get him to a pickup parked a little ways away. He seemed to stumble trying to climb into the back of it; some people helped him and someone in the pickup handed him a microphone.

"Okay, think about it: If you were planning an assassination — you wanted to make sure you got the job done — wouldn't that be your best chance? You put sharpshooters in two or three buildings to get a crossfire; your target's wearing a starched white shirt; the hillside's steep enough to give you an angle down on him. You even — à la Oswald — station a sacrificial lamb who thinks he's the lone assassin, and have him blast away too.

"Of course, that's not what happened. From where I was standing, I saw Colosio jump down from the pickup — there were hands stretched out to help him — then I couldn't see him anymore. Remember, he was a short man — shorter than most of the people around him. Whoever was in charge of the sound system put on music and cranked up the volume. I was watching the crowd — not just where Colosio was, but all around. You could see the general movement of the bodyguards: The crowd kept giving way and filling in behind them.

"Then there was what looked like a whirlpool of people right in the middle, where Colosio had been, and ripples rushing outward from it. The music stopped abruptly. Around where I was clinging to the windowsill, people still were shouting, '*Viva!* Colosio for Mexico!' — things like that. It took a long time for them to realize what had happened. And nobody heard the shots.

"The scene has been going around and around in my mind ever since. I keep thinking about Aburto. How did he know he could get through that crowd to get close enough to shoot Colosio? Hell, maybe he didn't know; maybe he just had the wild idea that he could pull it off and was determined enough to try it.

"You know, he had time; if he started shoving his way through when Colosio started to speak, he would have gotten close enough, and he could have been, you know, fighting this way and that way to get within a few feet of the man. He could have been rebuffed several times and still made it.

"You see, if he had help, if it were planned, why would he try to do it then? I mean, wouldn't it seem suicidal to you? An assassin with only a handgun, in that crowd: What chance would he have to get away?

"Unless — now listen, I don't know anything, not for sure, this is just Quintin Medina's speculation — but suppose whoever planned it had four or five Aburto Martinezes in that crowd, each one with a *pistola*, each one on a hero's mission — or paid assassin's mission, or martyr's mission, whichever you prefer — and each one thinking he was the only guy trying to shoot Colosio? They're all trying to close in on him, but Aburto gets there first? Bam! Colosio's blown away, the other would-be shooters disappear. Mission accomplished.

"Now, what's wrong with this is — what's wrong with all the scenarios you read about, it seems to me — is that Aburto still is alive. If somebody had wiped him out — like Lee Harvey Oswald was wiped out — but instead of Aburto, it's the police chief who is shot a month after the assassination.

"Did the same people who had Colosio killed kill him?

"You've finished your beer? Ah, mine's gone, too — no matter, I'm staying here at the rancho tonight, I can drink all I want. I'll drive back to Rosarito tomorrow. Now, what was I... Yes, okay, I've talked to lots of people. Ordinary people. Nobody — I mean nobody — believes that Aburto planned the whole thing and carried it out by himself. Not with the other assassinations that have occurred since.

"Some say it's drug dealers. Some say it's jealous old-line PRI politicians who didn't trust this Colosio. Some say it's a fanatical left-wing group — although really, if you think about it, that makes the least sense.

"Now, if it were a party job — an old-line PRI politician wanting to get rid of Colosio — the very men who are guarding the accused killer, Aburto, in the federal prison really could be his protectors, no? Keeping him from contact with the outside, feeding him the lies he's telling. Then, sometime in the future, he escapes — or is shot trying to escape, or somebody is shot and he gets a new identification and winds up in a mansion in Panama, or Columbia, or Spain?

"Hey, let's face it, it's happened before. This is a very romantic country, this Mexico you're writing about, and this is Tijuana — everything seems like a plot in Tijuana.

"No, I tell you, that's the truth. Nothing is easy here, nothing is simple. Nothing is like it appears to be on the surface. Business deals, real estate deals, government appointments — they involve a lot of money changing hands in the twilight. A rich man wants to acquire the land next to his, what does he do? He meets with an official. He buys lunch. He buys dinner. He locates fur coats for the official's wife. Jeeps for his business. Parties for his friends. These gifts, they all say: 'Do it, but don't tell me how you do it.'

"The official meets with one, two, three people. Like the rich man, he spreads gifts. He promises future rewards. 'Do it,' his methods indicate, 'do it — I don't care how.'

"That's the process. That's the plot. All the way down the line. The rich man acquires the land he wants — he doesn't know if anybody got hurt, he doesn't know what politicians were involved, he doesn't know what the bankers manipulated, he doesn't know if the police made threats. He just knows that the system works and none of it shows up on the surface.

"Okay, a rich man wants a presidential candidate shot? He meets with someone — someone he can trust. Gifts start to spread. Promises are made. Way down the line, there's an Aburto. What does he know?

"I'll tell you what he knows: He knows how to shoot a revolver. Past that, he knows what you know. What I know: Nothing.

"Or everything, eh? He is wise in his knowing that he knows no more than he does.

"Write it down, my friend. Write it down and say, 'This is Mexico.'"

The pistol shots that abruptly ended Donaldo Colosio Murietta's life shattered an already cracked picture that millions of Mexicans were clinging to: a picture of a land of peace and beauty, beset with problems but proud of its ancestry, customs and accomplishments.

Less than three months before that fatal day in Lomas Taurinas, a well-trained band of indigena insurrectionists had yanked control of Mexico's southeastern-most state out of federal government control. The photogenic and pizzazzy leader of the Chiapan insurrectionists, *subcomandante* Marcos, came across as a romantic cavalier in a country that for nearly two hundred years had worshipped revolutionary heroes.

The Army came across as a bunch of frightened youngsters led by bureaucratic nincompoops hopping around with their feet in their mouths. And the gunman who shot Colosio came across as a confused Lee Harvey Oswald saying what he thought people wanted to hear as he was hustled from prison to prison, allegedly beaten, threatened, compromised and bribed.

Television cameras showed arresting officers and prosecuting attorneys, governors, private investigators, administration flaks and purported eye witnesses falling over each other to relate or invent new accounts of the crime. They showed police lying about their whereabouts, arresting purported accomplices and then releasing them.

They showed Mexico's attorney general announcing that the crime was "the work of a single assassin," a haunting reminder of similar statements made after John F. Kennedy's assassination. They showed a private investigator's comparison of two official photos of purported assassin Mario Aburto, one showing him standing against a tape that measured him at 1.64 meters (5' 1/2") and the other showing him standing against a tape that measured him at 1.73 meters (5'3 1/4"), a full three inches difference.

What they showed was all glittering surface, not the dark undersides. They did not explain why Aburto was questioned by various sets of interrogating officers, some of whom had no connection with each other. They did not explain his whereabouts, before or after the shooting, and did not divulge lost tape recordings and memoranda about his supposed confessions.

They only reported, but did not explain, other killings, like that of former senator Jose Francisco Ruiz Massieu and Catholic Cardinal Juan Posadas Ocampo. And they only reported, but could not explain, the massive dissatisfaction that affected every Mexican in every walk of life.

No one ever will know the full story behind the assassination of the presidential candidate, just as no one ever will know the whole story about who killed John F. Kennedy, or why. Time gradually sweeps away the details behind killings and coups, wars and elections, but feelings remain, and the joy or the sadness that these changes generate seeps into the beings of generations to come.

The blood that was spilled touched all of Mexico.

Closed Eyes

"The federal police? Yes, I was one of them. For many years, until I retired. Dishonest? I would say that I was not. Explain to your American friend, señora, that within the system one cannot be totally virtuous. I was well-thought-of, always. But sometimes one has to close one's eyes to things one cannot do anything about."

Tetsuhiro Nomura pressed the tips of his fingers together, pausing as he considered each neatly clipped nail, the heavy rings on the third and fourth fingers of each hand, the slight protrusions of the veins along the backs of his wrists. Then he slowly opened his hands and peered at the three of us sitting with him in the darkened, almost vacant cocktail lounge.

"Wait; yes, it is true, within the organization — the federal police, the PGR — there were...how to explain it? Clubs, there were clubs, little groups, and you did not always know what secrets they had. But, hear me now, hear me, as police we did what police are supposed to do, we made arrests, we investigated crimes, we risked our lives."

A sturdy, compactly built man with thinning hair and a penetrating stare heightened by the lenses of rimless glasses, Nomura lifted a speck of dust from the rim of his whiskey glass. His friend Fermin Karim Beltran, who sat with us, had explained that "the *agente*," who was born and reared in Tijuana of immigrant Japanese parents, didn't "drink like he used to do" and Nomura had laughingly confirmed, "The hangovers aren't as fun as they used to be." The fourth member of our group, Victoria Agundez Alonso, had negotiated our get-together through Beltran, who had known both Victoria and Nomura for a number of years.

"So, like me, like all of Mexico, you want to know what really happened on that fateful day? The man who was supposed to become president is dead, his campaign manager has taken his place, a half-nuts mechanic is in jail for the crime? There must have been a cover up, you think? By whom? Ah! Of course, you say! The federal police!

"So, there is a cover up, and for no one to come forth and expose it, this cover up must exist on a grand scale, that's what you're thinking, right? Ah, but here, you see, here's the rub, here you should know something about police — all police. It is typical — here in Mexico, in the United States, everywhere in the world — for one police group not to let other police groups know what it is doing.

"Now, you see, within the various police groups, the members stick together. I can tell you, from my own experience, of a *comandante*, all right? This *comandante* has charges filed against him. *Denuncias.* Not for minor things. I mean, this is not a nice man, you would not invite to a poetry reading, eh? The charges were for rape. For homicide. For torture. He is put on what we would call 'administrative leave.' He is an embarrassment to his *delegación* in the Federal District. They need to get rid of him.

"So, what happens? I'll tell you. Two years later I run into him. Here, in Tijuana. How did he get there. Ah! I will tell you.

"It turns out that the high muckamuck he had worked for in the Federal District had been transferred here. Now this muckamuck, what did he want most in his new position? He wanted his own...henchman, no? So he 'arranged' that the problems that this *comandante* — his old henchman — was having were taken care of. How? Yes, well, money, of course. But not just that. In the police, you see, sometimes someone owes someone else a favor.

"Suppose — as has happened — there had been an 'arrangement' with, say, a well-to-do politician. A big property deal. A kidnapping — well, you know, whatever. To make sure this is not exposed — exposure would ruin the important politician's career and ruin the muckamuck as well — this muckamuck needs a trusted officer right under him to undo any type of investigation. So there is a bond created between the muckamuck and the henchman. Almost like father to son. A dependency.

"And so, of course, the henchman, well, he has the same situation. He needs 'his son.' With each promotion, each transfer, he takes 'his son' with him. It doesn't matter that 'his son' is dishonest, what matters that 'his son' does the job of protection. Even if it means 'taking a fall,' going to prison, killing somebody for the 'father.'

"You see, this process keeps building. Each father has a 'son.' Or 'sons.' Like knots, they form. Beneath the knots, more knots. It becomes like a lot of ropes tied together. Finally, it is impossible to undo any of them."

"Impossible!" Fermin Karim Beltran confirmed. "Impossible, because you cannot unravel them from the bottom. I mean to tell you, it is the 'sons' who have their 'fathers' by the b—s!"

Round-faced, round-shouldered, his features so smooth and regular that they nullified any point of singularity, he looked past rather than at us, a habit that he seemed to have developed and been unable to alter. Although not trained as an agent or investigator, he worked in an administrative capacity for the PGR, auditing, assessing and cataloguing properties that had been confiscated by the various agents.

"Okay, I am sorry for the language, I apologize," he reacted to Victoria's wince. "But it is true. I happen to know the *comandante* he is talking about.

"The facts about him really are, well, ugly; I would say very ugly. I happen to know because the *denuncias* followed him here, to Tijuana.

"It happened this way. Okay, now, as I understand it, a policeman who had worked for him in Mexico City was brought up on a lot of charges. They included 'depriving someone of his liberty.' You understand, no? Well, okay, this sort of is like kidnapping, you see, or it can be for arresting someone without filing proper charges against them.

"Anyway, okay, the person making the charges filed accusations for both a recent and a past occurrence, you see. The *denuncia* for the past occurrence also listed this *comandante* we are talking about. Then another person added another *denuncia* for the past occurrence, naming the *comandante*.

"Okay, now as the story unfolded, this is what happened. This *comandante* and his police took into custody some accused contrabanders. They took them to their offices in the *delegación* and separated the men from the women. According to the *denuncias*, while some of the agents 'interrogated' the men, some of the rest of them decided to, well, okay, I don't want to say anything offensive here, but what they did, you see, they violated the women. How many times I do not know but that, okay, that's not important.

"After they were through, well, okay, whenever that was, they told these women that if they tried to file any charges about the violations, well, the agents told them that they would cut important parts off of their husbands' bodies. Okay, now, the women, the women were timorous, frightened, they wanted to protect their husbands, they wanted out of the situation however they could get out of it.

"Okay, so maybe the charges against the men were reduced, I don't know. But one of the women did file charges. Perhaps her husband fled, or was not arrested, I don't know. I do know that this *comandante*, immediately he brought her into custody again and kept her there until she dropped the charges and said that she had come into his offices of her own free will.

"So, okay, five years later this woman signs a declaration telling what really happened. In this declaration she also described that the *comandante* tortured those that he arrested for other crimes in order to get confessions from them.

"So, this is the kind of 'son' that turns up in Tijuana. Even after he leaves the federal police, he has friends and influence. You think he would be capable of assassination?

"I tell you, *señor norteamericano*, he could do it and enjoy a good meal, a few drinks, right afterwards."

He also could cover his tracks. The 'father' for whom he had worked would have to continue protecting him or risk having his own malfeasances exposed. And though the men under him might have him "by the balls," they not only would lose their 'father' if they reported him, they would have difficulty making any charges stick because his connections to his own 'father' would provide him with everything from counter charges to perfectly conceived alibis.

More than one mid-level police official has been the recipient of a phone call or a visit from someone much higher on the totem pole telling them in no uncertain terms to drop a prosecution or a complaint. Failure to immediately conform could cost them not only their jobs but their lives.

This interweaving of protective knots becomes so extensive that every official virtually has every other official immobilized and, by the same token, has dozens of fingers squeezing his own. These knots strangled every step of the investigation into the assassination of president-to-be Donaldo Colosio Murietta. Each strand of evidence, each word of testimony, became so contaminated, so intertwined with other strands, that it no longer had any relevance.

Nor could it be seen by the many who'd closed their eyes.

The Gay Side

In Tijuana, "You don't ask if they have it, you ask, 'How much?' And when you hear the price, you say, 'I'll give you half that.' Especially if you're talking about sex.

"Or you just take, and don't pay at all."

Dave Shuler grew up on Chicago's South Side. His father, a construction worker, drank heavily; his mother "hung plastic images of Jesus and Mary everywhere in the house and prayed to the saints when she wasn't watching soap operas." After four years as an Air Force clerk, he went to college "and nearly graduated," he laughed, snubbing out his cigarette and, with detached amusement, watched the overfilled abalone shell he was using as an ashtray tilt sideways and coat the unfinished wooden shelf on which it was sitting with ashes and butts.

Like most cities, Shuler maintained, "T.J." is a complex of separate social and ethnic groups wrapped around each other.

"There was a painting here, in one of the galleries — I met the artist, a Mexican. The painting was all muscle and sinew, each of a different color, and each one had a different texture, you know, fabric and things like that worked into the paint. Like there was a farm worker muscle, you know, dark, glistening, like it was covered with sweat. And what looked like a burro's neck — I think it had real burro hair worked into the gray paint. And what looked like a whore's body. It was twisted, like it had been forced open.

"But the amazing thing about this picture, I mean there were, I don't know, thirty or forty of these shapes — the whole picture was shapes — was that none of these muscles seemed to connect with any of those twisted around them. I mean they were touching, but just the way this guy did them, the way he painted them, they all seemed to be separate, like something a huge storm jammed together, you know, so they were stuck where they were, so twisted up together that they couldn't get apart, I mean no single one of them could get loose, get free, they were that, you know, interlocked. But at the same time they didn't merge or blend, they were separate and, like, protected from each other.

"I think he called the painting 'Tijuana,' I don't know. But it was so, so....man, I don't know, so 'right on!' like we used to say. He had it down the way this place is. Look, man, look at those *colonias* where the Oaxacans live, the 'little Oaxacas,' man. They don't even speak Spanish in them. And, hey, look at the gays — the 'Gay Side' — they've got a Tijuana of their own. You come in from outside, you might not even know it existed. But it's big — there are a lot of them."

Shuler's contact with what he called "Gay T.J." was extensive but circumstantial and not, he insisted, "participatory." Like many gay communities, he suggested, "Gay T.J." attracted a diverse group that included many bilinguals and a swirl of artists, models, actors, photographers and college professors.

Many in this swirl did not live in Tijuana but in the United States. Some of them owned houses or cabanas in the nearby beach resorts like Rosarito; others came down for short or extended vacations, shared flats or condominiums or rented apartments or rooms from permanent members of Tijuana's gay community.

"Hey, they're tight. They do their thing and I don't knock them. What the hell, what do most men come to T.J. for? To get drunk and screw a whore. They're no different — maybe just more refined."

Surveying the splotched, chipped plaster walls of the apartment's main room, whose dominating feature was a wall-length bookcase filled with half-finished attempts at sculptures, books, pottery, crates, stacks of newspapers and old magazines, conch and abalone shells, bongs and a cow's skull, Shuler admitted his own "sense of refinement" might leave something to be desired. Nevertheless, I understood what he was trying to convey. Tijuana offered a different ambiance to the gays coming down to party than it did for the thousands of single (and married) men who swarmed across the border every night to head for the bars, brothels and pick-up joints in Tijuana's big red light district.

The gays stepped almost immediately into a familiar world marked off for — and by — them. Gay life in Tijuana is not radically different from gay life in New York, Hollywood or most other cities in the United States. As in the painting that Shuler described, it is connected to, but separate from, the rest of how Tijuana lives.

It has its own boundaries, identity and rules of conduct. It developed as a "sub-visible world," more clandestine than open. Chicano writer John Rechy describes this world as a shadowy, subterranean network of imitation and nuance where prostitution is easy, impersonal and approved of.

The "hunters" come to find young bodies and socialize with old friends. Their hangouts — night clubs, restaurants, baths, street corners — are exotic, fanciful, camp, but physically safe and not open to public scrutiny. Because Mexican law generally has chosen to disregard homosexuality rather than prosecute it as a vice or regulate it as a business, neither federal nor local authorities interfere with the "Gay Side's" goings on as long as it sticks to the shadows and doesn't trigger any media exposés.

This is quite different from what heterosexual singles find in the red light districts. "Boys Town" throbs with glitz and noise. Panderers line the streets. Cabbies hawk the "prettiest," "youngest" and "mos' fon" girls. Brothel doors swing open to everyone, from high school first-timers to scarred and drunken petty officers.

Women are everywhere — pretty women, many of them just recruited from the maquiladoras, or from financially strapped towns in the interior; they wiggle and beckon and paw and beg. As barmaids they bring beer and tequila, cadge drinks, solicit tricks. Nothing in Las Vegas compares with it, nothing along Sunset Strip.

The "Gay Side," too, has its sad and seedy aspects. Rechy describes young men caught up in "*La Vida*" ("the Life"). Many, like the central character of his novel, *City of Night*, grew up tyrannized by dictatorial fathers and over-nurtured by compensating mothers. This protagonist and young prostitutes like him fluctuate between a carefree giving over to "experiencing everything" and a paralyzing fear of forming emotional attachments of any kind.

Some of them define their homosexual participation in curious half-tones. Rechy describes young Chicanos who adopt only the male role in homosexual relationships and do not think of themselves as "homosexuals," but merely as men participating in "incomplete" sex acts.

Gradually, however, most of them get drawn into an obsessive predilection for a lifestyle they feel has chosen them, rather than one they have chosen to join. Many of those who are drawn in struggle against their own feelings; at the same time, they find a sanctuary in the identity that enables them to share their fear and alienation with others who, like them, sense only hostility in the world that surrounds them.

One only has to walk a few of Tijuana's streets at night to understand how important a sharing of that kind can be. Drivers who've just avoided collisions curse and wave their fists at each other. Clusters of young workmen, sharing paper bag-wrapped *ballenas* of beer, crowd other pedestrians off the sidewalks. Armed uniformed policemen accost teenage girls. Bands of children, their T-shirted arms impervious to cold or heat, dart among parked cars, assailing tourists and threatening ambulatory hot dog and taco vendors.

Eyes glare out from every doorway; vicious dogs growl behind every fence. The tired, the poor, the drunk, the weak, huddle in alleyways, beside trash can fires, around useless and abandoned vehicles. There is no way of telling in how much danger one might be — no way but to glare suspiciously at everything that moves, as everyone around you is doing. In all likelihood nothing will happen — but you don't know that. You can't be sure.

Not far away, the "Gay Side" exudes a different feeling. The danger is still there — and perhaps a heightened sense of contact and expectation — but something stronger, a sinew, seems to hold things together. It seems to give identity to those who belong.

If part of this identity is based on a need for shared secrecy, and on a cognizance of real or potential repression, it binds its members that much tighter. Even those who otherwise have little or nothing in common find a locus in that identity and they cling to it. Often, while they do so, they turn their backs on the heterosexual world.

Even as a separate sinew, a part of a painting that doesn't meld or merge with any other parts, Tijuana's "Gay Side" has more contact and finds easier acceptance with the hostile heterosexual world than many gay communities in the United States. Bisexuality long has been condoned (if not actually accepted) in most of Mexico.

The double standard that tacitly permits married men to have affairs but denies the same to married women considers seeking gratification from a homosexual prostitute the same as from a female prostitute. (The standard has many deviations: Married women often do have affairs; more men are killed by wives or mistresses than by any other familial acquaintances — and many who are not killed are stabbed, scratched or poisoned; young male prostitutes are held up to public ridicule; to call a man a *maricón* can trigger a fist, knife or gun fight from which there's no backing down, just as calling a woman a *puta* can set off violent reprisals from friends, relatives or customers, even if the allegations are true.)

Not every person of homosexual bent necessarily is part of Tijuana's gay community, however. Many are lost in "No Man's Land," Dave Shuler believes.

Twisting his shoulders uncomfortably, lighting a cigarette and putting in down, he again surveyed the littered apartment he shared with a sometimes girl friend who, like him, was American and who, like him, was a dabbler in things artistic and hallucinogenic, and mumbled, "You see, that, you see, is where the painting didn't work. I mean, yes, it worked emotionally, but on a factual level — on a factual level it should have had a lot of little loose threads, snipped off threads, that don't fit any of the sinews."

Everyone in Tijuana is looking for something, Shuler believes, and "nobody is finding it. Not all of it, at any rate. Or they're finding — finding so much misery spread around so thick that it makes them feel like their own misery isn't so great.

"Maybe that's what makes 'The Gay Side' seem so together. Maybe they know something that the rest of us are just beginning to learn."

A Few Extras

Seafood is an integral part of northern Baja California's diet (though it trails chicken and beef in poundage consumed) and it is the only major food source generated within commuting distance from the city. Tijuana lacks protected deep-water harbors (it straddles the river that bears its name, an ugly smarm that meanders through a corner of California before it reaches the Pacific) but the irregular coastline that wiggles southeastward past Rosarito to Ensenada provides a livelihood for thousands of amateur and professional food fishermen.

For many of them the great tuna boats that pull thousands of tons of bluefin from the depths far offshore for the processing plants in Ensenada and San Quintin are mere shadows on the horizon. Sea life closer to shore feeds families and fills the tile counters of fish markets and the ice chests of street-corner vendors.

Many of these markets buy from distributors for licensed professional fishermen, most of whom debark from Rosarito and Ensenada. Mexico's federal government has pumped money into the fishing industry, primarily by providing loans for vessel and equipment purchase, but many of the fishing boats "are rusty equivalents of Model A Fords kept together with axle grease and soldering rods," a long-time Baja area fisherman described some of his competitors.

Seldom do Baja fishermen discard anything from the catches their nets drag in. Their boats wallowing through sometimes blustery currents, they maneuver against piers strung along the coast northward from the Bay of Ensenada to disgorge the contents of their holds.

Many of them shovel their catches directly into the concrete troughs of open-to-the-weather corrugated-roofed gutting and filleting work stations. The filleting crews stand elbow to elbow, spattered with gore and blood, their knives clicking as they clean and sort the fish, their shouts barely audible above the cacophony of squawking gulls and bleating pelicans that surround them.

Refrigerated vans, panel trucks and pickups haul these catches to Tijuana. Those that don't deliver directly to markets or the larger restaurants hawk their catches from street corners. So do small-time unlicensed and non-union fishermen of all ages, who technically are fishing for "sport" but who surreptitiously seine perch, sea bass, sardines and bonito, or venture further off the coast to cast for groupers, bass and albacore.

Although many of these smaller operators go out every day, they may keep, sell or barter their catches, depending upon their daily needs. Some, like Carlos Cruz, have developed their daily fishing trips into family businesses.

A thin, patient man whose face is twisted by a scar that pulls one eyebrow into a cleft just above his cheekbone, Cruz and his oldest daughter, Maribel, a tomboyish thirteen-year-old, push their panga into the water just as the sun is coming up. Four hours later they chug back onto a landing just outside an abandoned resort.

Cruz's wife meets them there; together with their two younger daughters, they clean and sort their catch of twenty to thirty good-sized fish. While Cruz baits up for a second trip, the women bag the cleaned fish in plastic and catch the bus that will take them back to Tijuana, where they sell them to neighbors and to a couple of markets close to where they live.

His income, Cruz says, is sufficient for his family, provides them with a few extras and lets them live at a much more tranquil pace than most of Tijuana does.

Many Tijuanans who do not have boats also depend upon the sea for part or all of their incomes. They fish from the rocks and piers. Others sift tidal pools and beaches for crabs, clams and other mussels. Legally, Mexico limits the taking of shellfish to certain seasons, but scavengers comb the shallower bays and inlets for anything they can catch every day of the year. Some of the hardier — and more knowledgeable — scavengers know where to find abalone, which bring a good price in the city.

Many individual restaurant owners purchase seafood brought to their kitchen doors by fishermen coming in with fresh catches. More than a few throwaway orphans get money that way. So do would-be border crossers who learned fishing skills on the coasts of Oaxaca, Guerrero and Sinaloa.

Throughout the day, on the back roads that lead from Tijuana to the ocean fishing spots, one can see stooped grandfathers trundling along with their catches of perch, *amas de casa* carrying snapper or gar to boil in soup to supplement tortilla and bean diets, young men bicycling to the beaches before or after work, their fishing gear — a few hundred feet of line wrapped around a plastic Clorox bottle — dangling from their handlebars. Those who do not eat what they catch can trade for everything from gasoline to child-care to cigarettes.

MARCOS IS HERE!

"They came after dark. Right after dark. The store owners, of course, they live right here, just behind the store. Their son was behind the counter, right there — I mean, there's hardly room to turn around.

"He said he heard a vehicle stop — an old pickup, he said, from the way its engine sounded — but he didn't think anything about it, out here in the Valley of Guadalupe there are a lot of pickups. He looked up and just where you're standing, right there, he saw this figure, this *encapuchado*, he had a ski mask over his face, a soldier-type cap, he looked just like the *zapatistas* they show on TV.

"`Subcomandante Marcos is here!' the figure shouted, waving a pistol — a big pistol — and laughing. Thank God I wasn't there! As you can see, I'm rather nervous, I get frightened easily, I would have fainted, I would have been afraid he'd come to try to rape me.

"It wasn't just one robber, of course. There were four or five of them. They had pistols. They took what they wanted. Money. Beer. Food. Then they ran out, laughing, the son of the owner said. He was so terrorized, you see, he didn't try to run out to see what the pickup looked like.

"This is not the only place that they robbed. They robbed other places in the Valley, and right here around this town, Francisco Zarco, they did robberies, and all along the way to Villa Juarez. Not always at night, either, sometimes they came in the daytime, too. Really, they are very daring.

"I went to the police — you know, to talk to them, I mean, everyone here in the Valley knows my father, and my mother, dear departed soul, they say that I, Angelina Reza, look so much like her, except that I am skinny, sickly, and the police told me, well, they did not know anything, that they were as afraid of the *encapuchados* as we were. They said that they did not have the guns the *encapuchados* had. It is true, you see, here the municipal police have only their own pistols that are very old and some of them do not carry pistols, just night sticks, and these policemen are not, as you would say, 'professionally trained.'

"No one knows whether the *encapuchados* are old or young or where exactly they might be from but they cannot, I'm sure, be from very far away or they would not be doing their robberies around here. For I'm sure that, well, you can see that here there is no great wealth, the people here in the Valley, in the town of Francisco Zarco, do not have a lot of money here that can be taken from us.

"Perhaps these robbers are farm workers from somewhere else or *cholos* from up north or drifters from Ensenada — there are a lot of riffraffy people in Ensenada. Wherever they are from, they are not *zapatistas* — real *zapatistas*, I mean. They just are imitating them with the ski masks and all.

"But they are dangerous. Really dangerous. Who knows when they might use those guns?"

State police — *judiciales* from Ensenada — eventually responded to the complaints coming in from the Valley of Guadalupe. They made some arrests, more to flash a warning that depredations would be dealt with than to actually break up the gang of Marcos imitators.

Rumor had it that some of those who were arrested only were guilty of appearing on the roadways when the *judiciales* were passing by, or had indulged in jollifications that that made them easy to haul in, or presented a demeanor that the *judiciales* disliked. Nevertheless, that particular band of pistol-waving brigands vanished from the valley, though theories about its membership continued to provide a topic of conversation for months afterwards.

Francisco Zarco wasn't the only little Mexican community to suffer attacks from masked bandits like the Valley of Guadalupe gang. Subcomandante Marcos became an instant hero/villain after his appearance in Chiapas in January, 1994. Masks like those he and his rebels wore were easy enough to knit (or could be cut from old stocking caps); bandit groups from throughout Mexico adopted his disguises, just as, decades earlier, they had donned Pancho Villa Zapata apparel.

The cry, "Just tell them [the police] Marcos has struck!" left truckers, stores, warehouses and even banks bereft throughout Mexico. It even was rumored that certain police groups carried the disguises, either to wear for their own depredations or pull over their victims' faces after a shooting or an arrest. For who would doubt that someone — anyone — so disguised was a dangerous threat?

Now or Never

The 1,200-mile-long waterway that separates Baja California from Mexico's mainland has been, within the recordable memory of many who've fished its waters, one of the richest sources of marine life in North America. Until well into the latter half of this century, schools of sardines turned the shallow waters among the islands silver with flashing undulations that stretched for miles. Hungry amberjack and dorado pursued them, and dolphins roiling the waves as far as one could see pursued the dorado and amberjack.

The sands of the coralloid interior beaches, and the thick mangrove swamps tucked alongshore among them, yielded so many clams and scallops that you had only to walk barefooted along the water's edge to pick up all that you could eat. Shrimp were plentiful. So were sea bass and porgy, squid and lobsters. Turtles darkened the quieter waters, sea lions covered the rocks. Residents of the sparsely populated peninsula refused to eat less desirable catches like parrot fish and mackerel.

All that has changed. No longer is the Sea of Cortez the treasure trove that it once was. From the bottom of the food chain — the one-celled organisms — to the sharks, marlin and dolphins on the top, the sea is losing its rich store of marine life.

Sport fishermen crisscross the waters, using everything from electronic fish-finding gear to high-tech navigational equipment to fill their holds with catches they photograph but seldom eat. And commercial fishermen — especially the big rigs from the mainland — pull tons of cabrillo, of snapper, of sierra, of flounder, from the waters every day.

Shrimp fishermen, using trawling nets that scrape the sea floor, systematically comb up tons of baby fish and shell fish, along with juvenile shrimp that never will grow to adulthood. The shrimp harvest has declined dramatically over the past ten years, at the same time that the demand for fresh shrimp has soared. In this, as in so many things (including drugs and cheap labor), Mexico is servant to its neighbor to the north. Less than 10 percent of the shrimp scoured from the Sea of Cortez is consumed locally. The rest goes to the United States.

For centuries the Sea of Cortez's isolation prevented large scale intrusions onto its way of life. Only the wealthiest American sports fishermen ventured along Baja's bleak Pacific coast to enter the Sea of Cortez. The roads that connected northern Baja to sparsely inhabited Arizona and New Mexico were primitive at best, and there were no landing strips, gas stations or docking facilities anywhere along the peninsula.

Transporting fresh shrimp, scallops, abalone and other shellfish virtually was impossible since they spoiled so easily in transit. And the North American public, due largely to the geographical settlement of east to west, was accustomed to North Atlantic flesh fishes such as halibut and cod rather than the Pacific Coast/Sea of Cortez varieties.

But the '70s brought new technology — and new appetites — to markets north and south of the border. To encourage tourism, the Mexican government built roads and airports. American manufacturers began to produce sea-worthy sports fishing vessels at affordable prices. Mass market distributors whisked refrigerated catches by air to "fresh seafood" markets throughout the United States. And the great banks off Newfoundland, which had provided cod and halibut for generations of Americans, began to play out. The rush to the Sea of Cortez was on.

Laws theoretically protect depredations, but the laws irregularly are enforced. The huge commercial fishing concerns who operate with Mexico City capital and individual fishermen, lobstermen and sports boat concessionaires pay who they need to pay off to avoid being charged with infractions. The attitude, shared by commercial and sports fishermen alike, is: "If I don't get my catch now, I'll have lost my chance forever."

Forever may not be far away.

No One To Show It To

"In a story I wrote, I described my protagonist this way:

"`She loved the stark land of southern Baja, the gray hills above the beryl-green bay that was punctuated, even at night, by the upraised arms of lonely cardon, she loved it and needed it and was nurtured by it but at the same time she knew that a part of her, a gay, laughing extrovert part, was lost to her here, and that without it she was only half of her real self, and the real self that was here yearned for the part that was not.'"

That fictional character, admitted Laura Verdugo Cota, was more than coincidentally autobiographical, "although," she laughed, "I made her more attractive than I am, much more petite."

Not that Verdugo Cota wasn't attractive. She was tall and wide-shouldered, the type of woman who would have appeared domineering if not for a ingrained reticence that seemed to seek apology for her physical size. She had been a championship swimmer when she was in her late teens and early twenties, and even in her late forties she reflected that economy of movement that good athletes invariably develop.

"Please, give me your glass, I'll refill it." She glanced around her immaculate living room, with its decorative tile, walls of book shelves and balcony doorways that opened onto a sunset view above the bay, then shrugged, "It is not that I find life in Ensenada unrewarding. But this — Ensenada — is like a beautiful exile, a Never-Never land that has floated off by itself and is only superficially connected to the rest of Mexico."

There are advantages to that, I started to suggest, but a couple coming in from the balcony interrupted and I let the thought slide. But the theme obviously remained on Verdugo Cota's mind. She returned from the kitchen with my refilled glass of Chilean wine and, addressing both me and a woman her age whom she had introduced as a singer and musicologist, she continued:

"It's so different in Mexico [City]. I have a number of friends there — writers, poets, artists. The last time I was there I stayed with one of them, a good friend; she and I won fellowships to the same writers' retreat years ago. I hadn't even unpacked and she was showing me something she'd written. Not published; it still was in manuscript form.

"It was good — unlike what I'd have done — and I got caught up in it. We stayed up half the night talking about it. She wanted to know what I'd brought to show her. 'Nothing,' I admitted. You see, that's the way Ensenada is — that's the way rural Mexico is. You write in isolation. Paint in isolation. You never think to show your work to anybody because there's nobody around to show it to!

"But it wasn't just her story. We were interrupted I don't know how many times while I was there. By some friends who were upset — an issue over copyrights. Everyone was making phone calls back and forth, comparing, complaining, giving advice. There were invitations to an art gallery opening. A poetry reading. My friend and her friends — some married, some single — met in a bookstore-coffeehouse, then went to see a play in a little experimental theater.

"Then someone burst in with some books they'd been loaned by the proprietor of a foreign bookstore. Another friend — a very good writer — asked my opinion about some poems. I was flattered! 'I really can't...!' I said, but he insisted that I read them.

"You see, that's another thing about Ensenada — the hierarchy is very set. In Mexico it isn't. There's so much energy there! I was so overcome with new ideas that I stayed up until dawn trying to write them down. Then — being from

Ensenada — I apologized. My friend just laughed at me. 'That's what you're supposed to do!' she said. 'You're supposed to write! Whenever you feel like it! Whatever you want to put down!'

"Then, coming back here, it is — it is so *calm*. Once or twice a month a big *norteña* band comes down from Tijuana to play. There are art galleries that no one goes to. And if you tell someone that you write, they reply, 'Oh! For the newspaper?' They don't know that the magazines that I publish in even exist.

"Sometimes I stand here, just stand here, and watch the sunsets — the glorious sunsets! — and I tell myself, 'I should be getting filled with inspiration!' 'My spirit should be bursting with joy!' And I reach out — I reach out like the protagonist of the story I was telling you about — and I realize that only half of me is here."

"But that other half...ah! That other half can get so mauled!" The singer-musicologist met Verdugo Cota's momentarily surprised stare, then shook her head. "I'm sorry," she apologized, glancing toward me, then towards Verdugo Cota's husband, who had come in from the balcony to join us. "But there's a nasty side to all that bounding about from party to poetry reading. It's called..."

A self-conscious giggle forced her to hesitate and she stepped back, glancing quickly — almost shyly — at each of us. An attractive woman, perhaps a few years younger than Verdugo Cota, she seemed to be restraining an impish urge to jump up and run.

"Some of us call it 'the real world,'" she sighed. "Some of us..., well, I've lived in Mexico City, too. *Cielos!* You can't imagine! A casita no bigger than a closet! I think it once had been a maid's quarters. The patio was not much bigger — pure rock. Behind walls four meters high, spikes everywhere, and topped with jagged glass. Three locks on the doors — my young daughter and I, like prisoners, I mean it! That's what we were!

"Here, look! You have the view, okay, well, I don't, not like this, but even from Maneadero where I live it's pretty, okay? I want to walk on the beach, fine: I walk! Go anywhere I want. Hang out by myself. My daughter, I could leave her to play. She could walk to school.

"Listen! In Mexico I didn't get phone calls. Why? Most of the time I didn't have a phone — I couldn't pay the damn bills! I didn't go to galleries, to readings, to...what did you call it? Experimental theater? Why? I'll tell you! I had to work! I can't tell you how many jobs I had there in just a few years. But it was never enough. When I could, I took my daughter with me. When I couldn't she stayed with friends. The energy there? Yeah, energy. It was exhausting. I was exhausted all the time.

"That kind of thing — that kind of life — only works if you've got money. The theaters. Coffeehouses. Poetry readings. It's not for a single parent, like I was when I lived there. It's not for the common person. It's, what do you call it? An, uh, 'elite' thing, no?

"That's why I like it here. I don't get paid very much but I don't have to work so hard, either. And I can enjoy going out. I can speak to people and they speak back to me. Not about big intellectual things, maybe, but the sunsets and the weather and the best kinds of fish to eat.

"So, you see, for me it's just the opposite. Than what you said. That is for you. For me, I'm all of myself — here, I'm complete. There — there, I was all splintered. Mauled.

"There, I was someone I didn't want to be."

For all of the difficulties imposed by living in Mexico City, it continues to be the country's cultural hub. Each region has its own art, its own culture, both indigena- and European-based, and each region has writers, artists and musicians who achieve local notoriety, but relatively few of them are nationally recognized, and many regional capitals, like La Paz, import their culture — speakers, dance troupes, sculptors, theatrical performances and magazines — from Mexico City rather than patronize local efforts.

"To become known in Baja California," a local writer once confided to me, "one has to first has to become well-known in Mexico [City]. I think because, in the provinces, the people do not trust their own taste. They need to be told what — and who — is good. Then they will come running with all kinds of praise.

"And the longer you stay away, the more they will claim you as one of their own."

CHAPTER 7. DOWN THE MOUNTAINS TO THE SEA

STOOL PIGEON

It was a street that I had known but forgotten, some thirty blocks east of the Cathedral, a street narrower in appearance than in reality, sunless and gray because of the smog, and heavily trafficked even though it dead-ended a few blocks past an abandoned factory that once had produced huge sheets of window glass. I had lived near there, briefly, nearly twenty years earlier, and once or twice a day had crisscrossed its pitted asphalt seeking restaurants and liquor stores, bakeries and electrical repair shops.

The area that surrounded it, like many of Guadalajara's urban barrios, was thickly residential, with dwellings crammed one atop each other above the street-level shops. Push-cart and bicycle vendors peddled fruit, hot dogs, watches, posters, scantling and magazines and at night old women wrapped in ragged shawls slept among the tamale wrappings and discarded plastic bags in the darkened doorways.

At a corner where once I had bought sizzling tuna-stuffed jalapeños, I paused to ask directions of a woman who was selling lottery tickets. She scowled uncertainly, eyeing me from beneath brows whose wispy gray hairs undulated as she rocked to and fro on a little three-footed stool. The side of her mouth opened to emit an indecipherable snort, then abruptly she turned away. I shrugged, willing to slough off her hostility, but the man shining shoes beside her snapped his rag to get my attention.

"*No habla!*" In language typical of Guadalajarans — terse, profanity-laced phrases accompanied by gestures so rapid and exaggerated that the sleeves of his faded camise snapped as he spoke — he described how the woman's lips were sealed on one side of her mouth, the consequence of a machete slash that had been sewn back together badly. I nodded and he told me that the place that I'd asked about had closed the year before.

Again the woman pushed a series of harsh angry hoots through the corner of her mouth.

"She says there are better places," the shoeshine translated. An exaggeratedly high forehead gave his face an apprehensive urgency, as though he just had witnessed some other-worldly phenomenon. "Don't mind her. She is a good person, despite how she sounds."

I told him I'd once lived just around the corner and had asked more out of curiosity than out of need. The woman twisted around to face us, with gestures indicating that she, too, had lived close by. Her children had grown up playing in these streets. I asked about them and a series of violent shivers tangled her wispy eyebrows.

"Most of them are dead," the shoeshine confided. "Those who are not have gone away."

I bought a lottery ticket, more to encourage a conversation than with any hope of winning anything, and would have had my shoes shined if I had not been wearing bedraggled running soft tops. The neighborhood had changed, both the woman and the shoeshine insisted. It was more crowded now, fewer people knew their neighbors, there was more crime and more people prone to violence. I asked if either of them had been victimized by thieves or muggers and the woman shot some kind of incoherent curse through the opening beside her stitched lips.

"What more can they do?" the shoeshine asked. "They know who she is. They know she is the mother of German Angulo."

"German Angulo?"

The shoeshine crossed one knee over the other to pick at twisted, hammer-toed feet curled into dilapidated huaraches. German, he explained, had been the youngest and strongest of the lottery seller's sons. He had played baseball with the best in the barrio, had fought with the best, had had his pick of the pretty young women.

But he also had been the most impressionable, the most susceptible to movies and cars and money. He'd fallen in with a bad crowd, although opinion in the barrio was divided as to how bad they actually were, for they brought prestige, gifts and power to the people who surrounded them. German quickly rose from being a tag-along to becoming a full gang member. He openly displayed a pearl-handled .45 — the gift, he said, of El Chapo himself.

"El Chapo, the head of the Sinaloa cartel?"

Vehemently the lottery seller nodded. The beers that I had bought were making it easier for me to understand her snorts and gesticulations. She and the hammer-toed shoeshine explained that German had become one of El Chapo's personal bodyguards. When he came back to visit the barrio, he spent freely, helping people to forget their strained circumstances by setting up the tequila, the musicians, the food that would permit them to enjoy themselves.

When El Chapo went down, German transferred his loyalties to the brothers Arellano Felix of the Tijuana cartel. His visits to the *barrio* became less frequent but even more flashy. He bought an apartment for his mother and had hired a full-time maid to work for her. He gunned through Guadalajara in a new car and boasted about the parties that he had attended — parties that had included "the richest, the most influential, the most elegant" of the city's citizenry.

On May 24, 1993, Catholic Cardinal Juan Jesus Posadas Ocampo was gunned down while his limousine was delivering him to Guadalajara's international airport. Eye witnesses reported an immense amount of gunfire — automatic weapons going off in all directions — but details about the assassination varied. Many insisted that a car stopped in front of the Cardinal's vehicle, setting up the ambush, but federal officials released a report asserting that the clergyman had been caught in a crossfire between rival drug cartels.

"We didn't know what to believe," the shoeshine admitted. "We only knew that German, he didn't show up. Not right after the shootings, not later."

German didn't show up, the pair explained, but state and federal officials did. They questioned German's mother and threatened to "right some wrongs" if she didn't divulge his whereabouts. She protested that she had nothing to tell them, that she desperately wanted to know where her son was. She told them about German's contacts with the cartels, and how generous he had been with her.

Three weeks later a band of ruffians showed up. Though she could not prove it, she insisted that they'd been hired by the police. When she failed to satisfy their demands for more information, they ransacked her apartment, shredded her furniture, destroyed all her personal belongings and threw her into the street.

Destitute and grief-stricken, she'd returned to the barrio where a few old acquaintances helped her find shelter and catch-as-catch-can domestic jobs. One night a bunch of young toughs assaulted her. They left her among overturned garbage containers in an alleyway bleeding from blows to her ears and cuts across her mouth. A drunken doctor had tried to repair the damage but mangled the stitching and left her with a paralyzed mouth.

"And German?" I asked. "Did you ever...?"

The lottery seller twisted away to avoid the question. The shoeshine blinked sadly and peered at me, the dim illumination sent out by the corner streetlight making his high forehead seem almost translucent, as though the outer skin had been peeled away, leaving the mesoderm exposed.

"Yes," he whispered. "We..." He pretzeled down to pick at his hammer-toed feet, then slowly, muscle by muscle, squeegeed up to face me again. "A man came — he came from the prison, the most terrible prison, the one at Puente Grande — he said that he had seen German." This man, the shoeshine winced, was not the kind of man that one could trust. He was a thug, dissolute, the kind who would do anything for money. "He could have been sent, you see, to tell us lies."

What he did tell were accounts of other assassinations. They occurred in Puente Grande, the maximum security prison. One of the first persons arrested after Cardinal Posadas Ocampo's assassination was a *gatillero* called "El Spunky." Federal police pulled him off a Tijuana flight, found the automatic weapon he'd jammed into a garbage can outside the airport terminal, interrogated him and sent him under guard to Puente Grande.

"He was a *soplón* [stool pigeon]," the shoeshine insisted, a squealer who would put the finger on the guilty parties. But he never got a chance to give his evidence before a judge. Three months after he was incarcerated, El Spunky was found dead in his cell.

"Who killed him?" I asked. "Did this 'thug' know?"

A derisive burst from the lottery seller interrupted the shoeshine's "...said German was involved." The shoeshine backed off while the mother berated the inferences about her son.

"You know who did it! You know!" she almost upset her tray of lottery tickets as she lunged towards him. "The police did it! The police did it all!"

The shoeshine twisted away from her. "That also the thug said, that also," he conciliated, whether truthfully or simply to appease, I wasn't certain. "He said the guards found this 'El Spunky' dead. He said the prison officials reported that he had died from 'bad diet and strenuous exercise.' But those inside the prison, they knew better.

"El Spunky, they said, had been beaten to death. They said his mouth had been taped shut before the beating had started. They said it would have taken three or four attackers to kill him that way. Yes, and they said three or four prisoners, they could not have gotten together to do it, not at night, not in the maximum security prison. Unless, well, unless the guards helped them."

"The guards did it themselves!" German's mother spat.

"He was not the only one who was killed." The shoeshine acknowledged her indictment as he hobbled a curtailed semi-circle around her. "There was another who was arrested. The thug, he said this other *gatillero*, he had given some investigators some facts about the Cardinal's murder. What this information was, hey! the thug didn't know. What he did know was that the gunman didn't live long after that. The prison officials said he died in a fight that started over an inside-the-prison drug deal with two other prisoners.

"But the thug said, he said no one was punished. He said no one that he knew saw the fight. The thug said there were others killed too. He said that all of the supposed testimony that these informants had given no longer existed. Somehow, he said, it had gotten lost."

"And German? How do you think he was involved?"

"German." The shoeshine repeated the name with reverence. "Yes; perhaps he is not even there in that prison," he conceded to the mother before she could object. "But he has not appeared. For a long time, here in his old neighborhood, he has not appeared.

"That is bad, you see. In my opinion that means two things. He is dead. Or he is afraid."

Again the mother objected. I edged out of the crossfire as they flung recriminations back and forth. Tears spattered the old woman's cheeks and nose; she swiped at them with the sleeve of her dirty sweater. The shoeshine leaned towards her to touch her shoulder as he explained why he had come to that conclusion.

The drug cartels, like those of El Chapo and the brothers Arellano Felix, were so rich and so strong that they could control almost anything that they wanted to, including local politicians and local, state and federal police officials. If German were alive, and in the good graces of the cartels, he never would have allowed his mother to be thrown out of her apartment. If he could not appear in person, he would have sent others with money, gifts and information.

The shoeshine picked at his translucent forehead. German's disappearance, then, must mean that he had run afoul of the *capos* and either become a stool pigeon for the police or gone into hiding, probably in the United States. If he were a stool pigeon for the police, he might be in some kind of protective custody and not have the freedom to contact anyone in the barrio. If that were the case, then the police who broke the mother's furniture and threw her out of her apartment must have been working for the cartels. Whoever they were, they desperately wanted to find German Angulo, either to shut him up or to get revenge.

"Someday, *pues*, someday, if he is alive, he will get in touch with you," the shoeshine answered the lottery seller's interruption. "Perhaps he even will do some heroic act to help you." But, he continued, many people who'd been connected with the *capos*, and with the Cardinal's assassination, no longer were alive.

Not just the criminals, he gesticulated, but the police as well. No one was safe, no matter what his connections or status. The Cardinal hadn't been safe. Neither had the attorney general investigating his murder. He was by gunman in front of his wife and children, right here in Guadalajara. If he wasn't safe, if the Cardinal wasn't safe, what could we hope for? German, if he was lucky, had a new name, a new face. Otherwise he could be buried somewhere in an unmarked grave.

I nodded, again backing away from the mother's protestations. It now was almost completely dark. Neon Modelo and Corona logos glowed in the windows of some of the stores along the street. Charcoal braziers tended by indigena women in multi-layered shawls glistened here and there along the curb as huge, fumey buses geared stops and starts before turning down the intersecting thoroughfare.

"He was a good man. He is not dead," the lottery seller insisted.

"Was," the shoeshine breathed. He picked up his polish and rags as though intending to work on an invisible customer's black oxfords. His forehead glistened as though illuminated by some faint beneath-the-skin force as he peered towards the streetlight that just had gone on in front of us. The lottery seller brushed at the gray strands tangled above her eyebrows, then slumped back onto her three-legged stool, squinting upwards at him, then at me.

"You will see," she whispered. As she turned away, I noticed that she had locked her forefingers together and was pulling at them as though try-ing to break some invisible inner chain.

Street Dog

A vexed and frustrated Jocotepec developer described Arturo Ramirez as "a street dog that won't let go of my pants cuff." The developer was upset that Ramirez had stirred up a bunch of otherwise complaisant shantytown dwellers to demand payment for property that they legally owned. He was even more upset when Ramirez refused cash offers to abandon his opposition to the development of the golf course resort that the developer insisted would "bring credit and beauty to the community" — after evicting the squatter landowners.

"He growled at me. He literally made sounds like a dog growling at me!"

Ramirez could growl, no doubt about it. He also could bark, rant, coax, post petitions and file citizen complaints. A small man, sturdily built, with a wide face and thick, slightly protuberant lips, he was not a native of the quiet little town on the northern shores of Lake Chapala. The prospects of non-agricultural jobs in Guadalajara had lured him away from rural Veracruz when he was in his teens.

He'd loaded gondola cars, cleared vacant lots, installed water tanks, then wound up with a business of his own repairing, re-finishing and renovating tile floors. He'd fathered a couple of sons out of wedlock that he more or less diligently helped to support, then in his early forties finally had married. He and his wife had worked together, carrying their only daughter with them when she wasn't in school. They'd saved money, bought a house, furniture, a car, and struck up acquaintances with a number of the musicians who played at the various fairs and bars.

Sure of himself — and more than a bit spunky and belligerent — Arturo had sold the business and moved to Jocotepec with visions of becoming a promoter of singers and instrumental groups. The promotions fell through, a circumstance Ramirez blamed on the inability of *norteño*-lovers to appreciate good music, but a lottery ticket he'd purchased on a whim put hundreds of thousands of pesos in his pocket.

His wife, increasingly absorbed in her monthlies, estradiol and thinning hair, freed him for new adventures by choosing to care for her aging parents rather than continuing her marriage with him. Their daughter, bright and precocious, went away with her, promising, "I'll finish *prepa mamá*, then I'm gone, long gone!"

Over the years Arturo had experienced more than a few run-ins with public officials. He'd once lambasted Guadalajara officials for mistakenly jailing a young man Arturo had hired to help him. Neither police nor prosecutors had bothered to have the victim identify Arturo's employee as the man who'd tried to rape her before sentencing him to six years in prison. Arturo bounded from one official to another, badgering, remonstrating, browbeating, until he finally convinced someone with authority to re-investigate the crime and vindicate his employee.

A year later, as Arturo was driving to Jocotepec, a state policeman stopped him on the pretext of looking for stolen merchandise. The officer threatened to arrest him for carrying a pistol in the glove compartment. The officer not only rejected Arturo's offer of payment, he called for reinforcements. The *policía* who responded to the call stripped Arturo, whacked him in the testicles with their billy clubs, threatened him with electric cattle prods and sashayed off with his watch, wallet, rings, spare tire and new shoes.

Bulldog that he was, Arturo didn't let the matter lie. He found out the names of his tormentors by talking to everybody who might know them: the janitors who worked at police headquarters, gas station attendants, cafeteria waitresses, prisoners behind bars. Police officials threw away his protests but even that didn't deter him. He kept gathering statements and clippings that he filed in folders marked with the offending officers' names.

When one of them was arrested for shaking down a tourist from Mexico City, Arturo muscled his way into the prosecuting attorney's office with a sheaf of incriminating documents. He did the same thing after police broke up a protest march of Mixes coming down from the mountains near Tula. Bystanders photographed the police pistol-whipping several marchers. Local labor leaders demanded that the offending officers be prosecuted. Arturo recognized two of them and added his protests to those being processed.

The police might have retaliated had Arturo not developed liaisons with so many influential Jaliscans. Even those who disliked him often accommodated him, or went out of their way not to rebuff him. He browbeat the alcalde of Jocotepec into installing drains and paving the streets of a low-income barrio and badgering local DIF functionaries to institute a free breakfast program for farm worker and fishermen's children.

He wrangled PRI party money for a children's gymkhana and, when prison authorities refused to investigate the deaths of two inmates, apparently from starvation, he fired a tersely worded telegram to Mexico's President Miguel de la Madrid — and in reply received a holographic message delivered by personal courier.

The rise of the Partido Revolucionario Democratico (PRD) under the leadership of presidential candidate Cuauhtemoc Cardenas temporarily provided Arturo with allies who, at least outwardly, advocated social and political views similar to his. One of them, the co-organizer of a rural farm support coalition, brought several recently displaced campesinos to Arturo to describe how they had been evicted from their squatter homes. Both they and the coalition co-leader claimed that their choosing to affiliate with the PRD and its Cardenas-for-President movement had triggered the storming of their community by a group of machete- and sledgehammer-armed henchmen of a PRI party organizer.

Arturo, as always, jumped into the fray. He banged out complaints to take to state officials, charged into the chief of police's office to demand arrests and met with the head PRD organizer to urge that they organize a march through Jocotepec carrying banners.

The PRDers liked Arturo's moxie and enthusiasm. They had him organize and lead the march and invited him to Guadalajara to bring him in on state-wide voter recruitment demonstrations.

The co-leader of the squatter movement, Raymond Díaz, his wife, and two other PRD recruiters went with Arturo. Díaz ran a sometimes-open, sometimes-closed open air restaurant and was known as the best man to hire for a barbecue. His wife was one of the town's few trained nurses. She had treated Arturo's ex for a variety of ailments and the two of them had gone to a few social gatherings together.

None of the little contingency knew Guadalajara as intimately as Arturo did. He got them to the evening meeting just after it began, argued details that had no bearing on the PRD's campaign needs and, huffy and feeling unappreciated, led the Díazes to a restaurant with open air windows and a huge grill packed with sizzling *carne asada*, peppers, tortillas, garlics and roasting ears.

The Díazes didn't drink, and both of them obviously felt uncomfortable in the noisy, stranger-filled asadero with its scurrying waitresses and blaring television sets. They sat close to each other, Teresa de Díaz with her alpaca sweater pulled tightly around her shoulders, her husband stiff and erect, as Arturo flirted with the waitresses, re-arranged where he was sitting and insisted that they eat more peppers and drink more cinnamon- and sugar-thickened coffee.

Their two other Jocotepec companions had merged into a vociferous discussion about soccer with customers at an adjoining table. When a mariachi band began to set up in the corner farthest from the grill, Arturo bounded over to introduce himself.

On his way back to the table, he bumped into a group of middle-aged women, only two of whom were with their husbands. He complimented their clothing and their manners and when they responded positively he began to joke with them. A few minutes later, recognizing one of the mariachis' tunes as an old favorite, he asked one of them to dance.

The first dance led to a second, then a first and second dance with another of the women. They asked him to join them at their table and he invited them to join him at his. A brief but jocose debate ended with him bringing the two women he had been dancing with to share more peppers and *carne asada* with him and his companions.

Teresa de Díaz's face tightened into a dense, disapproving scowl. In whiny, vocalic tones she complained that it was late, that she was tired, that the night air was bad for her lungs. Her husband diffidently nodded but he spoke cordially to the newcomers. Arturo, insisting that they all eat more of everything, diverted the conversation to good beef and good peppers and how to judge and prepare them. He wasn't drinking — or was drinking very little — but he was exuberant and, as always, chattering incessantly.

Teresa de Díaz stonily repeated that she was tired, cold and catching disease and had to be taken back to their hotel. Since neither Arturo nor the two other Jocotepecans were ready to leave, Arturo hailed a taxi for her and her husband. Teresa de Díaz archly reminded Arturo that their meeting the next morning was scheduled to begin at eight o'clock and he laughingly told her he'd be there, "alert and obnoxious," just to please her.

Please her he didn't. On her way from her room to the little breakfast café, Teresa ran into him. One of the women he'd been dancing with the night before had her arm twined through his. Arturo greeted Teresa with unapologetic candor and re-introduced her to his companion. Teresa sniffed a terse "good morning" and strode away.

She did not return Arturo's salutations as the morning meeting was beginning. At mid-day, during the three-hour break for a meal and siesta, Raymond Díaz stiffly told Arturo that he and Teresa would not be driving back to Jocotepec with him, that they were going to take the bus instead. When Arturo insisted on knowing why they had changed their plans, Raymond only would say that his wife "felt too ill" to stay in Guadalajara any longer.

"No, it's such an inconvenience, I don't need to stay, I'll drive you back!" Arturo volunteered.

Raymond, wincing, muttered, "No, no, that would not be possible." Then he sighed and explained that Arturo was the cause of his wife's illness, that she considered him crass and immoral and didn't want to be in his presence or associate with him in any way.

Arturo protested that he was a single man, unattached, that his wife had been gone for years, that the woman was a very generous person, that she, like him, was single, that he had not "seduced" her, that it had been a mutual coming together and that he planned to see her again.

Raymond Díaz gnawed at the inside of his lower lip but only could respond that his wife was very religious and felt that Arturo's conduct had made a mockery of the mission they'd come to Guadalajara to accomplish. "I'm sorry," he offered; but Arturo strode away muttering that the two of them could do whatever they pleased, that it was of no concern to him, that the "mission" was all so much propaganda and he had better things to do with his time than to brownnose politicians and worry about some menopausal woman's misguided priorities.

Arturo located the two other Jocotepecans who'd come with them to Guadalajara. He was leaving immediately, he told them; they could come with him or take a bus like the Díazes were doing. Both quickly retrieved their overnight bags from their rooms. As Arturo was pulling out of the hotel parking lot's narrow driveway, the Díazes crossed in front of him. Raymond looked away but his wife, startled by the car's proximity, turned and found herself face to face with Arturo.

Arturo opened his mouth, as if intending some conventionally appropriate apology, but she stiffened her neck and stared at him, lips trembling and forehead drawn into a menacing scowl. Slowly she lifted her fingers and, still staring, drew the sign of the cross, almost as a priest might during mass, as if only that could save her from becoming contaminated by the evils incarnate in Arturo.

"Blessed Virgin, help me!" he heard her whisper before she wheeled away.

Arturo denounced her, her looks, attitudes and self-righteousness all the way back to Jocotepec. He remained so infuriated he not only refused to speak to her, he refused to allow anyone to mention her name in his presence.

But he didn't let his colic interfere with his political watchdogging. When the developer who'd accused him of growling tried to circumvent the restrictions on his proposed golf course by rigging long-term lease agreements from the legal owners, Arturo led a group of demonstrators to the site to force a stop to the excavations where the proposed club house was going to be built. Climbing the berm above a recently dug trench, which had become muddy and soaked by recent rains, he ripped up the duplicitously-worded leases.

"Nothing!" he shouted, "Nothing will make us back down! Not the mayor, the governor, not the President of the Republic!"

Just then he caught sight of his nemesis at the edge of the gathering. "Not...! Not...!" he blubbered, in sudden confusion, losing his train of thought. "Not even...!" he raised his voice, gesticulating towards Teresa de Díaz, "Not even her!" and, stumbling backwards, he lost his footing and tumbled into the ditch.

For the first time that the citizens of Jocotepec ever could remember, they saw Arturo Ramirez run away and hide.

Getting Rid of the Squatters

The mountains are not as steep around Iguala as they are around Cuernavaca and Taxco; there is more green on the slopes and a brighter blue to the sky. It is a historic place, best known for the "Plan of Iguala," the document that laid out the tenets of a new revolutionary document in 1821. I didn't intend to spend the day there, but on impulse I jumped off the bus to see what the town was like. I didn't have much money and I really didn't want to compete with the tourists in Acapulco.

It seemed like a quiet, pleasant place, its old houses hidden by faded stone and concrete walls and separated from each other by rutted narrow streets that exuded the odors brought to them by roasting corn ears, taco and bírria vendors. I strolled absent-mindedly, not quite hungry enough to sit down to eat, pausing here and there to look at a building, a cascade of spring flowers, a bullfight notice.

Just past what seemed to be the edge of town, I came across an unpaved road winding uphill past the walls of an old mill. A dog lying in the middle of the road eyed me sleepily as I passed a cluster of newly built cement block houses. I stopped to catch my breath and heard chatter and laughter coming up the road behind me. Four children, one pulling a wagon, one inside it and two others toddling along behind came towards me.

The girl pulling the wagon looked up inquisitively. She had a round face and surprisingly fair complexion. A mother of pearl barrette pinned long dark-brown hair over her ears. I greeted her, commented on the pretty day and asked her her name. She told me it was "Graciela" and said she had taken her sister and a neighbor's daughters to the store to buy some things for her mother.

I complimented her industriousness, then turned back to help her when the little wagon bogged down in a swath of loose sand that dissected the road. Her lisped "*Gracias*" was cut short by the sudden roar of motorcycle engines coming up behind us. Together we pulled the wagon and toddlers off the road into ramose vegetation. A flotilla of motorcycles, three abreast, vibrated past, followed by a posse old trucks carrying fatigue-clad men in their high, slatted beds. The motorcyclists all were wearing the uniforms of the Guerrero state police.

"What's happening?" I asked Graciela.

She shrugged, unconcerned, and I helped her get the wagon and her companions back onto the road. A huge cloud of dust traced the convoy's progress through what seemed to be scrub-covered fields less than a kilometer in front of us.

I started to ask again what was happening. Before Graciela could reply, I heard shouts and screams crescendo towards us. Leaving the children, I scrambled through a sagging barbed wire fence up the ridge to the point where I could see down the slope towards several hundred clumped together little houses. Most of them seemed to be made of cardboard, car parts and crudely trimmed tree branches. Many were thatched with palm.

The motorized police spread out to form a semi-circle facing the houses. Men and women scrambled out of the crude dwellings to confront them. A stocky, phlegmatic officer stepped into their midst and with deliberate forethought lifted the pistol he held in his right hand. For a moment, like a statue, he paused, the barrel pointed straight overhead, then he pulled the trigger. The cannon-volume explosion quieted everything but a flock of raucous crows.

He announced something—I was too far away to hear what he said—then motioned his men forward. They moved quickly, with clubs, hatchets and machetes tearing down and trampling the flimsy walls and flimsier support beams. The trucks moved in and the fatigue-clad invaders hurled butane tanks, stoves, beds, tables, chairs and wash tubs into them while the armed motor policemen, hands over their guns, held the residents at bay.

I was so startled—and engrossed—I temporarily forgot about my little companions. Suddenly I caught a glimpse of them. Graciela, pulling the wagon, was stumbling along a barely discernible path towards the melée, her two younger companions in ragged pursuit. A woman broke through the police cordon and rushed towards them, arms extended. She clutched Graciela with one arm and pulled the baby out of the wagon with the other. All three of them seemed to be crying.

The policeman nearest them looked over his shoulder, then casually picked up the little wagon and threw it onto the bed of the nearest truck.

Diarrhea Syndrome

It was a simple funeral, and a simple burial in a hillside plot carved out of thick tropical vegetation. As relatives of the dead teenager shoveled gravel and stones across the plain wooden casket, I intercepted the priest, who had closed his recitation book and was shambling down the slope towards the rutted dirt road.

"A small contribution, perhaps to help the family?" I offered a fifty peso bill (the equivalent of six or seven dollars), then asked, "What caused his death, do you know?"

The priest twisted the bill between his fingers. "God's will," a satirical wince threatened his languid demeanor. Slowly he forced his chest and shoulders around to face me. "Diarrhea, they say. He woke up one morning very sick and by evening he was dead."

In that sweltering little community of mud and decay tucked into the side of a barranca a dozen miles east of Acapulco, "diarrhea" is a common cause of death, particularly among the young and the very old. But medically speaking, "diarrhea" is a symptom, not a disease. Many things can cause diarrhea: bad food, bad water, viral flu, etc. In the tropical villages that surround Acapulco, contamination from flooding, seeping sewage and erosion periodically stricken laborers and their families. The result, according to official sources, is "a diarrhea syndrome."

Those better acquainted with tropical infirmities call the outbreaks "cholera."

The teenager's funeral wasn't the only one that the priest had conducted in the months preceding my visit. But state health officials denied that any incidents of cholera had been reported within 150 kilometers of the resort metropolis of a million and a half inhabitants. There had been, they said, various outbreaks of *la gripe* but they refused to elaborate on that term, which in Mexican usage indicates everything from a head cold to a hangover to the Asian flu. The health officials blamed the poor hygiene practiced by rural and shantytown residents for all of the incidents of death-causing diarrhea.

A year after I stumbled across that funeral, an English homeopathic practitioner, Wendy Owen, told me about "dozens of cases" of cholera in Las Plazuelas, a shantytown-crammed community where many Acapulco minimum-wage workers live.

"I was horrified," she said. "The tiny clinic there was jammed. There was one little boy, maybe four or five, curled up on the floor. His mother had wrapped him in blankets—rags—and they were all stained. She couldn't get his diarrhea to stop. She'd try to pick him up and he'd scream—a little tiny piercing scream. She was crying and the health worker kept telling her to *please! please!* be patient."

Cholera typically strikes humid lowland areas where poor sanitation allows the *vibrio comma* bacteria to breed. The hurricanes that lash Mexico's southwest coasts, particularly coastal Oaxaca and Guerrero, periodically inundate rural farms and villages, leaving thousands of areas of stagnant swamp land, broken sewers and rotting vegetation in their wakes. Federal clean-up efforts focus on high-income tourist areas, leaving the outskirts villages to muck their way back to normalcy as best they can.

Temporary houses cram the hillsides and barrancas, overflow through matted swampland and lean precariously from vine-tangled cliffs. Hundreds of new residents pour into these *colonias populares* every day—men, women and children seeking work as dishwashers, hod carriers, servants, peddlers, prostitutes.

"The government's only concern is that the tourists don't see how bad the living conditions are," a shantytown resident, Mauro Dominguez, complained to me. "They don't care what goes on inside them."

Clean ups after the massive floods of 1997 confirmed Dominguez's allegations. Work crews, utilizing heavy machinery and financing from Mexico's federal government, poured into Acapulco. Selectivity was based on appearances, not the needs of low income citizens. The clean-up crews spruced up the beaches and repaired the damage to the exclusive tourist hotels but ignored the devastated *colonias populares*.

Public service broadcasts paid for by the President Zedillo-run federal government extolled the clean up and later used clips of the repair work during election campaigns to demonstrate how quickly the government responded to citizens' needs. But even as it did so, residents of the devastated shantytowns still were patching their flood-destroyed houses with lamina and cardboard, unaided by any federal money or materials. Not only were they worse off than they'd been before the flooding, but the danger of damage from new flooding was increased, for levees and natural barriers had been destroyed and safer, higher grounds had been taken over by speculators and entrepreneurs.

These flood victims also were experiencing what federal Health Undersecretary Jaime Sepulveda admitted were "diarrhea-associated symptoms." A communique issued from his office in Mexico City warned residents about drinking non-treated water and suggested that precautions against eating from street vendors' stands were "advisable" until the "problems" had been solved.

But, though residents of the *colonias populares* were warned, the contaminated areas were not quarantined. Hundreds of thousands of shantytown residents converged on the tourist and business high rises every workday. They prepared food, made beds, swept streets, sold trinkets; they hawked newspapers, washed windshields, hauled cement blocks, shined shoes. Emerging as they did from cramped slums without running water, without drainage, without flush toilets, without garbage pickup, they carried all the problems of their daily living into the tourist centers with them.

Despite being potential carriers of the disease, they have yet to infect significant numbers of tourists. Cholera can be misdiagnosed, but it is a severe enough disease that American doctors would recognize its symptoms if they detected its presence among tourists returning to the United States. That this hasn't happened would seem to confirm Mexican government insistence that the disease doesn't threaten the city's residents or visitors.

But cholera isn't a disease that one contacts casually. Doctors that had come to Las Plazuelas told Dominguez that a healthy body would fight off small doses of the cholera bacteria, but that people living where water and food supplies were infected would be overcome because "everything we'd touch, that we'd drink, that we'd eat" would shove more bacteria "into our systems and finally we'd, you know, señor, we'd no longer be able to resist. We'd fall ill, not just one of us, but many, all at once."

That's exactly what happened in 1997. Hurricanes battered the coasts and surged inland, drenching the once lush forest land with rain. Down the steep hills the torrents swept. Barrancas became raging rivers roiling the debris from clear-cutting lumber operations with them towards the sea. They tore away the temporary housing that thousands of Acapulco newcomers had erected on their banks, then spread outward, covering hundreds of thousands of acres with sewage and chemical and agricultural waste.

Washed-out shantytowners, isolated on hillsides and protrusions of higher ground, had no choice but to drink what water and eat what food they could find. Bridges, roads and wells had been destroyed. A group of villagers who'd fled the flooding of their makeshift homes became isolated by a swirling water-filled gully. Beyond it, carved into the higher hillside, they could see cars and trucks passing back and forth on the Acapulco-Chilpancingo highway. Without water or food, drenched and shivering, they hunched together for nearly four days before helicopters ferried them to makeshift accommodations on an abandoned concrete basketball court.

"When they began to die," a Mexican visitor to the area told me, "medical authorities prohibited anyone from coming near them." They were whisked away, possibly to some facility miles from Acapulco, "where it would be all right to treat them for what really had infected them."

"Cholera?" I tried to read the grimace on his face.

"Hell, yes! Everyone knew it," he spat. "But in Mexico nothing exists unless the authorities say it exists. Sometimes even death."

He compared the rhetoric to that which often surrounds the issue of police brutality. If a problem doesn't exist, he argued, there's no need to do anything to correct it. The refusal to admit the continuing existence of cholera in and around the resort city made it unnecessary to take any official steps to contain or eliminate it. Why spend a lot of money to eradicate something that doesn't exist in the first place, particularly if such a campaign would negatively affect the flow of tourist dollars?

When Owen talked to doctors from Acapulco's government-subsidized social security hospital, she learned that they had specific orders not to document cases of suspected cholera or to use the term when discussing the disease with patients or visitors.

"They had a special isolation ward in the hospital, with a military [or special security] guard at the door. They would not tell me, but I learned from some of the relatives waiting outside the hospital, that at least two people in the ward had died and that the others could not receive any visitors, even from their parents, brothers and sisters or children."

A few miles away, in the bright post-hurricane sunshine, tourists were running along the beaches or reclining beside crystalline swimming pools, unaffected by the secret plague that was killing the families and friends of the hotel employees who were shining their shoes, washing their clothes and bringing them ice cold piña coladas on carefully disinfected serving trays.

The Winning Side

"They were not people I wanted to know. Well, sh— yes, they were, I guess. They were flashy — they had money to spend, they liked having women around.

"Women like me, I mean. American women with moxie, with class. Hey! I grew up having everything I wanted. Penthouses, tennis clubs, yachts were nothing new to me.

"Neither were drugs. I'd done them all by the time I was seventeen. They liked that, these Acapulco wheeler-dealers, these mafiosos pulling their strong-armed sh—; they liked hanging around with somebody who'd seen as much as they had. Somebody like me, who could talk their sh—, snort their sh—, rock their sh—, show them things they'd never seen!"

Cheryl Sabelman swung her legs from one side of the beach chaise to the other, rubbed her bare toes in the sand and squinted at the sun-shaded balconies of the Hotel Las Brisas. Though in her mid-thirties, "a little worn around the edges" by her own definition, she had a gymnast's trim figure that the scant fabric of her bikini did nothing to hide.

"That was their trip: power — power and wealth. They didn't care whose toes they stepped on to get it. They never were going to cut me in on their thing but, you know what? That didn't matter. I wasn't looking for money. I was just there to have a good time."

Again Sabelman swung her legs over the beach chaise. She had the unnatural dark beach tan that comes from extensive sunbathing and wore curved black-lensed sunglasses that obliterated the expression around her eyes.

"Emilia knows. She lived through it, too." She nodded to the woman on the chaise beside her. Sabelman's age or perhaps a year or two younger, she had the sloppy posture of a carelessly attractive woman who didn't put a lot of effort into her appearance. She blinked, then shrugged a scarcely audible "*Claro qu'sí, yo sé.*"

The *it* they'd lived through, Sabelman explained, was the transformation of a middle- and working-class sprawl of houses across 50-year-old *ejido* land into high-roller condominium resorts owned by some of Mexico's highest-ranking politicians. The appropriation began in 1989.

"Salinas — the one with the big ears — had just become president. His buddy Ruiz Massieu, the Ruiz Massieu that later got shot, was the new governor of Guerrero. The state capital's over in Whatchamacallit? Chilpancingo? but Ruiz hardly ever left Acapulco. The ruling party, you know — the PRI — gave him the state for past services rendered. Hey! Let me tell you! He sacked it good!

"Okay, Ruiz has got Salinas' backing, right? He can do whatever he wants to do. What he wants to do is get rich. So do his buddies. The way to do it, they decide, is to start building luxurious new beach clubs, marinas, villas, hotels, race tracks, you name it! So where are they going to do this? Yeah, all the land worth having's already owned.

"Well, hey, not quite. There's this section of houses—a subdivision, what was it called? What, Emilia? Yeah, 'La Copacabana,' that was it. Nice houses, a lot of them, two-storied, a lot of them had swimming pools. Behind them, stretching along the land that bordered the beach, were a lot of, you know, *viverias*—nurseries, plant nurseries. Bougainvillea, hibiscus, lianas of all kinds.

"Well, Ruiz and his crew aren't big on flowers. They wanted land. So what did they do? I'll tell you: They took it. Just like that. They confiscated it.

"See, Ruiz had the state legislature in his pocket — I heard him brag openly about this, 'my boys,' he called the elected officials — so 'for the good of the country' the land becomes a 'Designated Tourist Development Area.' They appropriate it for the government, then give title to themselves. Las Brisas, Joyas de Brisamar, Club Britania, the big Pemex building, what else, yes, the Extravaganza — the land that all of them is on were part of the package.

"I heard some of Ruiz's henchmen brag about taking it over. They offered the people who lived there a pittance for their houses, their land — I don't know how much, next to nothing, I heard — then whanged anybody who objected.

"This one guy — his name was Javier, he could dance, oh! he could dance like something off the New York stage — told me that Ruiz Massieu told the residents, 'Hey! I'm concerned, I'm really concerned that if you don't sell it now, later you might not have anything left on your property that's worth selling.'

"He meant it. The people who lived there, he didn't care about them, he didn't know anything about them, they could have been Laplanders or Patagonians as far as he was concerned. That people had to give up their houses so these mafiosos could build clubs like the Palladium and the Extravaganza didn't bother him a bit. Like Javier once said, 'There's a winning side and a losing side, and I know which one I want to be on!'

"He's probably got yachts and mistresses and more gold chains than he can wear right now.

"Or else he's dead. Like Ruiz Massieu. Or in prison somewhere, like his brother. Mene, mene, tekel, upharsin, you know? Maybe the bastards get what they deserve when the final count comes in?"

Sabelman's friend Emilia interrupted my "I doubt it..." with a tittered laugh that she immediately tried to cover up.

"I'm sorry," she said, then reverted to Spanish. "I was thinking of what they deserve, I guess."

Sabelman explained that Emilia's parents had owned a house — "a nice house, two stories, with a swimming pool, right?" — in the "La Copacabana" suburb. Her father, a doctor, "a quiet sort of man, very Mexican in some ways, but not a drinker, not a fighter," had joined the coalition that formed to oppose the takeover but soon afterwards, through contacts in the medical community, he had arranged to meet and negotiate with some of Ruiz's henchmen.

"You would have to know my father to understand. He was not political. He very much believed in making things comfortable for the family. He was not the type to make strong assertions. He was, I don't know, he had a way about him, a way of getting what he could out of a situation.

"He arranged something. He got a house in the Parque Ecologico Viveristas, a very nice house, a very nice lot. I already had left home by that time, I was married — I have children, did you know that? My husband and I, well, he is a musician, we live a little differently than my father does.

"And my father, he goes on doing what he was trained to do — medicine. He doesn't mess around in politics. He just looked the other way when the bulldozers came in and destroyed the houses of the people who had refused to sell. And he said nothing when some of those people who were dislocated tried to get their land back and were arrested and accused of despoiling property.

"I'm like him, I guess." As though seeking confirmation, she glanced towards Sabelman. "I come here to the beautiful tourist beach, even knowing what it was before. Even knowing about the evil thievery that has made it what it is."

A few days after an assassin cut down former governor Jose Francisco Ruiz Massieu, friends and sidekicks attended a mass in his memory in the elegant ballroom of the Hotel Vidafel. According to the president of the opposition PRD political party, Juan Garcia Costilla, as governor of Guerrero Ruiz Massieu had financed the building of the hotel, then sold it at a fraction of its worth to a group of buyers that included Jose Francisco Ruiz Massieu. Others supposedly involved in Acapulco Diamante's development include former conservative party (PAN) presidential candidate Diego Fernandez de Cevallos, Mexico's ex-president Ernesto Zedillo and ex-president Carlos Salinas de Gortari's jailed brother Raúl.

The music goes on playing behind the high walls that separate Acapulco Diamante from the rest of Acapulco. Sabelman and her friends are there to hear it, even though Ruiz Massieu and many of his are not.

Practicing for Bigger Things

Centuries away from the touristed beaches, the high-rise condos and luxurious yachts that hundreds of thousands of tourists photograph every week in Acapulco, a caravan of armed riot troops form the Guerrero state police descended on a little Mixteco community tucked into three fingerlike *cañadas* at the base of the Cerro de la Garza. According to descriptions overheard from the police group's Mexican Army escort, which included a tank and four helicopters, the strike force had orders to eradicate hidden opium poppy fields that local farmers supposedly were cultivating.

"They attack the little drug growers in order to practice for bigger things." Francisco Javier Higuera's self-conscious laughter turned his lean, large-toothed face into a rodent-like twitching. "They don't come here for *amapola*. Imagine how much a military operation like that costs! They come to show the mountain people how strong they are, how much firepower they have. They are afraid we might start another revolution."

The "we" that Higuera was talking about were Mixteca and other indigena groups that organized during the early '90s to oppose the unregulated clearcutting of thousands of acres of timber land and to end the arbitrary incarceration of indigenas without fair trials. A rural commissioner responsible for distributing federally-subsidized seed, fertilizer and pesticides to indigena communities scattered along the steep ridges of La Montana Tlachinollan, Higuera walked me and my escort, Francisco Javier Castro, through the scrap and stubble of what once had been a white oak forest a few miles from Metlatonoc, a remote — but rustically charming — center tucked in a tiny valley near Guerrero's border with Oaxaca among mountains that rise to nearly 10,000 feet.

Castro laughing called Higuera "*hermano*," because they shared the same very common first names. The rural commissioner, reticent at first to discuss the political situation in La Montana Tlachinollan, gradually pushed through his discomfort as he showed us the countryside around Metlatonoc.

He took us across half a mile of eroded hillside that had slipped mud, scrub growth and silt across several dozen maize fields and buried a cluster of Mixteca homes. He showed us places where the roads had washed out entirely, primarily because the clearcut areas no longer absorbed water, and he took us across huge swaths of timberland where lightning fires had ignited the scrap tossed aside during logging operations and burned out of control.

"To be *indigena* here is to be guilty of something." Higuera fussed with thick glasses that he seemed unable to adjust to his bony, almost chinless face. "Sometimes I think it is just to be guilty of not moving fast enough.

"You see, for years — hundreds of years — Mixtecos have cut trees. My people would clear an area, build a place to live, chop the lumber for fuel and plant where the trees had been. They did not sell much lumber because they had only machetes for tools. Besides — you see, it wasn't like it is now — if they did cut it, who would they sell it to? For them, the trees were not a product to be sold; they were obstacles they had to clear away slowly, painfully, in order to have land to farm.

"The lumber cutting, of course, worked its way up the slopes, little by little. Some Mixtecos — those who lived closest to where the lumbering started — even worked for the first lumber companies. They sawed trees down by hand, hauled them out with mule teams. It took a long time.

"That changed very rapidly. Now the lumber companies come in with bulldozers. Generators. Power saws. They devour everything — leave only rubble behind.

"In the time I am talking about, the last twenty or thirty years, Mixtecos could not do that on their own. They had no way to make an estimation of the forests' value. That takes someone from the outside world coming in.

"Listen, my grandfather, he was, what? nine or ten when he first came to Metlatonoc; he was so frightened he hid behind my great-grandmother's skirt — what a confusing, exciting world was Metlatonoc! and it was many times smaller than it is now.

"So you can see what I am saying: There was no way that people like my grandfather could conceive of forming lumber companies, or conceive of building furniture companies. He was not unintelligent — not at all — but I cannot picture him driving a car, or learning to use a power saw.

"Now, it is different. The outside world has come in: We can see trees like we used to see maize: something to grow and harvest. But the problem is — always the problem: We are a small group, starting almost from nothing. Much of the lumber already is cut. We have petitioned *La Secretaria*...what do you call it? *de Desarrollo Social*? [Secretary of Social Development] for enough money to build a sawmill that we would operate as a community, but — you know how this goes — the paperwork gets lost, or somebody sets it aside, or — *Fígate!* — the government runs out of money and we don't get anything.

"In the meantime, we have to fight to keep what little we have. You know what happened when we fought against the clearcutting...no? Let me tell you. The *maderero*, this *pinche* Olvera Medina [Luis Olvera Medina, a lumber magnate], began to cut on our ejidos. Enriqueta Juarez was there [Juarez was a Mixteca human rights advocate]. She went to hundreds of ejidos — she was passionate, this woman, mind you! this *vieja* whose whole life before this had been spent making tortillas and giving birth to little ones! — she said we had to stop him from cutting everything.

"Many of us thought the same as her. We blockaded the roads so the lumber trucks couldn't get in. Do you know what the lumber man did? He and his friends — *ejidarios* like ourselves, Mixteca Judases who sold out to him and worked for him — went to the police. They filed charges against us. Not for blocking the road, please understand. The charges were for rape. For attempted murder. For robbery. Things like that that were totally untrue.

"The police swept in — not just the local police, the *judiciales*; they beat up people and threw them in jail. Those of us who they didn't arrest — it was crazy! — we waited a week, longer than that, maybe, then we got together and we invaded the place they were cutting timber. We took over the trucks — seventeen, eighteen of them, I think — and blockaded the road until the lumber people had the police release our comrades they had arrested.

"That didn't stop it, of course. Every time we come up against something the lumber-cutters are doing, the *judiciales* arrest somebody. To be arrested, for a Mixteco here in La Montana Tlachinollan, is to be found guilty. Believe me, I am telling the truth. An *ejidario* — his name was Francisco Ferrero Ojeda — they were looking for someone else when they arrested him for stealing some cattle from someone who had leased some clearcut timberland from the lumber company.

"When he claimed that he was innocent, the police laughed at him. They said they didn't care. 'You're probably guilty of something!' They promised that they would make him confess, and they did; even though afterwards he said he never had confessed to anything.

"Of course, when he came before the judge, he had no lawyer and no interpreter. Paco — that's what we all called him — Paco spoke Mixteco and only a very little Spanish, not enough to understand what was going on. And it was difficult for us to get to Tlapa to help him — Tlapa, that's where the deposition took place.

"There was no defense. Someone from the court read the charges, someone else read the statements of the arresting officers, the judge asked Paco if he had any witnesses. A young law student who'd come over from the university in Chilpancingo asked permission to represent Paco but the judge said no, and sentenced Paco to a year in the jail.

"It has happened that way for many years. Many, many years. Only recently have we been trying to fight back in ways that Spanish law understands. We have organized committees in all the communities — not just the Mixteco, but the Nahua and Tlapaneco as well — to explain what rights people have and what they can do to get justice.

"The authorities, you see, the authorities do not like these committees, especially when the leaders of the local committees are in contact with each other. Several times the police have arrested this committee member or that one for being against the government. They say we support the rebels in Chiapas. They say we are planning armed revolt, just because we try to defend ourselves.

"So you see, the police come in and bring soldiers with them. But we are not so stupid that we cannot see what is happening. The *madureros*, they have just worked their way past Citlaltepetl and are clearcutting new hillsides. It is not coincidence that the authorities decided to wipe out a few poppy fields — do you have any idea how difficult they are to get to? — just when the tree cutting is in full swing. They think that we will not organize any blockades with the soldiers close by.

"Imagine, *hombre*, how much they are spending! For what they pay to bring the soldiers in on just one mission to wipe out a little *amapola*, they could provide seed and fertilizer and goats and drainage for every community in La Montana Tlachinollan! This campesino that I know told me about one of the gun battles. The growers set up an ambush for the tank and the trucks when they came in. They set off a landslide with dynamite, then with *cuernos de chivo* shot at the trucks.

"I think they didn't know that the soldiers had helicopters. The helicopters came in shooting rockets. It was like a movie, the campesino said: explosions and gunfire and men crying and dying. The campesino said that soldiers were killed — fifteen of them, maybe. Maybe more. When he went back a week or so later, he found cartridge cases — lots of them — and several wrecked trucks pushed to the bottom of the canyon, but he did not find any graves. Maybe the helicopters carried all the dead and wounded away, I do not know.

"When the police come, with or without the soldiers, they always find someone who has committed a crime. They snoop around and they threaten people and they find cattle or horses that carry old brand marks or they find some little patches of *amapola* or marijuana. Or they come, as they say, "to restore order." Restore order!

"That means that they use their guns and clubs to discourage any of us from insisting on our rights. One time, when the fertilizer arrived from the government, it was distributed only to commissioners who had cooperated with the authorities, not to any of us who had participated in the blockades. Many of us objected and they told us that we were not aligned with 'Solidaridad,' that the fertilizer only was for those who were members of PRI.

"That was a lie, of course. A *trampa* — a trick. Somewhere along the line, some government officials switched the distribution from the proper agencies to party officials.

"We had to demonstrate in front of the government buildings for three weeks to get the fertilizer, and then, after we got it, the police came in and arrested fifteen or sixteen who they thought were the ringleaders. We had to set up blockades to get them released from jail, but by that time the growing season almost was over, and many who were not PRI, were not what they called 'Solidaridad,' did not have crops at all that year.

"So you see why we have to stick together. We can't get a share of the lumber harvest, even though it is taken from land that was supposed to be ours forever, and if we object to anything that the authorities do, they send police in to arrest us.

"And sometimes soldiers to fight secret little wars that nobody ever thinks about.

"Except those of us who see and hear and know."

Like a Bird!

All too often, when writers — even Mexican writers — try to describe cities like Cuernavaca, they become entrapped by the emotions that architecture and flowers, fountains and vendors' cries evoke. Their prose vibrates the vivid language of the market place, the crisp mountain air, the brightly painted houses, the limousines of the rich and famous, the center city congestion that jams burros and chickens and Volkswagens and bicycles together with tourists and schoolchildren, prostitutes and movie stars. But behind the excitement and color, the barter and tours and pesos-for-dollars exchange, people like Romero Ibanez see nothing but the incessant boredom of the lives they are forced to lead. They despise their spouses, can't afford lovers, try to deny how cramped and overwhelmed with meaningless memorabilia their no-longer-sufficient living quarters have become. Month after month, year after year, they keep going on, blinded to the colors and noises, excitements and failures of the city around them. Until finally, like Romero Ibanez, some of them stop resisting what they really feel and, like him, go off the deep end.

Ibanez hadn't always lived among the trees and shrubbery in Cuernavaca's parks, a civil and contemplative dropout who spent most of his days watching flowers grow, birds mate and eat, clouds form countless figures overhead. Sensing his affinity with nature, children brought him candy and street vendors wrapped bits of the meals they sold for him to eat. He hadn't always lived that way, of course; some years before I first saw him in the early '60's, he had been a journalist, a husband and father, a man about town. Months after I returned to Mexico City, where I was living, I received a note in rushed but very legible script from a Cuernavaca social worker describing his sudden lifestyle change:

> I got this from a woman who lived in a building near the park. He came looking for an apartment, she said. He seemed tired and very nervous — he barely could climb the stairs. She said the concierge, who lived on the top floor, showed him the apartment. Apparently he told the concierge that his wife wanted something larger, something like this apartment, for it had a view. The concierge went up to her loft to get the owner's telephone number; Ibanez followed her. He began to talk about his wife, his life. Not to her, to himself, saying things like, "She's crowding me out." "All her things everywhere." "Besides that, she's fat." He lit one cigarette after another, smoking in huge gulps. Now he was saying, "Coffee in the morning. Brandy all night. How can I work?" "What do I get?" He gazed out the concierge's window, which overlooked the park. "Better to live in the trees," he told her. The woman I talked to said the concierge said his face suddenly changed. "Like a bird!" He stuck his face so close to her that he frightened her. "Like a bird! A bird!" The concierge said he tried to jump out the window but he couldn't get it open far enough. "In the woods! Like a bird!" He went running down the stairs.

As far as I — or anyone else — knows, he never, ever came back.

The Edge of the Volcano

If Mexico City — the Tenochtitlan of the Aztecs — is the country's heart, the throbbing masculine center that thrusts industry and control towards every corner of the nation, then Cuernavaca, some 55 miles to the west, is the elegant feminine soul. Red tile roofs overlook cobblestone streets, ornately carved doorways open onto extravagant gardens overflowing with bougainvillea, hibiscus and roses.

Elaborate grillwork encloses tiled hallways; stone aqueducts date back to colonial times. Through winding narrow streets marked here and there with monuments and old stone fountains, vendors of all descriptions trill offers of caged birds, wicker baskets, hot chocolate, hand-made brooms.

Since early colonial times, the rich, the famous, the talented, the opportunistic have built blue- and pink-walled mansions staffed by servants who scrub and polish and trim and dust. Once called the "The City of Widows" for the numbers of black-shawled mourners who emerged from protected gardens to go to mass (and occasionally to social events like concerts, dedications and parades), Cuernavaca escaped the rush and tumble of other mining region state capitals, in part because its proximity to Mexico City made direct shipment of the ore there possible and in part because the early Spanish *colonistas* erected weekend and summer homes among the hills and green canyons.

Diplomats, generals, silver, copper and sugar magnates retired to Cuernavaca to escape the smog that plagues the capital, to entertain their friends and write their memoirs. Maximilian and Carlota spend most of their short reign in Cuernavaca. Many of Mexico's presidents maintained residences there.

So did European and American writers, artists, sociologists and political refugees. They bought or built homes, learned Spanish together, discussed each other's books and ideas and expanded their habits and appetites to include local foods, local customs, even local problems that the residents of Cuernavaca faced. These residents regarded the outsiders as curious but acceptable co-inhabitants, just as they might have watched, talked about and interacted with small coteries of Asian jade merchants or Arabian camel drivers. Some even joined their discussions and projects, as much curiosities to the exiled intellectuals as the exiled intellectuals were to them.

One of the Cuernavacans who cultivated acquaintances with the foreigners was a policeman-turned-university student-turned-newspaper writer named Saul Gonzalez. I met Gonzalez in the early '80s during one of his perpetual parentheses (as he called them) among employments. He impressed me as a stubborn, pragmatic — perhaps even cynical — realist, outwardly affable but uncomfortable expressing personal feelings. Some inner energy — perhaps pain — seemed to restrict his ability to relax, let go, be himself. He seldom talked about his three years as a state policeman, nor about his father, for whom, I gathered, he endured a bitter admiration.

He did talk about his return to Cuernavaca after earning a master's degree at UNAM, Mexico's prestigious national university. As the correspondent for a Mexico City daily, he'd met and interviewed Ivan Illich, the prolific Russian sociologist, and Erich Fromm, already famous as the author of *The Art of Loving*. As impressive as each was, neither exuded the power of personality that a third member of their expatriate group demonstrated. Betsie Hollants, Gonzalez told me, put both of them — and everyone else — in the shade.

Swiping at his face as he talked, his fingers making little brushing movements across his cheeks and a sloping forehead given to alopecia, Gonzalez described one of his first encounters with the formidable Hollants.

"Ilyich had invited me to a sort of meeting or reception — I've forgotten exactly what the occasion was, something to do with the center [Centro Intercultural de Documentacion] and some studies it had done on differences between indigena and mestizo family life. This was back in the early seventies, right? I went, but I didn't know too many people there. Illich came over to ask me something: Did you read this or that or see this or that? I was about to reply, when he interrupted to introduce me to a woman who'd just come up behind me.

"It was this Betsie, Betsie Hollants. I'd seen her a number of times but I'd never met her. I responded automatically, politely — well, as polite as I get, you know, I'm a bit on the rough side. She held out her hand and said something — I don't think I heard her. She was a big woman — broad, heavy, with what she called a 'Belgian peasant face.' She was at least sixty, maybe almost seventy years old but there was real fire burning in her eyes. She squinted — scowled — with a 'just-who-are-you?' intensity. I...hell, I think I backed away.

"Illich mentioned something about my being a journalist. She wanted to know what I wrote. I started to say, 'News, some cultural events, some features...' something like that, but she cut me off.

"'Propaganda?'

"I felt — impaled by the word. I tried to brush it off, well, indicated I felt that I was conscientious, that I hadn't been bought .

"'I know about the conformist press in a conformist society.' She was smiling, but I could feel a toughness behind the expression. It pinned me to the wall even more. I don't know what I started to answer — something lame — and she cut me off again.

"'Don't bother. I know what it was like.'

"You see, I'd thought she was, you know, like Ilyich, like Fromm, a sociologist — professor. But no. She'd been a journalist. A war correspondent, back when there was no such thing as a woman war correspondent. She'd been in Spain, for Christ's sake, during the Civil War, a Nazi resistance fighter, a menace to the occupation. She'd been arrested, imprisoned.

"All this came out in our conversation. I was fascinated, but as she talked I felt like I was shrinking. I got this feeling, you know, that probably never would I do any of the things that she had done. 'Probably'? Hell—I knew I wouldn't.

And as I got smaller — as I felt smaller — at the same time I felt this swelling of admiration for her.

"She had what the press now calls 'a Presence.' She could do things that nobody else could do. Like make a totally macho-centered chauvinistic government that had no desire whatsoever to support women's rights cave in and help her. Anybody else would have been threatened with assassination, beaten up. Not Betsie. She was a fearless lobbyist. Mountains opened up when she approached.

"She was publishing a bunch of newsletters and bulletins, all of them about women and poverty and women and their subservience to men. Some of these things she was printing were translations of things sent her from here and there — Europe, the U. S. The press — or whatever it was, organization, I guess you'd call it — was called CIDHAL [*Communicacion, Intercambio y Desarrollo Humanos in America Latina*] but it was mostly her, her money, her work, her pushing it through.

"'Propaganda,' I chided her once, when she gave me a copy of one of the newsletters. She scowled, but through the fierceness — intensity — I detected a little dance of amusement.

"'No.' She had a strong deep voice — you could almost have pictured her having been an opera singer. "'Not propaganda. *La verdad.*'"

"'*Your* truth...' I tried to chide her, but I could feel my resolve starting to wilt.

"'It comes from here.' She pressed her big knuckled fingers over her heart, her eyes still fixed on me. 'Propaganda doesn't. Propaganda comes from here.' She tapped her forehead, just where her vividly white hair swished in a sort of curl beside her ear.

"'People lie.' She said it in a way that made disagreeing with her impossible. 'Lying is a social convention, you know that. You ask somebody how they feel, what do they answer. "Fine!" No matter how much they're hurting inside, that's what they say, right? Propaganda is the same thing. Just that the system is bigger. The individuals who speak for the system say, "This is prosperous..." "This is good..." "This is important..." and journalists copy down what they say and publish it as "fact." '

"'Propaganda,' she said, finally, 'is like the feed they give cattle in the stockyards. It fattens all the wrong cells. This is different. Read it.'

"I did read it. She — or one of her, you know, researchers, associates — had taken down conversations with some indigena women about how they lived, what they felt. What their daily lives were like. Their diets, their sicknesses, the trips they made, by foot, their pain over losing children, relatives.

"It stuck in my guts. I think more than anything I'd ever read, it got inside me. Finally I wrote a piece and sent it to *El Sol*, the Mexico City daily — I was writing for them at the time. The editor at first said something like — I don't remember exactly — 'Okay, let's not be playing around with this stuff, you're not there to write women's features...' but they wound up publishing it in a Sunday section. I didn't care. By this time, you see, I was hooked. I didn't want to interview political figures anymore. I didn't want the little paychecks they gave me to praise this or that. I wound up quitting — oh, it was some time after that; I went back into police work, private investigator stuff. It was dirty but it was more honest — at least I wasn't pretending to do something honest.

"Betsie, somehow, got hold of the piece I wrote. She reprinted it to send to all her outlets. And she thanked me. In a curious way, she thanked me. She sent me a tear sheet from the paper. Clipped to it was a bunch of white roses.

"I was never sure what she intended by it.

"And I was never brave enough to ask."

Betsie Hollants founded CIDHAL in 1969, a few years after she'd settled in Cuernavaca. Blanca Herrera, who designed and helped publish some of Hollants booklets and bulletins, called her the "generating force" behind Mexican feminism. Through CIDHAL, which she often had to keep going with her own money, she established outreach programs for women throughout Mexico.

In 1984, shortly before her eightieth birthday, she left the running of CIDHAL to associates and set up another social service association, *Vejez en Mexico: Estudio y Accion* (Old Age in Mexico: Study and Action), and a corollary, *Los Ancianos y Sus Amigos* (Senior Citizens and Their Friends). "Old age is not a disease, it's a step in our lives," her friend and associate Patricia Camacho quoted her as saying.

Betsie Hollants died in Cuernavaca in June, 1996 at the age of 91. "She did more after her 'retirement' than most truly ambitious people do in their lifetime," noted Rocio Suarez Lopez, who worked for and with her at CIDHAL. Few who met her ever were able to forget her.

Least of all Saul Gonzalez.

PART III

THE TORTURED SOUTH

The search for precious metals and the instantaneous wealth that they could provide thrust the sixteenth century Spanish conquistadors through the ore-producing slopes of the Sierras. Cortez himself led expeditions to the sources of the Aztecs' gold and to the Pacific, where the Spaniards established the seaport of Acapulco to anchor trans-Pacific trade to their holdings in the Philippines. They built regional capitals on the sites of indigena cities in Oaxaca and Chiapas, and fortified their Yucatan Peninsula settlements in Campeche and Merida, where access to hardwood forests provided lumber for building for cargo galleons and warships.

But the dense jungles and steep canyons of the southern selvas offered no great attractions. They installed regional governments and trade centers and gradually introduced large holdings agriculture in the accessible valleys and table lands, gradually pushing the native peoples higher into the mountains.

Rural chieftains — caciques[3] — manipulated the social, political and religious lives of their constituents. They paid homage to Mexico City but operated with little or no interference from the federal government, although the

3. In pre-Columbian times, the caciques were tribal leaders. The term now refers to a political boss, neighborhood honcho or non-elected leader who exerts control over certain groups of people and/or territory.

later had to repress bloody revolts in the Yucatan as late as the early 19th century.

Mexico's growing need for lumber, beef and export crops like coffee and bananas pressured further incursions into tribally controlled lands. Uprisings were quashed quickly and violently and many indigena communities broke up as their inhabitants left the threadbare land to become migrant workers or urban slum dwellers. The discovery of rich oil deposits throughout the Gulf Coast states of Veracruz, Tabasco and Campeche brought a new economy — and new problems — to much of the troubled south.

On New Year's Day, 1994, an indigena guerrilla force that called itself the National Zapatista Liberation Army took control of most of Chiapas. The fighting was brief but the uprising helped trigger an economic collapse and tarnished the country's self-image. Years of off-again, on-again negotiations, army incursions and vigilante raids have kept the area in turmoil as the rich in the southlands continue to get richer and the poor and dispossessed more indebted and more desperate.

Chapter 8. Where Trees Once Grew

Leave Your Women, Come!

Like many indigenous residents from the highlands of Oaxaca, Valentin Cortez Yilabe has a short-legged physique that makes his head seem too large for his shoulders. His heavy-lidded eyes have a sad milky tint and his wide mouth pulls his mustache into a drooping petulance.

I first met Cortez Yilabe one day when I stopped to buy a soft drink at a miscelanea among a cluster of stone and sheet metal dwellings where a rutted gravel road dipped through a shallow barranca a few miles north of Oaxaca City. A few weeks later I returned, with my landlord's 12-year-old handyman, Lorenzo, who, like Cortez Yilabe, had grown up speaking Zapoteco in a rural village.

As he talked, the 41-year-old Cortez stood with his hands shoved into the pockets of his hand-made jeans, the thumbs protruding and pointed inward. One pants leg was tucked into the top of a heavy work boot, the other hung loose. From the dwelling behind him, a wide, low rectangular structure built of loosely mortared adobe bricks and roofed with industrial sheet tile, children and grandchildren, most of them girls clad in frayed but scrubbed white dresses and white cotton sweaters, peered shyly at us before scurrying away to fulfill little chores that a beldam inside was assigning them.

Cortez had grown up in a beautiful small *poblado* named San Ysidro Alaopan, perched "in the clouds" above the rain forests, a torturous five-hour drive north of Oaxaca City. There, in a sloping clearing, 60 or 70 indigenous families had raised maize and herded goats around their bunched houses, single store and little church.

For centuries, they had lived in virtual isolation, seldom entertaining any visitors and marrying each other's children. Rarely did any of them leave until drought and a fungus that destroyed several successive crops of maize forced some of the men to seek work on lower land acreages.

Valentin Cortez Yilabe remembers the day one of the San Ysidro Alaopan villagers returned from a year's absence.

"'Come with me!' He gathered us together." Cortez spoke in a low rumbling monotone and stared towards the barren horizon. "He showed us new clothes that he was wearing, and a wallet thick with pesos. He told us that good jobs were waiting for us 'on *the Other Side*.'

"'Leave your women, come!' he urged. 'In a few months you will have enough to buy everything that you need and you can come back to your families!'

"I believed him. After all, he was a cousin, from the village. He said his *jefe* was holding 50 jobs. Our crops already were wilting. Even the goats couldn't find enough to eat. So I said, 'Yes, I will go.' A few days later, Cruz [the cousin] returned with two men and a truck. We had to walk to the highway [about four miles] to get into it because the truck could not climb the road to our rancheria.

"Carrying just our serapes, and with little to eat, we climbed into the back of the truck. There were so many of us crowded together that we barely could sit down. Sometimes the truck rocked so much on the mountain roads that we cried out, afraid that it would go over sideways into a canyon.

"We drove for days. The truck stopped only to let us urinate. When the truck driver would slam on the brakes, we all would crash forward, into each other. And we would slip and fall and bang each other when the truck went too fast around a curve.

"Some of the younger men were frightened. They never had gone so fast or so far away before. One said we would never get out of the truck. Others said we never would get back to our homes, ever again.

"We drove for three days. Maybe four. Then we stopped to spend the night in an abandoned warehouse and the next day *coyotes* took small groups of us across the border.

"On *The Other Side* another truck picked us up and took us to a ranch. They locked us in a large room. We did not know where we were, but we were so tired we all lay down. Hardly had we gotten to sleep than men came through to wake us up. They had us take showers and a man with an electric device shaved our heads. They said it was for 'sanitary purposes,' but I think it was to embarrass us. They gave us tortillas and coffee and wrote down our names and told us it was time to go to work.

"None of us ever had worked in fields like that before, tilling and cutting flowers and cutting and tying eucalyptus leaves. We suffered from the heat. Every day the *jefes* woke us up before daybreak and we worked until it was dark. At noon they would bring tortillas and beans to the fields so we could eat. When we got off work, they would drive us to the *casa grande* and they would check off our names and we would line up and get food to take back to the building in which we lived.

"All the way around the grounds around the *casa grande* was barbed wire. Behind our building was a little building made of cinder blocks. It was very, very small. In it the *jefes* would lock up anybody they wanted to punish.

"Why were we punished? I don't remember — no, for many things. For tearing a bag or fighting or taking too much time for lunch. One night, two of the younger men dug a hole and crawled under the barbed wire. I don't know what happened to them.

"We knew when it was Saturday night because that's when we got paid. Otherwise we did not know what day it was. The *jefe* giving out the money had a paper on each of us. On it was written how many meals we had eaten, how many other things we had had to buy. We could not buy anything, even a cigarette or a petate, except from one of the *jefes*. They said we owed money for our 'transportation' from San Isidro Alaopan and took out for that. At the end of three weeks, I only had about $11. Some had even less than that.

"I worked there for six months. After all the work was done, I only had $110 to bring back with me to Oaxaca. I had not been able to send any money to my family during all of that time. I would have left but I did not know where I was — or how to get back — and some of the workers said that if the *migras* caught us they would beat us or throw us in jail and take the little bit of money that we had.

"Out of the money that I earned, I had to pay my own way back to Oaxaca. When I got to San Ysidro Alaopan I was embarrassed and ashamed to see how much my family had suffered. Even so, the following year, when that *patrón*'s henchman Cruz came back, many from San Ysidro Aloapan went with him again. They worked so hard to earn so little, but still it was more than they could make staying home."

Life Afuera

For years in Apoala, nestled at the congruence of a winding canyon beneath the opening to a great cave once worshipped by the Mixtecas, the women's only money-making activity has been weaving palm fronds into hats that they sell for the equivalent of sixteen or seventeen cents apiece. "Just enough," a frequent visitor to Apoala, Luis Salomon, commented, "to buy salt or lime or a few little onions for their frijoles."

Although some of these women have migrated into the towns on the Oaxacan plateau — or even to the maquiladoras over a thousand miles away on the U.S.-Mexico frontier — most of them have remained in little clusters of dirt-floored thatched kitchen-sleeping rooms surrounded by sere gardens and a tiny stone or adobe church. They band together in communal groups to cook meals that they carry to their individual huts to serve to their families.

The only men present are husbands and fathers and brothers who've returned to the villages after working for months on coffee, chili and cotton plantations far away. From them, the women have formulated images of life *afuera* — life where everyone wears shoes and buys clothes and has things to do, life that they barely can imagine, much less aspire to.

But even in villages like Apoala, things are beginning to change. As one Mixteca mother of eight told Salomon, girls not only were going to school, but finishing *primaria* — "sometimes even *secundaria*." They did not marry as she had, when she was thirteen; they could read and write, they could work at something besides cooking and cleaning and weaving hats. They were not old women at twenty who only could marry widowers.

It was her belief (shared, ironically, by educators in Mexico City who never have set foot in indigena-speaking villages like Apoala) that her illiteracy — and the illiteracy of the wives and widows she lived among — had restricted her and her neighbors to the village and to the life that they lived there. For years, she explained, it had been a life of little to eat and constant child-bearing. It also had been a life of almost total submission — '*esclavitud*' — to a husband who left the village for months at a time to work far away to work and who returned with nothing but the torn shirt on his back, his muscles twisted from dawn-to-dark manual labor and his mind blackened by the mescal on which he'd spent his earnings.

To atone for his own failures — his having been used and cheated — he became arrogantly demanding and insisted that she wait on him hand and foot. He and other returning husbands often forbid their wives to associate with each other; they insulted them and beat them and even took the few pesos that the women earned by weaving hats to buy more mescal for themselves.

But there was no way that the mother of eight ever could have left the village. To migrate would have meant losing her little circle of friends — women like her who depended upon each other for nurture and support — and "How?" she asked, "would I have been able to provide for my children?"

For this reason, explained my friend Maggie Palacios Hartwig, many widows and "straw widows" in villages like Apoala refused to consider remarrying, even though they earned precious little from weaving hats, carrying water and doing laundry.

"They would tell me that life was hard enough without a crabby man around to make it harder," she acknowledged.

Eventually, even the villages like Apoala will dry up and disappear, believes Marilyn Eugenia Ochoa. An artist and art teacher who grew up in Queretero but who has lived in Oaxaca for many years, Ochoa predicts that the gradual exodus of younger women will leave the remote Mixteca villages with so few inhabitants — so few clusters of communal cookers and weavers — that even the last remaining holdouts will have to abandon a way of life that existed for centuries and follow their relatives and children to the already crowded cities that are absorbing so much of what once was indigena life.

Missionaries and Coffee Beans

As coffee plantations crept along the forested hills of the Soconusco in Chiapas and the foothills and valleys that dipped towards the Isthmus of Tehuantepec in Oaxaca, many small *ejidarios*, following the lead of the plantation owners, converted from corn and other seasonal crops to coffee production. Zapotecas, Mixes and Chontales, hired as temporary and seasonal laborers on the coffee *fincas*, returned to their hillside plots having learned enough about the crop to establish mini-plantations of their own.

Because their holdings were so small, these subsidiary producers marketed their coffee much as they had marketed other crops: by carrying them to the nearest town or city and offering them for sale. Gradually (with some government help) they banded together in cooperatives, many of which followed already established communal, ethnic and geographical lines.

Some of these cooperatives were very small — a dozen or so Chontales related by marriage who lived near each other on an arable steep slope, for example, or members of a rural municipality who agreed to pool manpower. Many fledgling cooperatives suffered growing pains — fights, recriminations, resignations and coups d'état — that forced the groups to disband, or fragment into even smaller groups, or consolidate around new leadership.

Instrumental to the formation of many of the cooperatives in the Isthmus were the organizing efforts of a team of Catholic missionaries. They convinced indigena coffee growers to band together, not just as agriculturists seeking markets but also as political-religious entities that could vie with the plantation owners commercially and with cacique-controlled police and security bands socially and politically. These missionaries encouraged the fledgling groups to put their new-found solidarity to work by demanding fair prices and fair treatment from the merchants who sold them grain, milk and tools, to insist on free access to roads and transportation, and to deal fairly and honestly with other indigenas, both individuals and groups.

Local reaction to the cooperatives depended on the economic and political structure of individual municipalities and the relationships that existed among indigenas, mestizo campesinos and the large landowners. Some cooperatives acceded to local political caciques and operated within their control; others expanded and became adversarial political organizations that challenged social and governmental decisions.

The latter frequently aroused the animosities of individual large landowners (and of some local political bosses who didn't want to see them upset the status quo). Luis Hernandez Navarro, in a *La Jornada* commentary, described depredations — including kidnappings and killings — in some of the more remote regions, particularly in the foothills of the Sierra Juarez.

Fluctuations in the coffee market and the difficulties that individual small cooperatives encountered in trying to transport and sell their crops prompted some of the cooperatives to form organizations that transcended their original ethnic and geographical boundaries. This coincided with the federal government's push to integrate indigena organizations into the existent political system. PRI organizers encouraged regional groups that had similar aims and functions to unite into large, loose "loyal" (to PRI) governing bodies.

These larger groups incorporated some of the cooperatives, and brought onto their governing boards the leaders of others. They helped the small growers to survive crop failures brought on by adverse weather conditions and to utilize some of the technical improvements being used on the larger plantations.

Like a number of other mini-producers in the foothills of the Sierra Juarez, Blas Millan's father began cultivating organic coffee beans in the early 1970s. A round-faced young man with heavy-lidded eyes and a wide-cheekboned face that seemed perpetually on the verge of breaking into a grin, Millan called the conversion to purely organic production "a godsend" because it pulled smaller growers like his father out of competition with the large plantations.

The organic growers not only created a niche for themselves in the overall coffee production picture, but also acquired an expertise that the large-scale producers often lacked. Millan and his brother-in-law developed several varieties of high quality beans and operated a small nursery as well as their mini-plantations, which they expanded onto some previously untillable steep hillsides.

In June 1983, the Union de Comunidades Indigenas de la Region del Istmo (UCIRI) formalized the organizing of nearly 2,600 Zapoteca, Chontal and Mixe coffee producers into a growing and marketing organization. As they hammered out of a constitution, Blas Millan, his brother-in-law and other organic coffee growers insisted on clauses that specified that the growers would develop, produce and sell only organically grown coffee.

"It was good," Millan commented on the successful campaign. "It gave UCIRI a clearly-defined purpose."

A clearly-defined purpose, but not necessarily an easy row to hoe. Though one of the strongest indigena organizations in Oaxaca, UCIRI still had to overcome the opposition of non-indigena landholders and politicos throughout the Isthmus. It had to develop financial resources, both as an organization and for its individual members, and keep the multi-ethnic, multi-lingual indigena communities from breaking away or caving in to local caciques.

The first step financially was to begin exporting directly to markets in Europe, a task made easier by using contacts that some of the growers already had developed. UCIRI then focused on bringing small growers — *ejidarios* — throughout the foothills and lower mountain slopes of the Isthmus into the organic coffee growing fold. UCIRI "missionaries" taught new skills as they tried to convince newcomers how nearly aligned their aims and interests were.

"It was not always easy," Millan admitted. "We were not experienced in union-type, government-type organization."

But Millan and his fellow growers soon had created both a state coordinating board for indigena coffee growers and had been instrumental in the development of a national board to share ideas and information and to lobby issues that affected the *cafetaleras*. They founded a school — the Centro de Educacion Campesina (CEC) — to teach organic gardening techniques to twenty or thirty rural residents a year and to send them back to their communities as on-the-job instructors.

As a lead group "kept in focus by its devotion to organic methods" of coffee and other agricultural production, UCIRI backed indigena organizations throughout Oaxaca that were struggling for autonomy and self-control.

"Outsiders criticized us for being more than a marketing coop," Millan admitted. UCIRI representatives moving into new territories incorporated new ideas about disease prevention, water purification and diet into their promotion of organic food production. CEC instructors returning to their native communities set up basic education centers to teach arithmetic, reading and writing as well as agriculture.

As the Catholic missionaries had done earlier, the UCIRI missionaries helped organize cooperatives and set up rural warehouses to store coffee harvests that couldn't immediately be taken to market. They even established stores — usually rural cooperatives — that provided isolated indigena communities with agricultural supplies and basic food necessities like sugar, powdered milk and flour.

For years the isolated farmers clustered in the virtually inaccessible valleys and meadows of the Sierra Juarez had been forced to depend on local control of trucks and shipping to get their products to market. In 1988, a UCIRI-forged alliance of Zapoteco and Mixe communities (called the Union de Pueblos Zapotecos-Mixes) acquired their own equipment and with picks, shovels and a little dynamite cut some new roads in order to get their coffee off the highlands into Coatzacoalcos and Veracruz.

"We wanted [the cooperatives] to be totally self-sufficient, to be in control of their coffee from the time they planted it until the time it left Mexico," Millan acknowledged.

For some local caciques, losing their transportation monopoly was the breaking point. Two dozen armed men intercepted a two-truck Union de Pueblos Zapotecos-Mixes convoy, forced the transporters into the brush, dumped their cargoes and set fire to the vehicles. The indigena coffee growers responded by sabotaging a road leading into the principal landowner's finca. The indigenas assembled a group of armed guards to accompany the next truckloads of organic coffee beans. They waited for stormy weather, and virtually had to rebuild the roadway as they rumbled along.

Twice the organic growers had to harness mules to pull barely drivable old vehicles out of *vados*. Local police arrested several members of the group as they returned towards their village, "for carrying concealed arms and for not having proper vehicle registration." The police confiscated the trucks, but UCIRI leaders forced higher authorities to order their release.

The UCIRI carried its protests all the way to the state government in Oaxaca City and the federal government in Mexico City. The union organized other indigena groups to support the Union de Pueblos Zapotecos-Mixes' fight to transport their own coffee.

"Finally," Millan smiled, "the caciques gave in — there were too many of us against them." Before they relented, however, cacique assassins had killed four indigenas, destroyed vehicles and manipulated numerous arrests.

Those incidents magnified UCIRI's reputation for militancy. In 1994, three truckloads of armed Mexican soldiers wheeled across the CEC campus.

"The students thought they were doing a typical grandstanding marijuana search," Millan observed. But the soldiers not only searched the campus, they interrogated the directors and faculty.

"They demanded to know what kind of military training the instructors were giving," Millan complained. "They looked for weapons and cross-examined students and teachers about supposed subversive activities."

That they found nothing was less pertinent than the attitude they reflected, Millan insisted. "It showed us how tentative our little bit of power is.

"And how easily everything that we have can be taken away."

A Living Experiment

In one of the poems in a ragged little book that survived the drying up of a tiny experimental school in the Sierra Mazateca, Jhon Maxwell Mayagoitia described himself as "an ugly bear" with "huge eyes" and a "face shaped like a shovel blade." No one quite knows exactly why he chose the nearly inaccessible cañada to establish a "school of art and growing things"; perhaps, as he mentions in another poem published sometime between 1934 and 1937, he did it "because in the deepest canyons, among the steepest hills, the plants, like the people, give off a kind of purity one can find nowhere else."

Despite his given names (including the transposition in "Jhon,") Mayagoitia had no English or American antecedents. His parents came to Mexico from Spanish North Africa in the late 19th century ("with their Spanish surnames and Mohammedan prayer rugs") and became bakers and candy makers.

In his poems he makes few references to them, but in a badly typeset and poorly bound book of "Reflections" that a friend of a former student saved, Mayagoitia mentions that his mother chose his first name "from some novel she'd been reading...a passing flutter, a bird's flight overhead, to which she gave permanence." In the same volume he describes shaving his invalid father — one of his duties as a young man living at home — as "a punishment, I sometimes thought, for my failure to go out in the world and become successful."

Mayagoitia's parents moved from Mexico City to Oaxaca City when he was a child. For reasons he never described in his poems, he became fascinated with the indigena cultures. Perhaps being a foreigner in a city where there were relatively few foreigners contributed to this fascination, for the indigenas, like him, were "different" and were treated with disdain by many of the mestizos. Or perhaps a quiet rebelliousness prompted him to make different choices from his parents and his brothers.

He must have been in his early forties when he started the school (which wasn't really a school, just a teacher and students who talked and wrote songs and stories while they worked in a communal garden). Mayagoitia refused to acknowledge that any altruistic motives guided him.

"I do it," he wrote, "for myself. I do it as a garden/Touching each of the separate leaves."

The leaves grew. An acquaintance of Mayagoitia's who visited the site described a "Garden of Eden...where twenty or more children sang as they tilled a verdant vegetable garden surrounded by enormous flowers and groves of fruit trees." For Mayagoitia, learning was a process, rather than a transference of knowledge from teacher to pupil; he regarded life as "an experiment...futile by definition, for it leads to death..."

But he discovered, through the processes of nature, that "there is a way of interacting...that brings one out of the personal self/Into the rhythm of things." A "rhythm of things" similar to that of the natural world evolved through the students' songs and stories into gardens not perceptible to the eye but nevertheless as real to them as anything they experienced through the outward senses.

These "gardens," as Mayagoitia refers to them, merged stories the students had heard as children, observations they made about the world around them and feelings that their activities aroused. Their daily work with plants and the soil influenced these shared inner gardens. They invented their own otherworldly creatures, anthropomorphic for the most part, not so much to explain the phenomena they were experiencing as to confirm how they felt about them with each other.

At some point, apparently early in 1934, a peripatetic priest trundled through the area, confronted Mayagoitia with an upraised cross and blubbered threats of excommunication for anyone who participated in his garden school, which the priest clearly recognized as "the work of Satan." Not being Catholic, Mayagoitia shrugged off the threat. Most of the Mazatecas spoke little or no Spanish and, though they understood that the priest was unhappy about something, they regarded his performance with the detached irony of mountain dwellers who forever are amazed by the events that unfolded in the hidden cañadas.

In a poem included in the ragged little book that one of his students retained, Mayagoitia quoted some distinctly erotic connections that his young students made between plant and human fertility. (Mazatecos become adults at ages thirteen and fourteen, so his students necessarily were younger than that.)

"They told how the plow/Plunged into the ground./They were there with the earth as it swelled/They were there as the young plants struggled to get sunlight/As they clawed through the earth for food/As they became ripe and proud/Filled with seed to thrust into the ground..."

No one seems to know how long Mayagoitia kept his garden school going, not does anyone seem to know exactly what happened to him. He had trouble with his eyesight, the acquaintance who visited his "Garden of Eden" remembered, and there is no record of his having published anything after 1937. The friend of his former student speculated that his students probably buried him in the garden when he died, and that some huge, ungainly foreign tree has grown over that spot.

He would like that, I think. After all, isn't living but an experiment in a temporary physical form?

The Brujo Bueno

At first glance, Joel Aguilar Aguilar appeared terribly unsuited for the reed-filled marshes that wound inland from the sandbar that separated the Parque Nacional Lagunas de Chacahua from the Pacific Ocean. Picking his way over the matted growth, his slender-legged movement reminding one of a shore bird stepping through an oil slick, he never lost his outsiderness, even after months of exploring the lush channels, the hidden estuaries, the huge pools of plant-clogged sludge that the national park had become by 1994.

To many residents of the town of Chacahua, a ramble of sea-stained walls and palapa-roofed houses half-hidden from view by palm trees and the masts of weathered shrimp boats, Aguilar Aguilar was witch and magician, a healer whose knowledge of native herbs and flowers exceeded those of any doctor or shaman between Puerto Angel and Puerto Escondido. To each other they confirmed stories about his conversing with crocodiles and standing among mangroves with a falcon obediently perched on one shoulder and an eagle on the other. They said flamingoes brought their wobbly-legged young for him to bless and huge manta rays surfaced to let him touch their muscled fins.

However fanciful and exaggerated the stories might have become, they did certify Aguilar Aguilar's love for the deteriorating marshlands. For years its lagoons had provided thousands of pelicans, herons, storks and other marsh birds with oysters, clams, scallops and squid, plus mojarra, pijolin, flamenco, cabezuda, cazon and many other varieties of fish.

Sunglasses riding the bridge of his thin, stirrup-shaped nose, the short, dark beard that he took pains to keep carefully trimmed accentuating a face that seemed both soft and somehow secretive, Aguilar Aguilar left the cabin he had rented on a hillside away from the town every morning and didn't return until late afternoon or early evening. One of the shrimpers had loaned him a little dingy and a motor — he was helpless with oars, never quite able to steer and row simultaneously or effectively — and he used it to get to places in the marsh that he couldn't have reached without it.

One day he returned with an injured duck in his little dingy. Its wing was too badly broken for it ever to fly again, but Aguilar Aguilar fed and cared for it and it followed him around like a pet on a string for months afterwards. When a flu epidemic swept through Chacahua, he went from house to house, sunglasses riding the frown that had settled over his eyes, prescribing and providing herbs and teas that relieved both symptoms and anxiety.

He was not, he told his patients, a medical doctor — they would have to go to Puerto Angel for that — but he was licensed to practice homeopathic medicine, his profession in his home state of Veracruz. Despite his demurrals, many whispering townspeople decided that he was, in fact, a *brujo bueno*, a status that they not only conferred on him, but on his pet duck as well.

In years past, the lagoon and the ocean had been connected and the tides had flushed through, keeping the lagoon water from becoming stagnant. Periodically, the long finger of sand that separated most of the lagoon from the ocean would close and the townspeople, with shovels and plows and sweat (and liberal doses of *caña*), would reopen it.

Aguilar Aguilar joined them. Though he proved inept with a shovel, and tired easily, he kept working, even after the townspeople had to admit that their efforts were in vain: They could not keep the channel open any longer.

Appeals for government help brought promises, but not the construction of a concrete jetty that would keep the lagoon connected to the ocean. Successful with neither his shovel nor the typewritten warnings he mailed to government officials and private entrepreneurs, to newspapers and to friends and acquaintances, Aguilar Aguilar delved deeper into the increasingly fetid swamp, adding to his usual apparel a bedroll, plastic tarpaulin and boots.

Townspeople noticed his absences — and eventually the fact that his little boat did not return to Chacahua. None of them knew for certain that he had not simply boarded a bus and returned to Veracruz. For many of them that was not a reasonable proposition, for (they said) they still caught glimpses of him far across the lagoon, eagles or ospreys on his shoulders, crocodiles and storks and all of the other creatures of the marshlands gathered around to follow him and his constantly quacking companion, the little duck.

Chapter 9. Too Soon for Some, Too Late for Many

The Guardian of Market Day

For centuries, through gaps in brush-covered hills marred by patches of burned stubble, along creek beds and over roads carved into the rocky earth by carts and burros and cattle and bare feet, little groups of campesinos, some indigena, some mestizo, headed for Oaxaca City for its big market days. As they arrived they spread across the cobblestones, an ochre- and clay-toned hub that seemed to have shoved its way out of the earth to absorb this pulsating flood.

Through them moved another flow, less defined, ununified, but singular in its awkwardness, its dress, its foreign ways of pronouncing words — tourists who came from Mexico City and Puebla and Guadalajara (and from even more distant places, like Philadelphia and Riverside and Denver, London and Amsterdam and Barcelona and Madrid). Like children edging along forest paths, they touched and peered and chattered to each other, haggled over pennies, posed in front of churches, looked for bathrooms among tiny eateries that smelled of burned tortillas, fresh-cut cilantro, rancid grease.

Eyes watched them; ears listened to them. Oaxaca City was not so big that its local commander of the federal police, Manuel Cadena, didn't know how long they were staying or what they were doing.

He seemed to be everywhere and nowhere, as though by some mystical formula he had created dozens of replicas of himself to move invisibly among the crowd, record their peccadillos, note their arguments and assignations, warn them when they had gone too far. He knew which ruffian's machete most recently had drawn blood, whose burro-bags were filled with illegal pulque, who was charging a few pesos to bang a sad-eyed teen-aged girl inside serapes thrown together as a makeshift tent.

He was not a large man, even by Oaxacan standards. Beneath his ubiquitous exterior, he was immaculate almost to the point of daintiness. His fingernails always were perfect half-moons, his straight black hair fell perfectly into place with just a touch of his fingertips, his never-seeming-new, never-seemed-used suits always were spotless and unwrinkled, as though the swirls of dust, the animal feces, the oily exhaust and crushed fruit and flayed straw of the market place never touched him at all.

Seldom did he draw a weapon, but its presence was subtly apparent. His jackets seemed to have been tailored to show the bulge of the holster that held the World War II American officer's .38 with its extra sets of clips.

He only had to slide his hand across his chest to stop a fight, or calm a drunk, or end a family argument. Many permanent residents of Oaxaca City — *imprenta* owners, university students, *amas de casa*, cab drivers — went out of their way to offer "*Buenos dias*" or comment on the number of tourists or ask about his wife and children but the campesinos, both mestizo and indigena, edged silently away or nodded stiffly, acknowledging his power and his presence, as he passed.

Market day in Oaxaca, outwardly at least, was a chaotic tapestry of shouts and colors and odors and flailing arms and shoving shoulders and pushing legs, of pig squeals and burning charcoal and taxi horns and church bells, children in all stages of dress and undress darting this way and that way and merchants and clerks and indigenas and drunks bumping and squatting and running and shouting. But beneath this clamor, this outpouring of energy, Oaxaca was an orderly city, and even during its fiesta days, when the market was busiest, both permanent residents and the immigrants from isolated mountain villages and ranchos conformed to established patterns.

Like most traditional country markets, the markets in the city of Oaxaca were loosely organized according to the types of products they offered for sale. Each little section, and each indigenous family group, had its spokesperson, its regulator, its decision maker. Manuel Cadena seemed both to understand and to encourage this social hierarchy. He only had to gesture to one of these rugged *jefes* and he would see that disputes were solved, encroachments regulated, excessive conduct quashed. His power gave them power and their authority provided him with lieutenants who would do his bidding.

As the city grew sultry and muggy from the thousands of bodies shoving and wriggling through the market place, most of the local residents retired to their houses for their midday meals and siestas. The vegetable and fruit vendors re-stacked their little piles of tamarinds and mangoes, chayotes and chilis and onions, and those who had not sold their chickens and ducks shoved them under little cornhusk pyramids to keep them out of the sun.

Dozens of dogs, bony-ribbed and showing patches of bare skin, sprawled among the flattened cardboard boxes and frayed petates, letting neither flies nor children delay their afternoon naps. Only among the tourist items — the blankets and blackened Oaxacan clay pots, the baskets and hand-made leather purses — did traffic increase, for tourists often were late risers and did not plunge into the early morning thrust and bustle of hot tortillas and ripe vegetables and headless chickens flapping through the dust.

The heat did not seem to affect Manuel Cadena, however — perhaps because he did not let it affect him. He took both food and refreshment standing up — an orange juice *licuado* here, a *taco al pastor* there — his face assessing each new noise, each darting figure, each pungent smell as he chewed or sipped or smoked a cigarette. At times, responding to some joke or remark from those around him, his lips would pull across his small even teeth in a smile that seemed to be undergoing some forced sudden pain.

His conversations invariably were chopped and succinct. He seemed to prefer gestures to words. By instinct, or by a constant processing of what he learned by watching and listening, he understood which fights were individual and which were tribal, for fights, like drunkenness, like fornication, free, purchased or forced, were part of the natural order of things, but conspiracy — organized, ethnic, armed — was not.

The mission that brought Manuel Cadena early to market day, and kept him circulating among its thousands of faces until the streets folded into dark bundles of sleeping, grunting, whimpering vendors, traders and transients, was not to dampen or thwart little moments of emotion but to preserve the thrust and surge that kept those moments within the boundaries that tradition prescribed. For Oaxaca, despite its Indian earthiness and Indian colors, was a colonial city, owned, manipulated and administered by families of status whose antecedents lay not in Mitla and Monte Alban but in the mansions and cathedrals of Mexico City and Guadalajara, Sevilla, Madrid and Rome.

As he sipped the last of his night-time brandies within the darkened, bolted and barred restaurant where he ended his day, Manuel Cadena would touch the bulge beneath his still unwrinkled and unstained dress coat, watch the patterns the clouds cast across the Zocalo as they drifted past the moon and with a slight tipping of his chin and forehead silently confirm the way things were and the way that things had to be.

I WON'T MELT

Above the earth-toned stone of the city of Oaxaca's first permanent buildings — the cathedral with its rubricated spires and heavy bell tower, the governmental palace and the parks and Zocalo they surround — the green-tinted windows of glistening skyscrapers peer down like imperious intruders. Built in the mid-'70s and mid-'80s, they monument a never-quite-successful attempt by the Mexican government to decentralize the federal bureaucracy by setting up regional administrative centers that not only would pull thousands of workers out of the congested and smog-clogged capital but would boost local economies as well. (The state of Oaxaca traditionally had been the poorest state in the nation.) But the result, insists American anthropologist Arthur D. Murphy, has been to "drag Mexico City's architecture, smog, *ambulantes* and corruption onto the Mixtec plain..." and, by doing so, "to sully and grime what always had been best about Oaxaca: its self-containment and identity..." that, despite cycles of poverty "permitted it to love and to take care of itself."

Of all the cities in Mexico, Oaxaca for centuries seemed the most immune to change. It presides over a high agricultural plain surrounded on all sides by precipitous mountains that, though not spectacularly high, are treacherous and in most places impassable.

"It is as though the two oceans pressing against Mexico's slender waist crumpled it into the thousands of ridges and canyons that isolate the Oaxacan plateau," an anthropologist who worked with Murphy in the mid-'80s noted. These mountains, which rise abruptly from Oaxaca's nearly 350 miles of Pacific coastline towards the Continental Divide on the south and from the Gulf plains of Veracruz and Puebla on the north, retarded the *mestizaje* blending of Spanish and Indian and insulated the state from the ravages of Mexico's wars and revolutions. The predominately indigena culture attracted tourists and the generally adequate rainfall and soil fertility provided the rural communities with just enough sustenance to keep their cycles of family life continuing generation after generation.

"All of that changed when the buildings [the government offices and banking institutions] went up," Luz Maria Tapia explained. A slender woman whose shoulders curved forward as though accustomed to lifting invisible burdens, Tapia stacked several large cardboard cartons we had unloaded from a cramped, fumy Volkswagen microbus on the sidewalk in front of us. Her fingers deftly loosened knots in the frayed clothesline cord that bound them together as she continued talking.

"The people they brought to Oaxaca were different from the people here. And at the same time, the indigenas moved here from the mountains. They too were different. The city became like three cities, each one different from the other. That's when all the problems began."

The "problems," said Tapia, primarily were economic. Oaxaca always had been poor, but before the banks and government offices arrived, it had been "poor with dignity." The newcomers brought demands for housing, transportation and modern construction materials. Government projects (like the expansion of Oaxaca's airport to accommodate major airline jet passenger planes) attracted thousands of minimum-wage workers, most of them from small- and middle-sized towns in other parts of Oaxaca.

Simultaneously, commercial expansion, particularly in agriculture and forest products, dislodged many Trique, Cuicateco and Mixe Indian families from their small self-supporting ejidos[4] in rural parts of the state. Many of these families sifted first to the towns, then to the city. They matriculated into the work force, but not as year-round or salaried employees.

"Before, on the ranchos, in the small towns, the families kept together. Now that is not true — not true at all." Tapia unfolded a metal-legged card table and placed it a few feet from the curb facing the government-subsidized ISSSTE supermarket. I helped her open the cartons — the largest first — as she arranged half a dozen sets of porcelain cookware on the card table, then, using the two largest of the cartons as auxiliary display tables, placed other sets on them.

Unlike several of the vendors arranging goods along the sidewalk beside her, she did not bring a folding chair to sit on, explaining, "It gives a bad

4. Essentially, land grants. They were given in perpetuity to families when the Cardenas government confiscated all land that wasn't being put to use by the big feudal landowners.

impression, like you're there but you don't want to be there. Customers like to buy from someone who seems eager about what she is selling."

Tapia was Oaxacan by ancestry, but not by birth. Her Oaxacan father and his family had followed one job after another to Zacatecas, where Luz Maria was born. He returned to Oaxaca when she was in her early teens.

"He had a good job, as a truck driver for a furniture company, but he got hurt in an accident." With the small pension that he received, he refurbished a little house and did odd jobs in Cacaotepec, a few miles northwest of Oaxaca City.

Luz Maria met her husband-to-be there. "Our first years together were a struggle," she admitted. He worked seasonally — agriculture and construction — until after their three children were born and they moved to Oaxaca City.

Gradually the night-time jobs he hustled cleaning offices and business establishments expanded into a full-time livelihood. Once he had "dozens and dozens of businesses" (particularly satellite services affiliated with government projects) for customers, Luz Maria persuaded her parents to move to Oaxaca and she worked with him and the three or four people they hired while the children slept at her mother's house.

"When he first got sick, he said it was just '*la gripe*' and he wouldn't do anything about it. He wouldn't go to the doctor. He just kept working and working." A violent shudder jerked Tapia's shoulders; as she turned abruptly away from me, I could see the muscles along her cheekbones twitch against her gritted teeth. "*Disculpa,*" she whispered, fingers flicking against her face as though physically trying to slap the intrusive feelings away, "I still am very angry. He —"

Potential customers browsing past her display pulled Tapia into a pleasant — if contrived — attentiveness. She and the other sidewalk merchants — there were just a handful — channeled those entering and leaving the ISSSTE *tienda* along a stretch of sidewalk ruptured by the roots of several old oak trees. Though *ambulantes*, Tapia and her vendor associates set up regularly day after day at this same location along the curb between the grocery and a row of taxis that maneuvered in and out behind them.

All in the little row catered to working- and middle-class permanent residents like themselves, not to tourists seeking native Oaxaca ware. Further down the street, grouped around the entrance way of a small parking lot still littered with cracked cinder blocks and fallen mortar of the building it had replaced, another cluster of *ambulantes* hawked fresh strawberries and steamed hot dogs, popsickles, lottery tickets, oranges and cucumbers.

"When he died, I couldn't help it, I was filled with anger at him," Tapia said, when the customers drifted away without purchasing anything. "I threw away all of my pictures of him, I didn't want to see him, I didn't want to think about him. It was stupid for him to die, do you see? Stupid! Stupid because he wouldn't go to the doctor. Stupid because he wouldn't listen to me! At the hospital, the doctors said, if they could have treated him, they could have....but he wouldn't go, he didn't want to spend the money.

"Spend the money! How much did it cost to lose the business? It was our income! It paid for everything we had — everything the children had. Our clothes. Our house. Our food. Everything!

"We had no insurance. We had no retirement. We lived on what we earned.

"As he got sicker, even though he forced himself to work, forced himself so hard that when he got home all that he could do was moan and try to sleep — he hardly ate, he hardly talked to me, he stopped being a father to the children — and then some nights he couldn't go to work and I would go and one of our sons would go with me but we couldn't do it all, we had to hire extra help but I couldn't keep them working the way my husband had, we couldn't do as good a job as he had and still he forced himself to try to go until finally he couldn't even stand up and I drove him to the doctor.

"For weeks they wouldn't let him out of the hospital. Then they let him out to go home to die.

"There was nothing else that they could do, they said."

Anger returned to the last sentence — anger that Tapia made no attempt to disguise from a slight, slender, shawled woman bending over one of the sets of cookware. And the woman with her severe face and nervous fingers took no more notice of either Tapia's words or tone than she did of other bursts of emotion along the sidewalk corridor.

Cab drivers made no secret of their politics, mothers of their domestic problems, stock boys of their differences with parents, police and girl friends. Passers-by listened and ignored the surges of anger, elation, discipline. It was an open forum — a marketplace, as it were, of emotion; those speaking seemed to presume that no one was listening except the person or persons they were addressing and, simultaneously, they seemed to assume that it didn't matter if someone else was listening or not.

Even after her husband's death, Tapia continued, weaving her descriptions between answers to browsers' queries, she had tried to keep the business going.

Both of her sons — one just out of *preparatoria*, the other still two years from graduation — had tried to help but both had other jobs (as stock clerks in the same ISSSTE *tienda* her vending display faced) and both had become short-tempered and antagonistic.

"I hurt for them, they were working half the night, working half the day, going to school, missing out on things their friends were doing, plus trying to deal with me — I was angry too, I hardly could sleep, all I could think about was my husband not taking care of himself and leaving me the way that he had.

"Then there were the men in the places I cleaned. It was very different with my husband gone. When he was still alive, if we found somebody still hanging around an office, doing some late work, my husband would joke with him a little, comment on things like tourists and weather and football, and that would be it. But with my husband gone, some of those men began to make comments. They would tell me to close the door. Say it was warm, wouldn't I like to take off my clothes? Suggest that I would have to do more than just clean if I wanted to keep working for them.

"It got to be too much. My daughter, too, was getting very angry; I was worried about her. Worried that she would run away and that something terrible would happen to her. From doing very good in school — good grades, and she was one of the best players on the basketball team — she started skipping tests, becoming a discipline problem.

"So I gave up the working at night to do this."

"Doing this" hadn't been just selling cookware. Her first vending job had been selling cheap imported clothing — blouses and skirts — dumped onto Oaxacan markets by importers who'd acquired huge lots of Asian-manufactured cottons and rayons they couldn't sell in the United States. The underground economy, she commented, was a world unto itself, with its own hierarchy and rules. As she became more involved with the people and products, she shifted from clothing to small appliances to jewelry before finally settling on cookware.

She belonged to an organization of *ambulantes* that guaranteed that her space in front of the ISSSTE *tienda* wouldn't be taken over by someone else. Her daughter sometimes helped her and her two sons contributed parts of their earnings to household expenses. Sometimes, to supplement her income, she picked up a case of tomatoes or oranges that a trucker was letting go cheaply, repackaged them and sold them door-to-door around her neighborhood.

Tapia's sales rap — low-key and conversational — attracted an eavesdropping flow of onlookers. Women with their hair pinned up in combs and kerchiefs leaned past children they'd propped in the ISSSTE *tienda*'s rickety shopping carts. Others, emerging from the store with more plastic bags than they could carry, detoured past to listen.

So did customers of the other stores nearby — a key-maker, a sports equipment store in a stone cavern that once part of a brewery, a *tiangui* bristling with brooms and pails and plastic dishes, a depository of native herbs and bulk grains. Now and then a browser would inquire about sizes or prices, or would touch or ping or rub or clang the pots of various sizes.

Although people want to buy from someone who is eager about their product, they back away from someone — "particularly a woman" — who pushes too hard, Tapia told me. And because her products were relatively expensive (the sets ranged in price from the equivalent of $15-$40 dollars), customers seldom bought the first time that they examined the cookware, or asked about its price.

"If they feel good about me," she reasoned, "they will feel good about buying from me. So even to those who I know will not buy anything from me, I talk, because I know that while I am talking others will come up to listen. They hear me say that I will do a layaway for them, give them receipts for their money, even give them the sets piece by piece as they pay for the whole."

Like thousands of other *ambulantes* in Oaxaca City, Tapia had to appear on her street corner every day in order to earn enough to pay her expenses. She seldom had money for extras, and no longer drove a car, "since the one I had, the one that my husband bought, threw an I-don't-know-what-you-call-it and stopped working. I could not afford to get it fixed, so I sold it to a man who wanted the parts out of it. That is why, now, I come here by bus, or sometimes, if it is raining, I take a taxicab."

A suddenly gusty breeze sent scraps of plastic bags, newspapers and leaves swirling along the sidewalk in front of us. As she had done several times before while I was talking to her, Tapia squinted skyward and exchanged speculative assessments with her vendor colleagues about the possibilities of rain.

"It does not drive me away," she boasted quietly. "I learned years ago that I won't melt, and neither will my porcelain — I only need to protect the boxes." A momentary irony brightened her dull eyes. She cocked her head and nodded, "They are very valuable to me, my boxes. Without them I cannot carry on my livelihood.

"We *ambulantes*, that is the first thing we think of. Sturdy boxes. To carry back and forth what we never sell. Think of it, *gringo*. Everything else we can do without. Food. Clothes. But our boxes, ah! Without them, what are we?

"Empty — empty, my friend. Without them we wouldn't know who we were. We might mistake ourselves for office folk. Or *amas de casa* just out for a midday stroll."

There Are No Fathers Here

"No, there are no fathers here. My sister-in-law and I live without them."

Martha Chavez smoothed her cotton skirt over her ankles so that its folds completely concealed the squat, hand-made stool on which she was sitting, then let her hands drop into her lap, the palms cupped as though holding a bowl of fruit. Her oldest son, a leggy teenager with sunken cheeks and myopia that caused him to crane his neck forward and squint at objects in front of him, rocked back and forth on the unevenly pegged legs of a stool beside her.

Now and then he would catch himself peering at my companion Elaine, who had made this trip to Oaxaca with me, and grimace self-consciously — a sudden spastic wince that exposed uneven, overly large teeth and darkened, purplish gums. Chavez's two younger children periodically peeked in and out from play in the rutted street, passable only to pedestrian traffic outside.

"My son, Ernesto, he is the only man," Chavez continued, the muscles of her rounded face twitching as though resisting a barrage of invisible insects. "His father has not been here for three years. He went north to find work. We do not know what has become of him.

"My husband's brother, he has been gone for three years too. Twice my sister-in-law heard from him, one time when she received some money that he sent to her, but that was — I don't remember — a long time ago.

"When we still lived in the mountains, on the rancho, my husband would be gone for weeks at a stretch cutting trees for the lumber trucks. We had melons and squash as well as beans and corn in our little ejido on the hillside. I took care of it when he was away. But the crops all dried up and my husband came to the city. He built this house, saying he would put windows in it, and a floor that wasn't just packed-down dirt. And a separate place to do the cooking, and a place for washing clothes.

"To make a little extra I started working — doing as I do now, selling little candies — because when he wasn't working we had no way to buy even masa or a few beans. Then his brother came, with his wife, my sister-in-law, and their little ones, and they moved in with us since they had no place else to go.

"My sister-in-law works too — she sells dulces but on Sundays, like today, she helps cook and wash dishes for *unos ricos* — and my son, my Ernesto here, he works too, every day and often at night; when there are parties at the big place where they hold dances, he parks the cars and scrubs the floors and cleans up everything afterwards.

"Yes, at times I think about the rancho. But, *ni modo*, it's gone. This is the life that we have now."

"It's hard," her son Ernesto confided. "It's a very small place, this house, for the seven of us. We talked about dividing it, one part for each family, but *mamá* and Tía Isabel could not agree on how it should be done. You see, there are four of us in *mamá*'s family and only three in Tia Isabel's, and my two cousins will not obey my sister, and my youngest sister and her cousin who is the same age fight. Now that my sisters are in school, my mother doesn't have to take the youngest one with her to the street corner where she works.

"When I was in *primaria*, I would take the bus from my school to the place that my mother worked and play with my sister. I would give her her sugar water and I would watch the candy tray for my mother when she needed to go on some errand. I would keep flies off the candy, and cover it to keep it from getting discolored from the car exhaust. Now my mother sells only candy and gum that comes in packages, but when I was little we sold mostly candy that was made in someone's home — little brown sugar molds and guava jelly cut into squares.

"After my father left, my mother would sometimes leave my sister with Tía Isabel. But my sister wasn't happy. Tía Isabel scolded her, and thought everything that she did was wrong and everything that my cousin did was fine. My mother was carrying my youngest sister, so I left *primaria* and took care of my older sister so my mother wouldn't have to both watch her and work.

"If Tía Isabel was here in the house with my cousins, one of whom was just a baby and cried all of the time, I would take my sister out of the house. We would look for things that we could sell or exchange for money or sometimes for *refrescos*, and I would ask people if there were any jobs that I could do, like wash their cars or sweep their sidewalks. Sometimes I would have to take my cousin with us, the one who is my older sister's age, but she did not like me and would not listen to me.

"If I did not treat her well, she would tell Tía Isabel and Tía Isabel would shout at me and if *mamá* heard her she would shout at Tía Isabel. Finally, Tía Isabel found someone who lives around the corner down the hill who would watch my cousin so that I did not have to do it.

"It was the same with meals. When we all tried to eat together, like one family, we kids would fight. I was the cause of some of it — I know that, now; I would want more than my share or I would take extra tortillas. Or I would bang my fists and complain that I didn't get enough to eat and that my cousins were getting more than I was. So now, almost always, we eat separately. If both my mother and Tía Isabel cook beans, they cook them at different times and we eat separately. It is easier for all of us that way.

"Not that there is nothing but fighting — that is not true. Tía Isabel took my mother to the hospital when my youngest sister was born and I stayed here in the house with her baby. Together she and my mother make piñatas for the birthdays. Sometimes when people that they know come by the street, *mamá* and Tía Isabel sit outside and they all talk together. And sometimes they all go to church together, although usually I do not go.

"Tía Isabel does not enjoy chatting the way my mother does, and she stays angry at things much longer. My mother says that everyone thought she was very pretty when she was my age, and that she did not want my uncle to move in with us when they came to Oaxaca City. Now that he has been gone so long, she does not want to talk about him, and does not like it when someone says that her son resembles him.

"I don't know whether she is more angry because he doesn't send her money or because she hates living in the city and wants to be back on the rancho. Maybe when she married my uncle she thought her life was going to very different from the way it is, I don't know. I do know that it makes it easier for us that she sells candy in the evenings, and works at the *ricos*' house on weekends; that way we do not bump into each other, and there aren't so many fights.

"Now that my older sister is eight years old and can take care of our younger sister, I don't have to interrupt my work to look after them. Still, it's difficult, because many times I work very late, especially on the weekends, and it is very hard to sleep if my cousins are making lots of noise. When my mother is here, it's better, because she helps keep everybody quiet, but when she isn't I think Tía Isabel encourages my cousins to wake me up because she is jealous that I bring home money.

"With it and what my mother earns, we can buy more things than Tía Isabel can. We have chayotes and zucchini to go with our beans, and we have chorizo or muffins sometimes. And I'm very good at getting little extra things from the places where I work. So I can understand that Tía Isabel gets upset. I don't mind. I have gotten used to her. I know it's hard for her. It's hard for us. There have been times when we have had very little and Tía Isabel has had more. I can remember leaving the house so I wouldn't have to watch them eat.

"I suppose I understand when they do the same. And it's not that we have so much. Just a little bit more. Just a little."

A Cloud Floating Past

A barrage of chattering birds shook pine needles from the trees above Jesus Enue. He braced his elbows against his knees, leaned back and laughed.

"It's nice," he gestured towards little rock-fenced garden quadrangles planted in nopal, aloe vera, tomatoes, strawberries and geraniums, then at the steep hillside beyond them. My companion Elaine had met his step-daughter Francisca in Oaxaca City several days before, and she had invited us to visit their foothills home near Zaachila, twenty-some kilometers south of the city of Oaxaca.

Elaine asked if the hillside had been virgin forest when he began to garden it and he laughed again, thick rich syllables that seemed to go inward, through his chest, instead of outward towards us.

"Not for centuries," he directed the words past her, towards the house with its winding rutted gravel driveway, palapa overhangs and vehicles in various states of polish and repair. "It was all ejido," the sweep of his head indicating the hills around us, not just his little *terreno*.

"Before that it was a rancho that some local cacique let his sharecroppers spot with little corn patches. Before that, whatever was left after timber harvests — scrub and a few huge old trees in inaccessible places — and before that, who knows? Some conqueror probably claimed it, hoping that he would find precious minerals and get rich from his mines.

"The house already was here when I bought the property. I put in the gardens and the sheds for my cars — I like to tinker with them in my spare time, they're all '*classics*,' as you would say in your country, not antiques but special for one reason or another. When I first came to my position with the Secretary of Public Education I lived in Oaxaca City, but originally I am from a small town in the mountains and I like having trees around me, and space to move around in.

"It was mostly by accident that I came to purchase this place. At SEP I was working to develop apprenticeship programs for the *preparatorias* — offset printing, computers, television, things above the mere vocational level for small industry and business application — and one of my coworkers was scouting Zaachila, thinking he might want to buy property and he came across it. I paid too much but at my level government employment is very secure and life here is so much better than life in Mexico City."

"For us, you mean — for us it's better than Mexico City." Enue's stepdaughter had emerged from the kitchen carrying an earthenware pitcher filled with fresh limeade, handleless drinking cups, sugar, extra limes and a bottle of brandy.

Enue had met Francisca's mother where he worked and they had become first friends, then lovers, then man and wife. A vibrant, excitable teenager with vibrant *I'm-alive!* eyes and an iridescent mane of raven hair, Francisca Sanchez had become involved in student movements for indigena rights and with musical groups that constructed and played traditional Mixtec and Nahua instruments.

"But where are the families who lived here before 'government employment' came? I'll tell you where, they are squatting on street corners holding their hands out for coins to keep them from starving to death! I know, I used to live in the midst of them when my mother and I lived in the city.

"Everything that is good about Oaxaca, they lost. Everything that worked for them for centuries changed and started working against them. Like my friend Rosa María. Her mother used to tell me about their house in the little village they came from. They built it themselves, the men and women working together. There were twelve in the family and all but the youngest children worked. Since they didn't pay rent — the house was theirs — they didn't need much, just enough for food, for clothes, their daily expenses.

"The men worked for ranchers, or in the mills — not permanent jobs, but jobs. Sometimes they'd go miles and miles away, a group of them working some harvest; while they were gone the other members of the family did little things to earn money. Rosa María could pat out tortillas faster than anybody I'd ever seen. And she knew all about chickens and gardens and how to make *pozole* and what herbs would make cuts get well.

"But in the city she and her family didn't have space to grow anything. Not that I had so much, but my mom was working and there were just the two of us — that made a difference. I used to give Rosa María things out of my lunch — she never would ask for them, but she only brought tortillas if she brought anything at all.

"When we had to learn dances for the May Day pageant, Rosa María helped me — we were the best in the class, maybe the whole school, she and I — but we had to have costumes. My mom complained, but she sewed mine — it wasn't very good, but it had little crepe paper wings and a little cotton cape with a headpiece that came to a point like a bird's beak.

"On the day of the pageant, Rosa María didn't show up. I was so mad at her I could have pulled her hair out by the roots — I thought she'd betrayed me. Then, at the pageant, just before I went out to dance, I saw her. She was standing way off to one side on the audience, clinging to her school books. Around her shoulders she had a funny little bunch of cut-up paper sacks. At first I didn't know what they were, then, as I was dancing, I realized she'd tried to make a bird costume herself and that was how it had turned out.

"In the middle of the dance, right then, I stopped and ran towards where I had seen her, my little wings flapping and my tiny voice calling her name. But she wasn't there. She'd run away and I didn't see her again that day. But when she came back to school I hugged her and told her next time my mother would make a costume for her too.

"While I only had to work at home, housework, laundry, things like that, Rosa María had to work outside, selling things — Chiclets, paper flowers, little bracelets that she and her mother and sisters wove out of strips of plastic. I wanted to go with her but my mother wouldn't let me. It was 'dangerous," she said. 'Then why does Rosa María's mother let her go?' I asked. 'They must need the money very badly,' my mother said.

"Although she was bright, Rosa Maria stopped going to school during *secundaria.* She went to work in a tortilla factory. I still tried to see her, but she pulled away and I didn't have the patience to pursue her friendship — I was doing lots of things, I had lots of other friends — friends I didn't really like as much, but they were accessible and we were doing things together. I still tried to see Rosa María, but she avoided me, and I began to understand how different our lives were going to be as we kept growing older.

"The last time I saw her, she was pregnant. She was wearing a huge faded T-shirt with American writing on it over her blouse and an old shapeless, colorless skirt. Immediately I thought of the May Day pageant and her paper sacks. She told me that most of her brothers and sisters had moved away, except for the youngest boy that she was taking care of. She seemed very distant when I tried to talk to her, and afterwards I felt very sad.

"Everywhere I go in the city I see people like her. Then I come up here where everything seems so, I don't know, so safe. And I realize that Rosa María lives in a different world from me. For a short time, when we were children, our two worlds came together and we connected; but now it's like I'm on a cloud floating past and she's way down there in a swamp and I can't reach down to her and she can't reach up to me.

"And I want to tell her, 'Please, Rosa María please, don't have lots of children! You're not in the village where the whole family works and everybody contributes!' I want to tell her, 'Take responsibility just for yourself! Have an abortion! Go it alone, like I'm going to do!'

"It's the only way, now, that works."

A Road Back

"The things that we Oaxacans say we value most about our land," Gustavo Robles insisted, "are the very things that have destroyed it. Oaxaca is like a person whose growth was frozen during childhood. It is beautiful — but at the same time doomed. It cannot function as a child in the adult world."

An "unimportant technocrat" who worked in a "bypassed part" of the state bureaucracy, Robles entertained Elaine and me on the patio of the turn-of-the-century house he had inherited from his parents in an older Oaxaca City *colonia*. Tucked against the curve of a winding hillside street among wide-leafed hardwoods and ornamental citrus trees, the patio encompassed a narrow driveway shielded from the street by a new wrought iron gate connected to stone walls topped with multi-colored shards of broken glass.

In his early thirties, at first impression reticent and insulated from the world around him, Robles had edged into a conversation that Elaine had been stumbling through with some indigena women peddling rag dolls and hairpieces on a mid-town Oaxaca street corner. Manipulating a limited but somewhat functional ability with English, he had managed to elicit answers to the questions she had been trying to ask the women. Then, curious, he had tried to get her to elaborate on her interests, but she had laughed and waved her hands and protested that she couldn't understand or communicate well enough — he would have to wait until she could come back, with me as a translator.

Elaine and I crossed paths with Gustavo Robles several times after that. We accepted an invitation to dine with him and his wife, and took the two of them and their four-year-old son to limeades and coffee in a newly opened glass-fronted restaurant a few blocks down the hill from their house.

Robles countered Elaine's New Age-tinted sentimentality for native peoples and their traditions with affable, non-confrontational demurrals. Although critical of his own parents' stolidly Catholic political conservatism, he considered the way that they slowly had pulled away from traditional roots as a positive kind of growth that bridged them from "the superstitious past" to "a workable present."

"There were no automobiles when my father was born — not in Oaxaca, at any rate. He grew up miles from train service. He remembered hearing stories about Zapata, but the revolution never penetrated that deeply into Oaxaca.

"When he was fourteen or fifteen he went to work in a plant that processed cochineal dye. He worked for a lumber processing mill, then for a cooperative that stored and distributed seed. He learned to operate machinery, to drive a car, to type and use an adding machine. By the time that he was in his 40s — when I was born — he had a permanent job with a major Mexican company that had come to Oaxaca in the '50s.

"I guess when they first were married, my parents' house looked a lot like the little houses in rural Oaxaca they had grown up in, but gradually they added all the new things being sold in the big markets. They cooked in aluminum instead of pottery; they bought modern furniture made in Guadalajara; my mother wore department store clothes. They never used credit cards but they had bank accounts and they pre-paid for their funerals and cemetery plot.

"So, you see, they moved the same way the world was moving. You say they lost a lot of their old traditions? That's true, but remember, they lost them slowly; there was no trauma. They replaced them with more modern things, but that doesn't mean they forgot the old ways. They talked about them. They identified with them at the same time that they were learning about telephones and tune-ups and 'I Love Lucy.'

"It's different for those who stayed in the mountains and resisted any kind of change, then found themselves thrust into a different way of life against their wills. They're trying to jump right from the sixteenth century into the 1990s. They have no tools — what can they do? Dig ditches and sweep sidewalks while their wives sell used clothing, make tacos and *birria*, peddle *pulseras*, become servants, take in washing. Everything they had — their *milpas*, their little neighborhoods, their holidays, their language even — has been yanked away from them.

"Let me tell you something: In a few years it all will be gone. Their children will be prostitutes and thieves speaking street language, not indigena, not even Spanish. Tell me about the *hongo* ceremonies and I'll tell you about desperate people who make a livelihood out of getting hit by cars in order to collect from the drivers who hit them.

"My parents passed on enough of the old culture that I have access to it if I want it. But also I have a car and a house and a way to make a living. I have something to pass on to my children — if they want it; they may want something else — and along with it I can pass on knowledge, awareness, of the old ways.

"Here in Oaxaca, we have to learn that we all are part of a process — not just tribal and animistic but urban and computerized as well — and we can't stop it. No matter how much we might want to stop it, we can't. Without knowing how they understood it, my parents understood that and kept pace with the process.

"That's what I'm trying to do, for myself and for my children. I feel sorry for those who resisted — they are losing everything, including their identities. I have a different identity — not rich with superstition and folklore like theirs, perhaps, but an identity nevertheless. And I have a road back to where I came from.

"So many have nothing but their memories of the mountains and the ranchos on which they were born. Their children don't even have that."

MA-ES-TROS!

The changes thrust onto Oaxaca in the late 1980s "surged through me like a lava flow." Ana Lilia Amador described her transformation from a dispirited and ineffectual public servant to an active unionist "driven by my new perception of myself" to confront — and change — the status quo. By her own admission, "rather lackluster in appearance, the kind of woman people remember as attractive without being able to recall a single distinguishing feature," Amador came to Oaxaca with the invading wave of urban professionals who followed a flow of federal money into the regional capital. Only three years out of college, with two years' experience teaching in a private Monterrey *colegio*, she almost drowned in the "educational cesspool" that served Oaxaca as a public school system.

Amador admitted that her impulse was to shrink away, shocked and disgusted, from the mis-administered stone shell on the outskirts of Oaxaca City to which several hundred listless, angry and anonymous students brought scraps of textbooks, old soccer balls and empty stomachs. For reasons that she later defined as "more fear of what my husband might think of me than bravery," she slid "as inconspicuously as possible" into her new role. The lack of teaching materials, the poorly maintained facility and the high degree of absenteeism precipitated a slide into a torpor that most of her colleagues shared.

Teachers' salaries hadn't kept up with inflation, and Christmas bonuses (the end-of-the-year *aguinaldos* that so many Mexicans depend upon to pay accumulated bills) had been suspended. Over a period of several years, most of the good teachers had quit, leaving vacancies that the administration failed to fill or filled with temporary and unqualified instructors. The campus itself was so bad the choosier students paid the *dueña* of an eatery a block away for bathroom privileges and a favorite morning recess game was seeing which student could kill the biggest cockroaches.

Nothing in Amador's background had prepared her for either the squalor or the overwhelming sense of defeat that both teachers and students shared. Her father, a Spanish-born banker, outwardly jovial, worldly, multi-lingual and materialistic, had presided over both Ana Lilia's and her older brother's educations, sending them both through private schools and tightly controlling her social life. She met her husband-to-be at a party hosted by her father and, acceding to his recommendations and encouragement, her husband accepted a promotion and transfer to a Oaxaca financial institution.

"I was dead. One had to be dead to teach under the conditions I stepped into. One of the jokes among the teachers was to recount how a former colleague had taken a job with the new city garbage collectors' co-op to improve his social standing.

"I remember how one student, an angry young man who I suspected was coming to class under the influence of alcohol, reacted to a correction I made on a test: 'What good are right answers? You want me to wind up teaching school? My father would kill me. He'd rather I die in a house of ill repute.'

"For the first time in my life, I wasn't special. My husband encouraged me to quit and find a 'more suitable' job, like running a boutique. I thought about it, but this was 1987 — the peso was going crazy; it was a terrible time to invest. I promised him that I wouldn't bring my school problems home with me as we looked into various little business opportunities for me.

"When the government withheld the teachers' raises — raises so small they didn't even keep up with inflation — the mood around the school became angrier. Talk about a work blockage, a strike, started to circulate. In other parts of the country — in Puebla, Monterrey, Mexico City — teachers were demanding not only more pay, but social reforms. One of the leaders of a dissident teachers' union came from Mexico City to talk to us. Our local organization — and the school administration — threatened to suspend anyone who attended.

"I wasn't going to go — I was afraid. But my husband remarked that it might be 'a blessing' if I got fired; and I went. Someone reported us to our local organization and their representatives started to hassle us.

"We hassled back. We demanded an open meeting and at the open meeting we demanded that we be able to elect new officers. The head of the organization ruled us out of order. We shouted him down. One of the teachers — not from my school, from a *primaria*, a mild-looking little man wearing thick glasses — rushed to the front of the gymnasium where the meeting was being held and grabbed the microphone. Those on the platform pushed him back. His glasses fell off and one of the officials grabbed them and snapped them in two.

"Immediately, eight or nine or ten teachers rushed forward. They helped the *primaria* teacher to his feet and jumped onto the platform to get the microphone back. Many more followed. Then everybody — men and women, even me — rushed forward. We took over the meeting. By voice vote we replaced the old officers with new ones. And we proclaimed that, should the election not be honored, we would form a new union that would stand up for our rights.

"I'd never seen such emotion, such jubilation. I didn't even hear the sirens until armed police came swarming into the gymnasium. The voted-out officials screamed that we should be arrested and we screamed that they should be arrested. We still were shouting as the police emptied the building and we all went home.

"The next day the city's school officials announced that they would not negotiate with us, either as newly elected leaders of the old union or as the representatives of a new one. We tried to meet with them to present our viewpoints, but they closed their doors to us. We met again that evening in a public square and voted to issue a strike ultimatum.

"The next morning, at ten thirty, all of us who belonged to the new union told our classes what we were doing and walked out. School officials confronted us: If we left, they said, they not only would fire us, they'd confiscate our benefits, including our retirement funds. As we strode past them, through a crowd of students who'd come out of the building to watch us, I saw the student I told you about, the one whose father didn't want him to become a teacher, leap on top of a car parked at the curb and pump his fist.

"'*Ma-es-tros!* he shouted, '*Ma-es-tros!*' '*Ma-es-tros!*'

"Immediately, almost all of the students joined in. They drowned out the school officials who were trying to shout at us through portable bullhorns. They ran past us into the street, chanting '*Ma-es-tros! Ma-es-tros!*' and they opened a pathway down the street for us to march through.

"I was flabbergasted. I couldn't believe that they cared that much. By the time we reached the park that faces the Secretary of Public Education office, students from the other schools whose teachers were striking had joined us. There were police everywhere. There were sirens. Somebody set off some skyrockets. While the students were shouting '*Ma-es-tros! Ma-es-tros!*' the main body of protesting teachers were shouting '*Huel-ga! Huel-ga!*' in counterpoint.

"The demonstration lasted all afternoon. There were speeches and shouting and roars of applause, with police reinforcements surrounding us on all sides. By the time we broke up to go to our homes, we all were totally exhausted, but exhilarated, happy. We absolutely were determined not to waver in our purpose."

The intransigent refusal of the government and former union leaders to negotiate or compromise actually helped the protesting teachers, Amador contended.

"Had they been more flexible, I think some of the teachers would have relented and gone back to their classrooms and gone back to the old union."

Instead, the municipal government tried to break the strike. It ordered police to arrest school picketers on grounds that their actions were illegal.

"But as soon as they moved against us, the students responded. They stormed the Secretary of Public Education building and, unfortunately, broke windows and did some other damage. It was one thing, the police found out, to arrest a bunch of poor farmers; it was another to arrest us, for suddenly we had status and a lot of the community was behind us."

Amador vividly remembered going to a neighborhood store during the picketing.

"It was just a little *tienda*, it sold only packaged goods, beer and sodas, tortillas and eggs. I'd gone there occasionally before the strike, and the *dueños* politely would address me, 'señora,' but always keep a distance. The first time that I went in after the strike started, they were all smiles, they addressed me, '*maestra*' and refused to take my money when I tried to pay them. '*Ándele!*' the owner called out when I turned to leave, 'Do it for my children!'

"Then, on the sidewalks outside the school itself, while we were picketing, some of the students who'd refused to cross our picket lines brought their books and held classes, teaching themselves. They also launched several demonstrations, and set a huge bonfire in the Zocalo to burn thousands of issues of the newspaper that carried an editorial condemning our actions."

Gradually, Amador began to assume a greater role among the strike leadership. After federal officials ordered school officials and the old union to negotiate, Amador took her place with the negotiating team.

"I had grown up among my father's friends — bankers, businessmen, political figures; I knew how to present myself. It was partly what you call in your country 'image' — some of our leadership was very radical, but very Oaxacan; they could not afford to dress the way I could. I looked like I belonged on the other side of the table; my fellow negotiators said that I commanded respect.

"And I can express myself. I was very factual, very clear. We conceded that ours had been a wildcat election, and we agreed to have it nullified, but only if the organization immediately scheduled new elections governed by democratic guidelines. The old union officials objected, but eventually relented, and the elections sent all of the people we nominated into office.

"I clearly remember my first day back in school after the strike ended. We teachers met to have breakfast together, then went to campus as a unified group. We found the entranceway decorated on either side with huge bouquets of flowers. As we stepped through them, the students formed a corridor around us and began to chant in unison, '*Ma-es-tros! Ma-es-tros!*' I was so happy I started to cry — and I wasn't the only one. I'd never felt anything so engulfingly wonderful before in my life."

Her experiences during the teachers' strike "changed me," Amador admits.

"I am a different person, I know that. While the negotiations were going on, my husband told me that I had changed so much it frightened him. I am a better person for it, I know that. I am very proud of what we did — what we achieved.

"And I am very proud of my profession now. Very, very proud."

The Curandero

From the crevices of narrow alleyways, from the corners of buildings set against stones pulled from the earth thousands of years ago, from the rasp of brooms sliding every morning across concrete and tile and stone, one senses something older and deeper than any of the civilizations whose traces remain on the City of Oaxaca's surface. This ancientness oozes up through the cobblestones, infiltrates the sunlight, drips along the little creases in the pavement.

It has a soul, this city does — a soul that pulls one downward into darkness that is livid and strange. Those who live with it accept it and reflect it, but visitors, able to sense it but unable to absorb it, often find that it frightens and oppresses them — even visitors like Heather Daly de Murillo, who'd married into Mexican wealth and knew and understood Mexican ways.

But the Mexico that Heather Daly knew best was Mexico City's salons and dinner parties and investments and real estate, not squawking chickens and black pottery and curanderos' *chozas* made musty with drying herbs. They frightened her, but even frightening her, they seemed to beckon her and she felt drawn — forced — to respond.

When she found out I was going to be in Oaxaca, she wrote me and told me that she would meet me there. She and I had been friends — though never lovers — in college in Mexico City seven or eight years before and had corresponded irregularly back and forth after her marriage and subsequent divorce. We'd taken, she'd joked, "different roads" — hers the "high road" (Mexican society parties, Acapulco vacations, pregnancy, fights, affairs) and mine the "low road" (part-time jobs, a first novel, hitchhiking through Europe).

Gradually her letters shifted from cant and braggadocio into descriptions of deepening depression, failed primal scream therapy, panic about the future. In the handwritten note setting up our reunion, she told me about a curandero who had the ability to "transform one's life." She was afraid to go to him alone, she admitted, but would meet me so I could take her.

Over a light meal that she ordered for me at her hotel suite (she was fasting for her interview with the curandero), we renewed what remained of our acquaintance while her Mexico City nanny put Heather's four-year-old daughter to bed. The three of them seemed to function as a unit and that gave each of them a sort of stability that none of them would have had alone. But when we separated, the nanny to take little Irma Murillo Daly to stores and playground while her mother and I climbed huge hewn stones to a raised sidewalk that had survived centuries of wear, Heather seemed to become increasingly tense and brittle.

Her fear became more visible as we threaded our way past chipped and re-plastered walls strewn with rusted car and bicycle parts, chipped *ollas* and scraps of cardboard. Heather showed me the instructions she'd scrawled on a sheet of her monogrammed stationary. Go down two blocks; just before the street deadends take the alley to the right and pass through the door that has the bones of an iguana on it.

"Maybe..." Heather's hand, groping for my shirtsleeve, seemed tiny and ineffectual. I was surprised by how small she seemed — and fragile, despite her resolve. There seemed to be two of her, one held captive against its will, the other desperately asserting outward control.

I suggested that we think through her commitment to the supposed miracle worker, but she shook her head.

"Just a little bit further. We don't have to..." *go in*, she left unstated.

The alley was so narrow the thatched eaves on either side rustled against each other over our heads. Heather glanced nervously from side by side as we sidled past doorways set so closely together that the rooms behind them couldn't have been much larger than sleeping cells.

The last structure on our left was nothing but a pile of rubble spotted with rusted cans and scraps of plastic, but in front of them shards of black pottery surrounded the spiny tops of pineapples that someone was trying to grow as ornamental shrubs. The hovel next to it, a stacking of gray stone blocks salvaged from some 16th or 17th century building, presented a half-ajar aperture — too small really to be called a doorway — covered with cardboard and bent strips of corrugated metal.

Heather shivered. "I — I don't think this is..." The rest of the sentence caught in her throat. "Oh G-God, look! Th-there..!"

Instinctively — protectively — I put my arm around her. For a moment, seeing nothing but cramped alleyway walls, I thought shadows had frightened her. Then a red-eyed serpent glare forced itself into my awareness.

"Oh!" I gasped, realizing as I did that the creature, though ugly and lifelike, was inanimate.

I relaxed my grip on her shoulder and squinted at the figurine. Its head, carved out of ironwood, protruded into a narrow passageway that separated the walls of two structures larger than those we just had passed. Glass eyes, irregularly chipped to refract light, peered from beneath a cape of dried iguana skin. The ribs — actual bones — were inset into the passage way with some kind of plaster. The tail, also a dried skin, coiled beneath the body and vanished into the wall. A scrap of canvas catching the breeze on the roof above the figurine sent light and shadows dancing across the eyes.

"Why? What does...?" Heather seemed to be trying to shrink into herself, disappear. I rubbed my hand across the figurine's carved smirk, trying, I suppose, to show her *See, it's nothing. It can't hurt.* Instead I mumbled, "This must be what we're looking for. How do we get in?"

Edging into the passage way, I detected the folds of some heavy fabric covering what seemed to be a doorway. Heather followed me, her breaths coming in short, anxious gasps. *No wonder she wanted me to come with her* I thought to myself, but when I hesitated, intending to ask her if she wanted to reconsider, she pushed me forward. Her pale blue irises glistened like hardened crystal and I realized that the determination that had brought her this far wasn't ready to crack.

The fabric curtains opened just as I lifted my hand to knock.

"*Pasen ustedes,*" a quavering voice invited.

I squeezed to one side to let Heather precede me into a dimly lighted, cool, L-shaped living space with tile floors and a few pieces of heavy colonial furniture. An ancient woman who in her youth probably had been broad-shoulder and sturdy, hobbled ahead of us to offer us places to sit. Before we could thank her, or inquire about the curandero, his greeting from somewhere out of sight acknowledged our presence.

"*Señora Murillo,*" his voice had the peculiar lisp that indigenas who've learned Spanish as their second language often develop, "I'm sorry if my totem frightened you."

Before either of us could come up with an answer, he stepped into the long end of the L from a curtained doorway. He was younger than I'd expected — but at the same time he seemed almost ageless: broad-faced, with thick shoulders and the muscular frame one would expect to see on an *albañil* or farm worker. Despite his physique, he conveyed an impression of softness rather than muscularity; his facial characteristics strongly resembled those of the woman who'd ushered us into the room and who seemed to have vanished without either of us noticing her departure.

Heather extended her hands — as though, she told me later, the curandero wordlessly had ordered her to do so. She pulled away slightly as he held them and peered into her face; the corners of her mouth and her shoulders twitched and she seemed unable to find a comfortable posture. Something momentarily must have diverted my attention, for the impression that they — or I — had left the room and gone somewhere else surged over me. I must have gasped or grunted or twitched, for Heather turned to stare at me. I stared back, but had difficulty achieving eye contact.

"It was generous of you to come." The curandero's voice seemed to come from far away. I wiped at my eyes and, in doing so, knocked my glasses askew. For a second — just a second — the impression that something had jiggled the flow of time persisted, but when I looked up the curandero was brushing something from one hand with the fingers of the other and Heather was asking me if I were all right.

"Not all friends would do what you are doing," the curandero continued. He seemed to know a great deal about us — or to sense enough about the dynamics of our relationship to have a picture of both our concerns and our differences. "It is appropriate for you to come and want to remain unchanged," he seemed to be talking to both of us, "just as it is appropriate for you to pass through to the other side," to Heather — but in a tone of inclusiveness that made me a part of the connection between them. Then, "Please come," he indicated the doorway through which he'd originally appeared. "I'll show you where we will be."

The drapes opened onto an exposed landing shaded by a piece of corrugated metal tacked to the frame above the doorway. A half-wall that once had been part of an adjacent building shielded a flight of rusted steel frames to which warped boards had been tied to form a staircase to the roof. His fingers barely touching Heather's elbow and hip, the curandero directed her upwards. The top step butted against a wall set directly on top of the rooms we had just left. Tree branches thick with leaves rustled above it.

The curandero tripped a hidden latch and pushed the doorway open. The opening was so small that Heather had to crouch sideways to squeeze through.

"Oh!" I heard her gasp — in surprise or pain, I couldn't tell which. As the curandero crabbed through behind her, I heard her gasp again.

"Are..." *you all right?* I started to call to her. The question dissolved as I wrenched sideways through the narrow opening.

Heather was standing, hands clasped at her waist, gaping at the foliage that surrounded us. Mango trees and lemon trees, their thin branches balancing still-green fruit, shaded ferns and snake plants. Bougainvillea wreathed the walls with bright pinks and pale orange. Everything — trees, shrubs, ferns, flowers — was planted in earthen vessels of one kind or another. Wild sparrows and finches flitted among branches whose thick vegetation also provided perches for parrots and two or three large macaws.

"Yes," the curandero led us along a path that wove through the *ollas*, "I find it peaceful."

The quirky vibrations that had marked Heather's anxiety seemed to diminish.

"More than...peaceful," she offered, twisting her shoulders as though ridding herself of uncomfortable outer garments.

The curandero gestured towards an alcove set among potted trees and a bank of flowers whose clustered yellow blooms toppled earthward like bunches of fecund grapes.

"Here, you'll be comfortable," he smiled towards me.

Heather's sharp, barely audible inhalation brought the curandero's smile back towards her. She seemed to want to reach out for someone or something —

me, the curandero, or something shadowing her imagination, I couldn't tell which. Again, as had happened earlier in the room below, the sensation that they or I had left the room, then come back without altering anything or without time seeming to have passed, came over me. I frowned, and was about to ask if something had happened — something that I had missed — just as Heather slipped forward and kissed me lightly on the cheek.

"Thank you," she whispered before turning away. I merely nodded, in echo hearing — apprehending — the curandero indicate to me, "Please, if you need anything..."

"Yes," I seemed to answer.

Seemed because, looking back, I have the sense that all of the dialogues that day hovered between spoken and unspoken. Whether I turned away from Heather and the curandero, or they just vanished, I'm not sure. I do remember making myself as comfortable as I could in the alcove. I inspected the various tropical and sub-tropical plants and the *ollas* that held them, and peered at the birds.

Despite the isolation that the walls provided, the rooftop garden allowed sounds and smells from the old section of the city to intrude. I heard the shouts of garbage men as they came along the street, the whistles of vendors' wagons, children calling to each other, dogs barking, *telenovela* passions rising and ebbing on distant TV sets. I saw airplanes overhead — and vultures; I smelled plastic burning, and the homey, acrid aroma of tortillas being fried in pork fat.

I also saw Heather, and in actuality — or by inference — saw her accept the curandero's ministrations, saw her share the ceremony of the mushrooms. I saw her bless and thank each one for its participation with her, its sacrifice. Memory tells me that I perceived all of this, but I may only have heard, or sensed, and built the rest from fragments of my own experience and imagination afterwards.

I do know that I was on the rooftop for a long time: I may have become entranced by the peaceful — I even could say mystical — environment. I also may have walked among the *ollas*, spied to make sure that Heather was safe — even fallen asleep briefly and dreamed. I both remember that the afternoon seemed to stretch on forever, and seemed to have passed in the blinking of an eye.

But despite the way time seemed to telescope in and out, vivid images have stayed with me. I clearly can picture the curandero sitting beside Heather. She is moving slightly — lifting her head, smiling, slowly brushing her hair away from her face with her fingertips — but he is motionless, so motionless that he seems to be a shadow of himself, an imprint left behind by a physical form that has gone somewhere else.

And I clearly can see the old woman puttering past to water the plants. I talked to her, I remember: She had lived in Oaxaca a long time, she said; she remembered when the city was much smaller, before there were automobiles or airplanes, when the people all would come together to discuss important events. She told me about Benito Juarez, who had been governor before he led the revolution against Maximilian and became president, and she remembered the sorrowing and pain after he'd been murdered.

I watched her as she talked, her voice coming in chirped little gasps as she twitched and jerked against the arthritis that twisted her limbs. I got the impression that the deeply socketed caverns around her eyes and her crackling, splotched skin were the outward manifestations of age that didn't seem to affect her attitude or her mind. It was as though a younger being peered through the hunched form and was challenging me to see through the old woman disguise. Why, I couldn't guess.

Nor could I divine what she might have wanted from me. Only much later did I realize that, even as old as she was, she couldn't have been alive when Juarez was murdered over 110 years before.

And I remember — most importantly I remember — that just as the setting sun sent shadows across the garden, I heard Heather scream. She had pushed herself to her feet — the curandero was nowhere in sight — and was holding her hands in front of her, her bent fingers groping at shadows and her mouth letting the scream go on and on without stopping, without changing its timbre or volume or intensity as she stared at something that only she could see in front of her in the garden.

"Heather!" I called to her, "Heather, are you all right?" but apparently she couldn't — or wouldn't — hear me. I had to struggle to get through the garden to her — perhaps I got tangled in the shrubbery, or couldn't find a way through the *ollas*, I don't remember; when I got to her side her scream had diminished and she was standing with her head bowed, her shoulders sagging, and her lips trembling, trying to swallow.

"Are you all right? Heather?"

She blinked and peered at me. "B-Bob..." The voice stammering my name seemed to come from deep inside the quivering shell I put my arm around. Her floating irises drifted past, then pulled back to focus on my face. "I didn't..." the words scarcely were audible, "how could I...? I didn't know. That — that thing inside, that oth-other me, it was so — so dark, it was like — like all the bad dreams I've ever had and I, then I was it, it was like I was it and I was looking, looking at this little dying me!"

"Heather," I tried to keep my tone steady, rational. "Listen to me. Things happen when you, you know, trip out that way. It's not real, Heather, it's just..."

For an instant — just an instant — I seemed to be looking into the curandero's face, not hers. Knowledge filled her eyes — more than knowledge, experience; the kind of experience that one associates with seers and gods. Then, as quickly as it had appeared, it vanished and she blinked, seeing me, I think, for the first time since I'd coming running up to her. She let her forehead sink onto my shoulder.

"I'm all right," a tiny voice — recognizably hers — whispered. "Just wait a little longer and then we'll go away."

I have no read on how much longer I waited for her, or what I did while I was waiting. I remember her fingers trembling in my grasp as I helped her squeeze through the opening onto the metal staircase, and I remember how small and dark the room beneath it appeared to be. As he had done before, the curandero seemed to materialize out of the shadows and step softly forward to face us.

And for a second, the most fleeting of seconds, the impression that they left the room and went somewhere else — to another dimension or another realm of consciousness — swept across me again. I whirled — or thought I did — but nothing had happened, nothing had changed. The curandero lifted his fingers as though offering Heather a benediction of some kind, then he turned to me.

"I think it is easier for those born here." His voice had that faraway chanting quality that I had noticed earlier. "For us, it is not such a frightening thing, this passing through to the other side."

"The other...?" But he disappeared behind the curtained doorway. "Heather?" I started to ask a question, but her wavering glance pleaded not to be asked or told anything more.

"This way," I guided her down the passage way towards the alley, keeping to myself, then and afterwards, the perception that it was not the curandero whom the drapes had covered, but the old woman who'd first shown us into the room, and who'd clearly remembered Benito Juarez and the circumstances surrounding his death over a hundred of years before.

Chapter 10. A Complicated Dream

Where the Magic Doesn't Work

A wizened human spider twisted through the converging lines of people in the Tuxtla Gutierrez bus station. He scarcely was four feet tall, and his lopsided face popeyed into a noisy snort as he stabbed his staff against the floor's worn tiles. His right foot, twisted inward and bound with rags, scraped the floor as he loped in my direction, cursing and swiping at the spittle that was dribbling onto his chin. Seeing that I was watching him, he stopped and tried to thrust himself into a more or less erect and challenging stance.

I spread my hands and glanced around the small, cramped station, then shrugged and told him quietly, in my foreigner's Spanish, "I am looking for the bus to San Cristóbal."

Around us I sensed a quieting, eyes turning towards us expectancy. Before he could speak, I shrugged again.

"I thought you might know. You seem wise."

His body quivered and he grabbed his staff with both hands to keep from falling. Thrusting his head sideways, he began to cough, the spasms shaking his twisted frame and causing his head to jerk sideways. I stepped forward, concerned, then realized that he was not coughing. He was laughing.

"*Sabio!*" he repeated when he had caught his breath. Playing for a wider audience, he Oliviered around the cramped, noisy room. A few commuters laughed — uncomfortably. They were *mozos* for the most part — coffee workers probably, short, tranquil men; most of them seemed to be waiting to board second-class buses that would take them out of this dusty commercial center back to their home villages in the mountains.

Again he laughed, chest-wrenching coughs that caused his shoulders to jerk. He let go of his staff and toppled to the floor. I curbed the temptation to rush to him and help him back to his feet. Out of the corners of my eyes, I caught glimpses of women crossing themselves. A puddle of misfit garments on the bus station floor, he peered up at me, his chest vibrating with the last of his coughing laughter.

"Buy me a drink," he gurgled. "I will tell you how to get to San Cristóbal on magic wings."

He was lying, of course. Not only did he not tell me how to fly, he did not even tell me which buses went to San Cristóbal. I bought him a drink — he directed me to a rickety stall that surreptitiously sold bootleg *caña* in addition to iced guayabana ade — and he told me that his name was Francisco Rivas. He was not from Tuxtla — "Nobody is from Tuxtla," he insisted, then added, "This is a city of strangers, where people come and use themselves up and are thrown away."

He himself had come from a place in the green mountains and had lived on a *milpa* which had corn and pigs and he had close relations who were priestess witches who could make stones move and water turn black and snakes swallow themselves whole. He had lived there until just a few years before, when the local cacique had driven him and all of his relatives off of their land and they had come to Tuxtla Gutierrez to work and to beg and to do magic spells.

In Tuxtla, he explained, the magic seldom worked. Banging his staff on the chipped, worn tile, he told me that Tuxtla had paved its spirits beneath asphalt and concrete. The city had no soul. Its inhabitants were fleas sucking its dog's blood and falling off to breed in the alleyways. Even its churches were evil. In his church in the place where he had grown up, he exclaimed, the floor was of dirt and live flowers grew from its altar.

I told him I would like to see the place that he came from and he began to wave his hands and cough and bark out directions that I couldn't understand. They seemed to contain descriptions of things that I'd never learned the Spanish words for — vernacular names for trees perhaps, or anthropomorphized geographical characteristics, or Indian place names. Again, when I suggested that I would like to see this place, to go there, to have him show me where he had grown up, he cursed and spat against the stained building side and muttered that it was impossible, no buses went there, he could not return, the place was evil, his sister's child had tried to go back and had been changed into a mad dog that slavered and bit at people and ate its own excrement, *did I understand*?

I nodded. Propped against the bus station wall, one hand on his staff and the other wiping at the drool on his chin, he described the *espantos* and *espectros* that haunted this remote, bucolic place where he had lived most of his life. These spirits would take revenge on the usurpers of the land, he assured me.

They would bring the cacique and his family bad dreams and illnesses and accidents would befall them and they would grow angry and miserable despite all their accumulated wealth. I asked him how he could be sure, and he twitched and spat and pummeled his stomach with his hands and replied that he knew because he could feel these spirits, they had talked to him.

They still talked to him, he said, in his dreams.

I bought him another *trago* and we trundled through dusty outskirts of Tuxtla Gutierrez to a field-side shantytown of tiny thatched concrete-block and stucco houses crammed with scrap metal, plastic, dogs and clotheslines. In a lane muddy with garbage and fetid water, surrounded by the silent, watchful eyes of children and women uncertain why their resident cripple had brought this intruder into their midst, Francisco Rivas and I stood opposite each other speaking the commonplace inanities of two people about to part ways forever. He started to say something more about the *espectros* but a fit of coughing surged through him and he dropped to his one good knee, cursing and spitting on the ground.

"You'll see!" he stabbed his staff against the muddy lane, trying to get to his feet again. "You will see that what I said, what I said, what I said..." but again, he couldn't finish the sentence.

From the juncture where the lane twisted away from the *colonia* and hooked up with the highway, I turned for one last look at the little cripple. He had pushed himself to his feet and was leaning against his staff, his head tilted against his shoulder. I waved, but he didn't return the gesture. For a moment, watching, I thought I saw shadows envelope him, shadows that he could merge into and, as he had promised, fly away on magic wings.

But he did not move. I had seen something that wasn't there. This is Tuxtla Gutierrez, I reminded myself. Here there only is dust and stained walls and plastic and mud. Here, the magic doesn't work.

BLANCURA

"He doesn't get his feet wet," residents of Ciudad Hidalgo said of Narciso Díaz. A big man, wide-shouldered, with a craggy head and an upper body that seemed to be too big for his delicate waist and hips, he didn't muck around in the mud and grime of the Rio Suchiate, smuggling cars and cornmeal and beer and bicycles from Mexico into Guatemala and people and guns and drugs from Guatemala back into Mexico. Others did it for him.

Not getting one's feet wet in Ciudad Hidalgo was an emblem of social prestige. So was the designation "a businessman," for it implied circumspection and success. In Ciudad Hidalgo, no one talked of smuggling or black markets or moneychangers, one talked only of "business" and how dollars or groceries or stolen Ram Chargers affected the stream of salable items flowing from one country into another.

Narciso Díaz thought of himself as a businessman — if he thought about himself at all. No one really seemed to know much about his thoughts or his feelings or his hopes and aspirations — although they did know (and talk about) the woman who had turned him into a dour, incommunicative hermit. If he was not so apt to lend money when she still was with him, not so apt to have politicians and policemen and truck drivers and *polleros* tapping at the entrance to his office — which wasn't really an office, just two rooms behind barred windows off an alley entrance way — then he was more apt to be seen in the restaurants and movie theaters, the barber shops and hotel bars and the tianguis that lined the Zocalo.

The woman was his wife. Her name was Rita Lorena, although everyone called her "Blancura" for the light complexion she'd inherited from northern European ancestors (and later for the irony of a character by no means pure). She was tall and self-possessed, a nurse trained in homeopathic medicine.

Ciudad Hidalgo seemed both to fascinate and bore her. She at first drew away from the coarse, constant comings and goings of "businessmen" of all descriptions — *chilangos*, Tapachulans, indigenas, Guatemalans — whose enterprise and negotiations made the town throb. And she drew away from the red-light district's prostitutes and their customers spilling into the everyday life of the permanent residents. And from the destitute illegal immigrants seeking work or stealing bread or chattering about the long trip ahead of them to the United States. And from the police who did nothing but pursue little bribes.

But gradually she began to find the hubbub invigorating. And to find Narciso, by contrast, boring. She began to be seen in various places without him, then be seen in those places with other men. Handsome men usually, wealthy men — but not always, for Blancura had a wild streak hidden within her and the more open her rendezvous became, the more risks she seemed to be willing to take.

Narciso, of course, knew what his wife was doing, although he may have been willing to ignore or avoid as many of the details as possible. Virtually all of his friends and acquaintances anticipated that sooner or later a confrontation would tear the marriage apart. This anticipation may have become a self-fulfilling prophesy, for one January evening several of these friends hurried to his office to tell him that Blancura was in a Ciudad Hidalgo restaurant with a big-time trafficker of stolen cars and might be in physical danger.

Reluctantly, Narciso let his friends persuade him to go after her. They arrived at the restaurant just in time to see Blancura and her companion hop onto a little three-wheeled bicycle taxi and head towards the Suchiate. Instead of following the main road towards the bridge that connected Ciudad Hidalgo with Tecun Uman on the Guatemalan side of the river, the *biciclista* veered onto an unpaved road that led to a popular smugglers' fording place.

Narciso chased down another three-wheeler and ordered the cyclist to head after the gallivanting couple. His friends ran back to get the pickup truck that one of them had been driving, but by the time they got onto the road both Blancura and Narciso were out of sight. Apparently Narciso's cyclist gained on his counterpart (who after all bore a two-person load) and might have caught up with him, but the car smuggler yanked a pistol out of a shoulder holster and began to fire, either at Narciso or in the air to frighten him.

Narciso's cyclist stopped pedaling (some say he abandoned his vehicle contraption and dove into a roadside ditch, leaving Narciso to pedal it himself). At any rate, when Narciso reached the ford, apparently on foot, Blancura and her companion already had boarded one of the ferries, a jerry-built affair constructed of tractor tire inner tube pontoons lashed together with bicycle inner tubes and topped by several *tablas* of balsa wood.

At the river's edge, Narciso stopped. He lifted one hand — to wave, some say, but whether "come back!" or "goodbye!" no one could ascertain. Despite the current, which was causing the fragile *balsa* to pitch from side to side, Blancura suddenly stood up — some say to wave farewell, other to signal for help. Her companion lunged towards her. The two of them seemed to struggle for a moment, then, just as Blancura started to rise again, a shot rang out. First she, then her companion, toppled into the water.

Boatmen from the far shore dived into the river. All of them were excellent swimmers and knew the quirks of the current. Jose Luis seemed to watch them, but he did not move. Even after his friends arrived, and maneuvered their pickup so its headlights would illuminate the river, he remained stone-like, staring towards the water, apparently not seeing anything.

He remained there, still staring, until his friends lifted him and carried him away.

Neither Blancura's body nor the smuggler's body ever was found, leading many on both sides of the river to conclude that they both survived and ran off together. But others said that the smuggler accidentally shot her, or that she suddenly repented her frivolity and turned the gun on him. Still others claimed that no shots ever were fired, and that swimmers from the Guatemalan side of the river rescued the pair. And some insisted that more than one shot, from more than one gun, was heard.

These last rumors increased as the story was told and re-told, and soon most of Ciudad Hidalgo came to believe that Narciso knew more than he ever revealed. He was, after all, a good "businessman" and good businessmen know whom to hire and when to act in order to get things done.

"He never gets his feet wet," people would wink as they re-played the fatal events. Could the smuggler have been a hired killer? The boatman? Someone on the opposite shore?

Every *balsero* who ferries passengers across the Rio Suchiate tells his version of the story, adding details of his liking about all of the characters involved. "It seems so strange," they always muse, "that nobody knows..." for in Ciudad Hidalgo everybody knows everything — except for the answer to this one mystery. And invariably the accounts end with a nod towards the place that Narciso worked, and the suggestion that perhaps he knew, and never told.

Singing New Songs

San Cristobal de las Casas is an ancient, self-contained, puritanical city surrounded by mountains and punctuated by churches, none of which is an architectural marvel but all of which are colorful and unique. Until New Year's

Day, 1994, few Americans had heard of the provincial capital in the highlands of Mexico's southeastern-most state of Chiapas, and few Mexicans seem to care that the coletos, as the residents of San Cristobal are called, blissfully ignored the poverty of the indigenas who huddled on the fringes of a way of life that resembled rural Alabama and Mississippi in the early part of the 20th century.

Even in daytime, life in San Cristobal seems muted. Most automobile traffic whizzes along the Periferico outside of town. The market is busy, but begging, soliciting, hawking and street vending is illegal. There are few cantinas and they close early.

Licensed vendors sell hot spiked pineapple punch on street corners in the evenings but they douse their charcoal fires before ten o'clock. If you are desperate, you can buy a bottle of tequila by stealthily knocking on certain locked portals after hours but, beyond that, night life securely is kept behind barred gates and tightly shuttered windows.

Government authorities passed a restrictive street-selling and begging ordinance years ago, but do allow indigenas from the various mountain villages to display and sell clothing on the grounds of the old basilica. The children of Chamulan refugees driven out of their mountain villages after they embraced Protestantism also are allowed to sell on street corners, but their efforts are limited to waving little woven bracelets and belts in front of tourists.

Serafin Rodriguez Anaya was one of those youngsters. Several times after I first bought a *pulsera* from her, I coaxed her into brief conversations.

A bright little barefooted greenfinch wrapped in colorfully tattered Chamulan skirt and shawl, she chirped brief, embarrassed answers to my questions about her well-being, her interests and her life as I sat on an iron bench on the shaded square and promised that, yes, someday I would buy more *pulseras* from her, but right now I had more than I could give away. I met her mother and sisters and one day, accompanied by my friend Maggie (Magdalena) Palacios Hartwig, I got to talk to Serafin Rodriguez and her family about their lives.

Margarita, Serafin's mother, sat bundled in shawls, a passive grimace pulling her high-cheek-boned face above missing molars as she directed little bursts of words in Spanish towards Maggie, rather than me. Half-a-dozen infants, two of them Maggie's, three of them Margarita's and the sixth Margarita's niece, clamored, crawled, bawled and pawed among us as we talked.

Serafin flickered in and out, giggling and twittering in Spanish to Maggie and in Chamulan to her mother. I poured lemonade from a big jar — my contribution — asked questions and listened. Even when I addressed questions directly to Margarita de Rodriguez, I noticed that Maggie had to repeat them, the Indian woman found the chasm so great between her life and mine.

"What does he mean, who are we? I do not understand...what? Oh, how did we become *expulsados*, how did it happen? I am not the one to tell you, I do not talk well. What? Tell you about my life. When I was little? I was....a girl.

"Shhst! Serafinita, it is not that funny. Yes, I was born in Chamula. In the hills. On a little place, we had our own corn, we grew chilis. Sometimes we had a goat.

"What was my life like then? No different from others. We had neighbors. We worked together. I worked in the garden patches.

"The church. Yes, I went to church. The Chamulan church. Yes, there were many fiestas, many, many. Every market day [once a week] was a fiesta. Yes, my parents, they did not know any different, they went to the fiestas. My father, *hiii!* he would be very drunk. The poor thing would spend whatever he earned on aguardiente. He would work until he would fall down and then he would take his money and drink.

"But never alone, you understand. That was not the way, in Chamula. The men did not drink alone. They did not drink at home. But if they met someone coming home from work, then they would drink. Or if they met in the market, or at the church.

"Yes, he would beat me, sometimes. And my mother. The poor thing, my mother, also would drink quite a lot. Everybody would be very drunk. Sometimes they would be drunk for many days. Nobody knew different then.

"Yes, shhst Serafinita! I would drink too. Not to get drunk, just to learn. I did not know different then. But I did not drink too much because I had to take care of my little ones [brothers and sisters].

"After the fiestas my poor father sometimes could not stand up. His hands would go like this [quiver violently]. He would pound his head to think of the things he had done at the fiesta, but in a few days, he did not know different; at the next fiesta he would do them again.

"Yes, in our village there was a municipal president. Everybody had to do what he said. He was in charge of the fiestas. Everybody had to pay him for the fiestas, a tithe of what they earned. Not the [weekly] market fiestas, but the big fiestas, like those in the church, or when a baby was born, or when someone died, or when they changed the clothes of the [statues of the] saints in the church.

"Sometimes my father would not have enough to pay the municipal president. My poor father would get into debt. Then he would have to pay everything he earned to the municipal president until the debt was paid off. We would have nothing to eat, only chilis.

"Only the municipal president could sell the aguardiente. It also was he who made all the plans for the fiestas. If someone was sick, they had to go to him to get aguardiente to use for medicine. He kept all the accounts. He also kept all the collections that came from [charging tourists to visit] the church. He also punished those who did not take part in the fiestas. Who did not pay their [prescribed] amount. Who did not get drunk at the ceremonies.

"Well and good, you see, nobody opposed him. Nobody could say no to him. Not until the good priests came. At first, no one listened to them. No one believed them. Then some of the women — yes, and the men, too — they started to listen. They started to understand how they always were in debt to the municipal president. They started to understand that they could use their money to buy food with. To buy corn and a goat and even shoes.

"My father was not the first to listen. Some of my uncles were. My uncles, they met with the good priests. The good priests did not belong to the regular [Roman Catholic] church. They showed my uncles and my father that they could say 'no!' to the municipal president.

"Soon, there was a lot of agitation. Many Chamulans, they were saying, 'No!' The municipal president, he was very angry. They were a lot of meetings. The good priests told us that to worship the real God we did not have to drink. The other priests said that we would lose our homes if we disobeyed the municipal president and the elders of the church.

"We chose our own municipal president. My father and my mother and my uncles did not go to the church anymore. We went to the good priests' ceremonies, instead.

"There were arguments. There were more meetings. Many people, they came to our ceremonies. At the ceremonies, we did not drink aguardiente. The good priests said to drink at the ceremonies was bad. The good priests showed us how to sing new songs.

"Many people became happy doing as the good priests said. Many people were happy not to do what the municipal president said. Because they did not go to the ceremonies, and kept their money from the municipal president, my father and my uncles came home from work with money to buy things. A goat. Two goats.

"Yes, there were fights. More fights. There were *gobiernos* [government officials]. There were priests. There were people from the pueblo saying our priests were bad. There were people from the pueblo saying that because we did not pay our share, they were having to pay more. There were the good priests saying we did not have to do what anybody said, that Jesus would take care of us.

"The municipal president had papers, saying, I don't know...I don't tell the story well, he had papers saying that we had gone against him, against...everything, against the rituals, against the community, against....Well, God...

"In the end, we left. A lot of us. We took just what we could carry. We came here. We cannot go back. Even to visit.

"They held ceremonies as we left. They took our land. They took our rights as Chamulan people. They expelled [excommunicated] us from the church. The municipal president gave our lands to those who stayed.

"Here to the edge of this place [San Cristobal de las Casas] we came. The government did not want us in the town. The government moved us here, then there, then over there. For some of us, at last, built houses — not the kind we were used to living in. The houses were close together, with almost no land, on the hill that won't even grow corn.

"Soon, here, I am married. I have my children. Sometimes our men, they go away to work on the coffee plantations. In the market. We make the little things to sell and the children, they sell them.

"Yes, we go to church. To a church of different priests [than the priests who first converted them to Protestantism]. We, the *expulsados*, we go to many different little churches now: *adventista*, *evangelista*, all Protestant.

"The churches tell us not to drink. We do not drink in the churches [as part of the church ceremonies]. Well, you understand, sometimes we cannot help it. Our men sometimes...

"Shhst! Serafinita, chica! That is not a bad thing that I am saying! Serafinita, she goes to the school sometimes. She has been to the hills [around San Cristobal de las Casas] but not to Chamula. When the people from there come into town, they do not speak to us.

"And when we see them lying drunk, we do not speak to them."

According to government records in Chiapas, the Chamulan expulsion occurred in 1976. As estimated 30-35 percent of the Chamulan population (about

6,000-7,000 persons) left (or were driven out of) their Chamula homeland. Most of the *expulsados*, like Margarita de Rodriguez and her family, have scraped out a meager living ever since by making and selling native crafts and by non-union manual labor, including migrant work on the coffee and sugar plantations of the Soconusco and central valleys.

Immediately after the expulsion, a number of government agencies provided housing and work-training assistance, but financing for those projects evaporated after 1982, leaving the Chamulan *expulsados* with a religion they understand imprecisely, stark concrete-block colonias in which to live and employment opportunities that are tightly restricted. Some work as servants in San Cristobal, but for the most part the city and its residents seem to prefer to acknowledge their history but to ignore their presence and keep them out of the center of town as much as possible.

A second group of *expulsados* who live on the outskirts of Tenejapa, a smaller town in the same high valley that includes San Cristobal, is only slightly better off. Their living conditions are worse, but they seem more integrated into the town, probably because it is smaller and their presence does not offend as many *colonialistas*.

Separate Dimensions

A thin young man whose thick glasses dominate an intense, bony face, Jesus Richter speaks with an occasionally passionate, but usually detached, acceptance of what life in the highlands of Chiapas is all about. Educated (he holds an advanced degree from the National Autonomous University in Mexico City), politically liberal but entangled in a kind of cultural cynicism that limits his participation in activist movements, Richter held a part-time professorship at the State University in San Cristobal when I met him a few years ago. He fancied himself a writer, but some dark, inner force seemed to pull the genius he felt that he possessed away from putting words on pages and into a gloomy and occasionally destructive self-indulgence.

Richter grew up in an exclusive Tuxtla Gutierrez suburb, the son of a businessman who had ties to wealthy coffee plantation families in the Chiapas highlands. (German surnames dominate the Chiapas coffee-growing industry. Early in the 20th century, adventurers with surnames like Luttmann, Bernsroff,

Pohlenz and Schwabe directed their money, assertiveness and ingenuity into developing highlands coffee plantations. These adventurers married into the reigning Mexican families to create a landholder elite whose plantations, attitudes and culture would seem hauntingly familiar to those acquainted with the ante-bellum American South.)

Both Jesus Richter's father, and Jesus, in stages, broke the family pattern. Richter's father left the highlands, intending to become a teacher, but his wife steered him into a family-grubstaked insurance business. He succeeded financially but indulged a lifelong bitterness about lost dreams. Jesus, perhaps unconsciously trying to proxy his father's wrong decisions, did become a professor, but he seemed indifferent about teaching and seemed rather passively satisfied to teach as few classes as possible and focus on a bucolic private life, much of which he was spending in the company of a young Peruvian artisan who crafted expensive bracelets and necklaces out of native Chiapas amber.

At the National University, eager, precocious and, by his own admittance "naive to the point of arrogance," Richter fell in with a group of equally precocious young would-be writers, artists and actors. Most of them came from backgrounds similar to his, rejected U.S.-influenced materialism, and were beginning to explore the idiosyncrasies of their own backgrounds, including the class distinctions that permeated Latin American society.

Richter says he returned home briefly after completing his degree work and a year of post-graduate study, but neither his parents' upper-middle-class isolation in Tuxtla nor his relatives' plantation life in the highlands appealed to him. After a brief fling at "student excesses" with old university acquaintances, Richter and a friend joined an INI (Instituto Nacional Indigena) project designed to help non-Spanish-speaking natives of eastern Chiapas develop communal food production and irrigation facilities.

A few months later, he began working with Guatemalan refugees at camps inside the Mexican border. He worked there for over a year — an "unhappy time," as he later described it, for he suffered from intestinal disorders all the time that he was in the selva.

Until he was in his second or third year at the National University, a fledgling poet who was reading history and psychology as well as literature and drama, Richter said he hadn't paid a great deal of attention to his Mexican-German heritage. But student experiences, including what he called "a deep sense of alienation" exaggerated by plunges into depression and doubts about his personal abilities and his sanity, triggered a brooding "anchored in blame" curiosity about his cultural past.

"Until I'd thought a lot about it, I didn't have much of a picture about the German-Mexican mix. Of course, for years I'd heard stories about my paternal forebears, their coming to Mexico, establishing the plantations and all. And there was a lot of intermarriage in the Soconusco Valley — I have German ancestors on both sides of my family. But the more I've grown to understand it, the more I've come to realize what a thrusting together of psychic forces was involved.

"For the Germans, I'm convinced, Mexico represented the dark side of the id. At least Chiapas did, Chiapas and Tehuantepec and the jungles and temples of the Yucatan. Not the dark side necessarily, but the id itself, with all its energy and flamboyance and sensuality. They were fascinated by this part of Mexico. Few of them went to the mining regions, or the northern plains, or Mexico City for that matter. But they came to Chiapas, they came to Guatemala, they came to Brazil.

"There was something here, something they wanted deep down inside. You've got to look at who they were — where they came from. One only has to read Freud to learn how repressed they were, how little they indulged their dreams. They were factual; they were disciplined; they were mechanical. They were obsessed with order — so obsessed that they didn't have any *duende* in their lives. In their minds, everything had a definition, a worth: Money. Morals. Even music.

"A lot of Germans were leaving Germany. It was the time of German expansion — you know, early in the century. They went into Africa, they went into the East Indies, they came here. Have you ever read Conrad? These ancestors of mine, they were Conrad characters, like Kurtz, like...like Lord Jim, like all of them.

"Once they got here, for them it was like stepping into a wonderland of the id. Everything that Germany wasn't, Chiapas was. It was green and sweaty and primitive and there were no boundaries of any kind. Even from Mexico City, there was little or no control. You could take anything you wanted to take: Land. Women. Even human lives.

"It was a psychic process, a primeval battle. By cutting the jungles, driving out the primitive forces, putting in the coffee plantations — miles and miles of beautifully regular rows of imported, exotic trees whose fruit couldn't be eaten, only drunk as a stimulant — these Germans were harnessing the id. They were impressing the German order on the jungle. They were inhibiting its wild natural state.

"But in doing so, they were absorbing some of the old Spanish *caudalismo*. They had harnessed the id but they still could indulge in it. The jungles, the primitive creatures — the indios — stayed within sight. The isolation allowed these immigrants a great deal of freedom. And they didn't have to touch anything they didn't want to — they always could get straw bosses to handle any dirty work.

"Oh, there were casualties. I think a lot of these Conradian characters didn't make it, harnessing the id. I think a lot of them lost themselves in it. They became corrupt. They indulged too much. They got lost in the jungles. They drank. They got eaten by the dragons that came out of the jungles — or out of themselves, I don't know which. The jungles absorbed them, just as they absorbed the old Mayan temples. Just as they've absorbed millions of Indians since."

Until he became immersed in university social and political movements as a young student, Richter said he never had pushed past a casual, somewhat sympathetic but generally non-critical awareness of Chiapas' indigenous population.

"I was no different from anyone else in my social group. Everyone in Chiapas lives surrounded by the poverty of the Indians. It's the way things are — you accept it. Once, at the university, a student I met — he was older than me — made a film, a sort of *telenovela* that he shot by luxury hotel swimming pools, under chandeliers, among Maseratis and Porsches. He washed it in pale colors — lavenders, aquas, golds — and transposed it over stark black-and-white footage he'd taken in Nezahualcoyotl and some other slums.

"By the time he finished editing it, it was terrifically powerful. The tinted characters moved over and among and through the black-and-white characters, just as though they didn't exist. Or existed in separate dimensions but sharing the same time and place.

"That's the way things always have been in Chiapas. We see the indigenas but we react to them as though they were in a different dimension than we are in.

"My parents and my relatives and their friends insist that it has to be this way. They drive around in their Broncos and pickups, right through the villages sometimes, and they look out and they see them [the Indians] and they talk about them as though they were parts of the plantations, parts of the forests.

They say things like, 'We should remove those,' as though they were talking about blighted trees. In Tuxtla the residents where my parents lived used to hire security guards to keep the indios off our streets, just as they paid *mozos* to carry off the garbage and wash the sidewalks and cut the weeds.

"I've heard *colonialistas* that it would be better if they [the indigenous peoples] were dead, if somebody shot them. I've talked to *landifundistas* from Guatemala who had no remorse about ordering or condoning the killings that took place there. They told me the Indians lived in such terrible misery they were better off being killed. Just like they would talk about sick cattle or goats or sheep.

"Even those who have an awareness, even those who try to make the [Indians'] situation better, believe that some kind of divine plan put them in the situation that they are in. They're not really religious — oh, some of them pretend to be — but they parrot, 'It's God's will,' just like the conquistadors of old.

"Myself, I think it is a problem of greater magnitude than anyone is able to face. I think a lot of people, like me, do not believe in government systems anymore and they do not believe in God. I think they pull away and just try to take care of themselves, build little lives of their own, enjoy little pleasures.

"They pass a street corner where an *expulsado* is begging, a little child at her feet and a baby on her nipple, and they'll give her coins, or buy something from her. Or they'll pay their servants a little better than other people do, or once in a while they'll drink tequila with the indigenas they meet. But that's all they can do, except try to live their own lives as best they can, and get a little pleasure out of doing so."

Richter admitted that his outlook was colored — "discolored," he wryly phrased it — by his own experiences. He admits that the year-and-a-half — almost two years — that he spent working with destitute Tzotzils and with Guatemalan refugees in eastern Chiapas eroded his naive youthful exuberance.

"We were way back in what had been rain forest. The lumber companies had cut most of it, leaving a lot of scrub and overgrown hillsides. The INI had worked out a traditional ejido system for the indigenas, you know, a plot of land for each small family group. But before the bulldozers and chain saws came in, before the INI and government reform, the indigenas had been migratory farmers.

"They would clear a space in the forest, plant their *maiz* and their vegetables, build little houses of sticks, and stay for a few years, I guess until the land was used up or had eroded; then they would move on and repeat the process and the forest would grow back over the places they had farmed before.

"They had no sense of what we were trying to get them to do. They had a communal sense, but no sense of ownership. Even communally, they didn't have a sense of working together. They had running feuds with each other. They'd get drunk and try to steal each other's wives.

"And they were sick a lot. Until I lived among them, I didn't realize how sick the indigenas are most of the time. Many of them barely could breathe, their lungs were so congested. Several of them, men, men not over 40, died of pneumonia while I was there.

"And they all had parasites. Of course, I caught them right away. I was so sick I hardly could move. For weeks, imagine! I can't tell you what my excrement was like. It had blood and crawling things in it. Nothing I tried to eat would stay on my stomach. The indigenas began calling me 'the skinny ghost.'

"The refugee camps for the Guatemalans were even worse. They weren't really camps; they were more like prison compounds. I think the government wanted to keep the refugees out of sight, so it set the camps up way out in the hills where there were no roads, nothing. The soldiers who built the camps strung barbed wire through the chaparral and they herded the refugees inside.

"There were at least 50 or 60 of these camps near the border. They had about 1,000 Guatemalan indigenas in each one. And not all the refugees were in camps.

"Some of them refused to eat the food we brought to them. Finally, we just gave them dried corn and let them make their own *masa* and tortillas.

"One woman — she couldn't have been too much older than me — turned old, really old, in a couple of months. Her eyes pulled inward and her face wrinkled and her hair lost its sheen and began falling out. Her fingers got so crippled she couldn't hold things with them, and she got all bent over and couldn't walk. When the doctors from Comitán came to check on those in the camp, we took them to her. The only thing they could diagnose was that she was wasting away from homesickness.

"As you can tell, I became very disillusioned. Never would I go back, believing that anything that I could do would have a positive effect. Because of the year-and-a-half I spent there, my health never will be the same. I would have been better off doing as I'm doing now, reading books, living in pleasant surroundings, with pleasant companions, going to Mexico City when I want to hear a concert or a lecture or want to buy some new books.

"I don't know what's going to happen [to the indigenas] but whatever it is, I don't think it's going to be very good, even here in Chiapas, where they still have some protected land. I am afraid that eventually Mexico will become two countries. One will be like the United States with McDonalds' burgers and computer screens and Santa Claus and the other will be a huge human garbage dump where all the indigenas and the refugees and the displaced and poor people will live.

"I hope I'm wrong, Señor Norteamericano; but I really don't think I am."

No Different from All the Rest

"I don't know how many we were, starting out together. My oldest brother, I remember, was with us, and there were a lot of children from a lot of different families, a lot," 11-year-old Enrique Castro pressed his lips together and peered first at me, then at my companion, Kevin Carrick, as though needing assurance that he was saying what we wanted to hear.

I nodded; so did Manuel Manrique Martinez, a squat round-faced loquacious man whose large teeth pushing against his upper lip gave him the appearance that he was on the verge of interrupting conversations, even when he wasn't. Manrique had been hired by the Mexican government to keep track of (and dole out) provisions brought to the refugee camp thirty-some arduous kilometers north of Comitán, near the Guatemala border in eastern Chiapas; Carrick was American, a nuclear chemist whose volunteer work with a church group from Oregon brought him with a truckload of medical supplies, food and clothing to the Guatemalan refugees in Chiapas. Only by getting special permission from Mexican officials in Comitán and Mexico City could one visit the camps (my previous attempts had been turned down), but the church Samaritans were allowed in, and I, for the day at least, was, like Carrick, one of them and, with Manrique as a go-between and interpreter, got to hear the stories that several of the older children and their mothers were willing to tell.

"We had to leave — this, others have told me — because some members of our community, some young men, left to find work in Huehue [Huehuetenango, Guatemala, a city on the southern edge of the *antiplano*, where most of the refugees had lived]. They did not come back. I don't know what happened to them. None of us did.

"Then one day soldiers came with the head and hands of one of them pegged on a board. They asked if he was from our community and when his mother burst into shouts and sobs, they said he was a guerrilla and our community supported guerrillas and they, they set fire to everything.

"We had to run away, to hide. Days later, when we went back, the soldiers took several of the older young men and told the rest of us, mothers and children, they would kill us if we returned. We had no choice but to climb over the hills to the next valley. But the community there had been destroyed too.

"We were crying, we had nothing to eat, just a tortilla at night that some mothers cooked over tiny fires. Some of them caught grasshoppers — in one place there were a lot of grasshoppers — and cooked them and we ate them. But some of us, the grasshoppers made us throw up. We were very sick.

"How many of us? I think, oh, a lot, sixty or seventy, but only a few fathers and grandfathers. We walked for days — seven, ten, twelve, I don't remember. Sometimes when soldiers would pass us in their vehicles, they would give orders, tell us which way not to go. Finally, we stopped outside a *ladino* place with walled buildings [*ladino* is a Guatemalan term used to identify ethnic non-indigenas, i.e. those with Spanish blood].

"We stayed there and some people brought us corn to make tortillas. The corn was bad but it was better than the grasshoppers. It was not so bad in that place, because it was not too cold and we pieced together some little shelters. More people from communities like ours came — they had horrible stories to tell, how the soldiers had taken away almost all of the men and had taken the women and hurt them.

"Then some other people came and told us we could not stay outside the *ladino* town any longer. They said we would have to move towards the river. We moved slowly. Very slowly, a line of us so long you couldn't see the beginning of it or the end of it. The walking was hard — we carried what we could — and we got very thirsty. Finally, we reached a place where there were a different kind of soldiers with big trucks. For many days — I don't know how many, ten, twelve, more I think — we stayed there, waiting. Then, at last, the trucks brought us here.

"And here we are. Here in this place."

"This place that is not a home: It is a pen in which we are kept like animals." Maria Cruz's voice, emerging from her tiny, frail frame, was surprisingly deep, full of hard edges and broken Spanish that Manrique had to translate for us (and which, for the most part, I had to re-translate for Carrick). Huge eyes dominated her lumpy, splotched face, as though they had continued to enlarge while the features around them had receded during her years away from the steep hills and little pastures of her highlands birthplace hundreds of miles away. Unlike many of the residents of the camp (which was one of nearly 140 such camps, each containing 100-300 displaced Guatemalan indigenas), Maria Cruz had been a refugee for nearly half of her life.

"The men who came first to take our land [in Guatemala] were not soldiers. They were big men, they rode horses, they were evil. One of them cut my brother's face with a whip. It made him ugly, like he had two mouths, and he could only see out of one eye. Later he was killed, because people thought he was a *brujo* and could make people sick.

"At that time I had been married only long enough to have two children. The first, she died when she was a few months old. The other, my son Marcos, was on my breast. The men brought young animals — cattle — and told us not to touch them. The animals broke into our little *milpas*, ate and trampled our corn. Two men — one of them my husband — caught one of the animals and killed it. The whole community ate it.

"When the men came back, someone told them what we had done. This one who told, he was named Jesus, he was one of our community, a bad man who was born crooked and spoke all the time about things that he did not understand. The men destroyed all of our *habitaciones*, then took my husband and his nephew and tore off their clothes and I cannot tell you what they did to them, but they were bleeding, and although we tried we could not save their lives.

"So we moved to a higher place beyond the steep ridge, but there the corn did not grow, so the men and the boys and some of the women moved back to near where we had lived to plant little patches of corn and melons. It took a day's walk to get to the patches and a day to get back. That summer we had corn and melons, but the next year, when the corn shoots were just green and growing, some soldiers found us.

"They said we were growing the corn for the guerrillas. We told them no, it was for our community. 'What community?" they laughed. They took me and another woman aside and did awful things to us. They took away the men who had come with us to work in the corn. We tried to find them, but we could not. No one ever found them again.

"Later, some of the guerrillas did find us. They gave us some beans and flour. They warned us not to tell anybody we had seen them. By this time, the one who had talked to the soldiers, that Jesus, he was gone — no one knew where — so we felt safe. But those horrible things that shake the trees — right, helicopters — they came, came roaring over our head.

"Then more soldiers came. We could not tell them where the guerrillas were — we did not know. But the soldiers said we were sympathizers because we did not run to tell them about the guerrillas when they brought us the beans. To 'teach us a lesson,' they said, they tied up two of the boys from our little community and in front of their mothers, they shot them.

"We were hungry and now, from our community, there only were a few men left. We had to leave the land that we knew. We followed some trails to a road that trucks moved along. Several times soldiers and men like soldiers, men with guns, stopped to question us. Finally, some of them made us get into a truck, all of us. They took us to a place like this one.

"There we had poor things to eat. Many of us — the children, yes, especially the children — got sick. But we stayed for a year — over a year.

"One time, some of us left to go back — no, not many of us, just eight or nine. We did not follow the road, but only trails. We collected wood and carried it with us and sold it where we could for centavos to buy corn. It took us a long time — I don't know how long, from the cold into the planting time we followed the trails. We just had planted a few things when the men, they found us again. They got their guns out to shoot us but they didn't. They called the soldiers and the soldiers took us in a truck back to the place like this.

"One time, a man from where we used to live came by the place like this and told us about working in a place where there were lots of buildings and roads and many things to do. He was a good man and he paid for some of us for the ride on the bus. We put together a little dwelling place — we were two men and five women. We did work, but not always — husking corn, making tortillas, gathering firewood. This place was very noisy all the time, and the air was bad.

"One time, I got very sick. So did two of the others. Holy María! I thought I would die! Some *ladino* — a doctor — came from I don't know where and gave us medicine. The medicines made us better. Then men in a truck came and took us back to the place like this.

"From there, after a long time, they brought us here. So that is my story. It is no different from all the rest."

The Mexican government established the camps for Guatemalan refugees in 1895 and 1986. They did it less for humanitarian reasons, claimed Guatemala's congressional human rights commission president Jorge Luis Archila Amezquita, than to stop the illegal flow of Guatemalan refugees across the Mexican frontier. Few of the refugees liked the camps, most of which were tucked into inaccessible (and otherwise unusable) nooks and crannies of the thickly forested selva.

The original agreement between presidents Miguel de la Madrid of Mexico and Vinicio Cerezo of Guatemala stipulated that the refugees gradually would be repatriated back to the Altiplano Occidental but Guatemala's Congress consistently voted down proposals to establish *aldeas model* (model cities) or *polos de desarrollo* (development areas) in or near the refugees' former homelands. In addition, Guatemala's federal government lacked the power to enforce repatriation in the big landowner-controlled rural areas of northern and western Guatemala.

The Mexican government, meanwhile, lost interest in the "refugee problem" after de la Madrid passed the presidential baton to Carlos Salinas de Gortari. A few refugees tried to make it back to their homelands on their own, but met fates similar to what María Cruz encountered.

Others sifted into *zonas de marginización* in and around cities like Tuxtla Gutierrez and Tapachula. Petitions to return periodically surfaced, engineered for the most part by human rights advocates or de facto Mexican government officials trying to nudge their Guatemalan counterparts into action, but as media interest in the "refugee problem" faded, the two governments let inertia take its course and the camps (and their residents) disappeared — as so many things before them have disappeared into the entangling branches of the selva.

Not by Magic!

Efrén Gissman never bought into the nostalgia about indigena ways. A pragmatist like his father, Gissman was born on a highlands plantation "surrounded by tropical orchards on hills rising above a green rain forest," the son of a young German immigrant and his Mexican wife.

Despite his short stature — he was just over five feet tall — Gissman, even at 80, emanated the kind of strength that one associates with a healthy physical life. As he talked, hands firmly braced on the arms of a ponderous baroque chair, his dark eyes, enlarged by thick, rimless glasses, probed distant corners of the dustless but relentlessly static living room. I spent several afternoons visiting him in this house set among pear orchards a few miles from Ocosingo, alone or with my friend Angel Gomez Sanchez, who was negotiating to buy a lot near Gissman's stream-side property. Now and then, his voice animated despite his fixed posture, Gissman would brush at the few remaining strands of hair that covered his square temples.

Unlike many of the immigrants so instrumental in developing Chiapas' coffee industry, Gissman's father had never intended to leave Germany. But older relatives and acquaintances who'd come to the highlands just before the turn of the century sent for him because they desperately needed someone with his mechanical skills. Unable to turn down the money they offered, the elder Gissman left his pregnant wife and a child and made the trip, intending to return within a year.

But Chiapas was a long way from Germany. The trip took forever, the work (which included putting together coffee bean processing equipment and building an irrigation system) took longer than expected and the dense green rain forests filled with jaguarondi and peccaries and ocelots and Mayan idols drew him into an earthly dream world from which he couldn't emerge. He stayed, married Efrén's mother ("the priests were understanding and cooperative" about his distant and now forgotten Protestant marriage), and he never returned to Europe.

Although Efrén's father gradually acquired coffee plantation land, Efrén grew up on the "have less" side of plantation society. Though quick-witted and energetic ("*muy listo*" he described himself), Efrén had little patience for schooling. Like his father, he had a keen sense of how things work and, despite a zest for adventure, he developed an instinctive recognition of the boundaries necessary for self-discipline.

As a teenager, he went with his father to Guatemala to set up plantation irrigation systems. He returned to Guatemala on his own a few years later, a technician who (by his own admittance) "could fix, rebuild, adapt or improvise" anything that had moving parts, especially the treasured automobiles, trucks and agricultural equipment that were being manufactured in the United States and were beginning to make their way into Mexico and Central America.

He repaired, bought, bartered and blended all of the internal combustion engine-driven machines he could get his hands on. As he did so, he gradually obtained newly planted coffee plantation land on the Pacific slopes of Guatemala's Sierra Madres. He didn't return to Chiapas to live for nearly three decades. He sold his Guatemala holdings shortly after World War II and moved his now sickly and dependent wife and his two teen-aged daughters back to the country in which they'd been born.

Gissman spent the next several years ramrodding gold-dredging operations, a venture he enjoyed more for the opportunities it gave him to improvise equipment than for the money it brought him, but in the early '50s he resettled into life as a small volume coffee grower in a Chiapas that was much more tranquil and tamed than the country he remembered from his boyhood.

"Your eyes don't see very far — into the past or into the future," he told me. "When I was a boy, there was none of this. The Angostura Reservoir didn't exist. There weren't any roads to speak of. Cars? No one around here even imagined them. There were no airplanes. Hell! Porfirio Díaz was running the country. Madero! Zapata! They weren't even fully grown!

"My father, my father's friends, they looked at the hills and they saw opportunity. All this talk about driving the indigenas out! How many indigenas do you think there were? I used to ride horses all through these hills. There was nothing but forest. Before the coffee plantations there was nothing but forests, wild animals, bugs!

"The indigenas, we didn't move that many of them. Little campgrounds, that's all they were, not even buildings really. And not very many of them. And even in those they didn't grow enough to keep themselves alive, not really.

"Coffee: Coffee was the best thing to grow. Those trees didn't march up the hillsides by themselves. The trees that were there before them didn't just fall down and disappear. Day after day, week after week, month after month, we would go in there, with mules; we would chop and dig and grunt and pull and plow and cultivate and plant, one little piece of hillside at a time. Then wait, wait for the trees to grow. This year, so much..."

Lifting one hand, he measured a little section of mountain that he seemed to be able to see beyond the room, beyond time, 50 years — or more — into the past. "Next year, so much more — growing year by year.

"It took some men's lifetimes just to make one small plantation.

"Other crops wouldn't have worked, you see. Not as well. The idealists, the radicals, they talk about — hell! I don't know what they talk about! — but this idea, this idea that we should only have grown crops that could be eaten here, that's not right, that's very wrong.

"Remember, when I was just starting out, in Guatemala — but here, too — there were a lot of debates about what to raise. Bananas, pears, grapes for wine, tobacco — all of these things we discussed. You see, you have to understand, when you are in the position we were in, with hills covered with scrub forest and the rainfall coming when it does, you have to figure out just how you can make a living.

"The thing about coffee was, the trees would grow well and the market was steady. It's not possible to grow coffee in the United States; it's not possible to grow coffee in Europe. They have to import it. So they would come to us.

"Coffee beans aren't perishable, like pineapples, like mangoes or bananas or pears. So you see, that was a consideration. There was a minimum of loss. The market was there — you have to understand that, too. We didn't invent it, we didn't just decide, willy-nilly, to grow something and then figure out how to sell it. No, when we came into the industry there was a demand for coffee. It was an industry we could get into that would pay off. It was something we could learn to do — learn to do well.

"We did. We transformed the hills. Not by magic — by work. Days and days and days and days of work. We created something — the plantations — where there had been nothing before. We gave the world something it wanted; we gave the highlands an order, a meaning.

"It was like a calling — a priesthood, being a producer of good coffee was. It wasn't an idle thing: It was a dedication, something we were proud of. It was something we devoted our lives to. It was our work, our identity, our....our, it was *us*!"

Us. Not just a livelihood, not just personality, but a way of life superimposed onto the highlands. But even in the orderliness, the uniformity, by which the coffee plantations have conquered the green Chiapan hillsides, one senses that all this controlled neatness is only temporary. That within the earth, moving through the darkness as soon as the sun slides westward towards Oaxaca and the Pacific Ocean, a dark, absorbing spirit moves.

You Are the Problem!

"You bring this, this cross, this 'God,' and what is it, really? A big thing, an invisible thing, but not a thing of nature. It is nothing but a 'super chief,' like your governor, your president, only bigger, no? And you say that 'He' makes rules but the rules, really, what are they? Human rules, that's all that they are. They are not about the earth. They are not about the sky."

The words ended in a piping squeak — the sound a drill press makes when it punches through metal — as Aurelio Rodriguez leaned past me to squint towards hills patched into swatches of dry corn and brush. Past them, gray and volcanic, the denser mountains beyond Las Margaritas lay wrapped in mist. For a few moments, the muscles of his lean, high cheek-boned face twitching with an array of tiny, independent movements, he blinked towards them, as though seeking something to confirm his descriptions of how his people, the Tojolabales, had worked in rhythm with the seasons for centuries in this deeply creviced land just west of the vast rain forests of the Lacandon.

"And you — well, not you, of course, personally — but those from your culture, who advocate the marvels of this 'super chief,' have created the problem that that you define as being the 'Indian problem.' What you don't understand is that we are not a 'problem.' We have a problem: You. You and your super chief-god are the problem. You and your insistence that there is something wrong with the way the Tojolabales have lived since long before your people knew about guns or engines or airplanes."

Several passers-by — like him dressed in work cottons, their crumpled straw hats pulled low over their eyes — drifted over to listen as he described how the Tojolabales and other peoples of the hills and valleys of Chiapas, considering themselves to be the earth's children, had remained in small communal groups, loosely linked to other groups who spoke the same language and followed the same customs, for hundreds of years before the Spanish conquest. These communities had considered entire valleys to be their "homes" and they had moved from one site to another, clearing land and planting corn before drifting on to let their farms revert back to grassland and forest.

"Because of this, this 'lifestyle,' you would call it," Rodriguez' features twitched more intensely as again he gestured towards the hillsides, "they could not effectively resist the Spanish conquerors. Nor, later, the Mexican army. These little communities fought back, of course, but not as an army, not with military tactics, just as a people wanting to plow and plant and grow their corn and raise their children."

Gradually the conquerors pushed the Tojobales out of the most fertile land and tried to impose a European system of towns, roadways and private property on the land they considered theirs.

"Growing up here," Rodriguez admitted, "I did not understand, at first, the conflicts. The education, you see, is all from the conquerors' point of view. To that point of view, we Tojolabales are 'backward.' We are 'primitive.' We need to be brought into the modern age. We need to learn the conquerors' ways.

"It took me a long time to realize that it was not 'backwardness' that afflicted my people. The way of life of the Tojolabales always has been very beautiful. Now, I know, for you, that is hard to understand, because when you come into the village here and look around, you see suffering on every face — poverty, hunger...for the love of God, man! I see it too! But that is not the way of life of the Tojolabales, nor of the other descendants of the Mayas who inhabit the canyons of Chiapas across the mountains from us.

"I know, I know, I am very passionate about this! What you are seeing is the result of people pushed out of their land, out of their way of life, away from their gods."

Throughout his late teens, Rodriguez said that he lived torn between two cultures. He wanted to read and learn; he liked school. But the more he studied the conquerors' concepts, the more he realized that his culture and the conquerors' culture could not blend.

"I was in agony. I could see no future for the Tojolabales — I even thought of them that way, as something outside of myself — I only could perceive that they would be destroyed. Then — okay, it was like waking up, waking up from a complicated dream — I realized that the people around me, the conqueror-type people — were afflicted with a monstrous hunger, and nothing that they ate satisfied that hunger. Nothing that they did — nothing in all their conquering — made them happy."

He came back to Las Margaritas, he said, feeling soulless and abandoned, feeling as though he belonged to neither culture. Then he met several other conqueror-educated Tojolabales struggling to forge meaningful identities in the violated valence shell that Chiapas had become by 1980. They talked constantly, both to each other and to those around them — migrant workers, displaced campesinos[5], struggling sharecroppers — and they came to the realization that, in order to survive, the Tojolabal villages somehow would have to form a larger union in order to have any kind of political power.

"Now this is important, it is something we talked about and talked about. Finally we understood that it was not to force those of the conqueror-culture to change that we needed to unite. What we needed to fight for — to resist — was their forcing us to become like them.

"Our struggle is not for conquest. We do not need to rusticate you. We do not care if you and your people worship your 'super chief,' even though we see that it only makes you angry, only makes you want more of what you already have too much of — oil, trees, coffee beans. It is to have back a way of life that is rich with contentment that we struggle. To live as we choose to live without bothering anyone — and without being forced to do things that we do not want to do."

Like the little communal *milpas* of the Tojolabales, the roads leading out of Las Margaritas vanish into the scrub brush that coats the hillsides. Trails seem to lead everywhere and nowhere. I chose one, then another, expecting to find little clusters of people, little places of habitation, here or there.

What seemed like jeep or truck tracks swerved through bristly vegetation and disappeared, only to reappear several hundred yards away, divide, rejoin and disappear again. Animal droppings seemed to indicate a route along a whaleback crest that gave me a view of deep canyons, a cloud-streaked winter sky and a green mirage undulating through distant mist that I thought could be a corner of the tropical rain forest.

From a denuded crest pocked by excavated stumps, obviously the aftermath of lumber clearcutting, I caught a glimpse of a Tojolabal family trudging along the spine of a ridge on the far side of a steep cañada.

The man seemed to be dragging something in one hand and carrying a hoe-like implement over his opposite shoulder. The woman, behind him, bent beneath a prickly nest of sticks almost three times her height. Behind her a child (a boy, I presumed by his attire) lugged a cloth-wrapped bundle in both arms. I lifted one hand in greeting but either they did not see me or chose not to acknowledge my presence. A few minutes later they disappeared beyond the crest down into a canyon on the other side of the ridge.

---

5. Originally peasants, but now farmers or agricultural workers. The word comes from "campo" which means "countryside."

I thought about them a few hours later when another young Tojolabal, more militant than Aurelio Rodriguez, recited a Tojolabal belief that he said a "very wise man" had told him.

"The earth is our mother, and from the earth comes the corn that we eat and because it comes from our mother, it is sacred. When we eat it we take that sacredness into ourselves and we take care of other growing things, especially the mountains and their forests. He told me that if there are trees, there will be water, and where there is water, there will be food, and where there is food, the people will be healthy. And healthy people, he told me, are both happy and wise."

I asked him if he believed what the very wise man had told him. He stared directly into my eyes with an intensity that released no emotion, but came from an imprisoning depth to which I had no access.

"Yes, *echa la chingada!* I believe it!" But, he added, it wasn't possible to achieve the happiness and wisdom that the wise old man had described when the Tojolabales lacked access to the land that was needed for growing corn, and the mountains with their forests were being destroyed.

I described the family of three that I had seen and the stare returned, opaque and angry, but again without outward force that I could sense or feel. So many Tojolabales, he said, had been forced away from their communal roots.

Instead of retaining their "one-ship" with nature, they had become subsidiary participants — migrant workers, wood gatherers — of the dominant conqueror culture. The further they were pushed into the dry hills, where the land barely would yield a meager crop of corn, the more scattered one from the other they became, and the less able to continue their traditional lifestyle.

To avoid extinction, he insisted, the Tojolabales — and other native peoples of Chiapas, Oaxaca, Guerrero and Veracruz — needed to retrieve some of what they had lost. They needed stewardship of lands that the Mexican revolution had granted them (and that recent amendments to the constitution were taking away). An organization to which he was a delegate, the Frente Independiente de Pueblos Indios, was bringing Tojolabales from all over western Chiapas together and inviting other native peoples and oppressed non-indigena campesinos to join them.

Seeking optimism (or perhaps hope) in his eyes and in his expression, I asked him if he saw a time in the near — or distant — future when the Tojolabales would again become the happy and wise people they had been before the Spanish Conquest. His imprisoned stare turned inward and he became so unblinkingly, breathlessly still that I thought for a moment that he had gone into a catatonic trance.

"I didn't mean..." I started to hedge, but he silenced me with a wave of his hand.

"It's not that, it is...too much has changed." He struggled to express contradictory thoughts, his gaze still fixed on some interior image. "It is that, to have what is our life, will not be easy. I know — we know — that Mexico is not going to disappear. We know that we are part of this Mexico that is here now.

"But we need — what we need is to have our life, to have our life as a people with a language that is our own, with a way of providing for ourselves that is different from what those who are not indigenas have for themselves. What we need is that which is in the land and in the water and in the forests and that which in us is the same as that which is in the land and in the water and in the forests."

As though overwhelmed by the effort of expounding deep-felt beliefs, in his second language — Spanish — the young Tojolabal thrust his chin upward. Again, he seemed to fall into some kind of a trance. As I turned, curious, I saw what had engaged his attention: a rainbow spreading from horizon to horizon, its spectrum of soft muted colors forming a halo over the beautiful, tortured land.

False Rumors

Whippets of color braided the trees that were clinging to the ravaged sola on the eroded Chiapan hillside as wild birds — tanagers and orioles — scattered in front of my 12-year-old companion, Lorenzo, and me. We stopped and turned to look back at the stubbly mead with its splintered hayrack and rutted wallow and heard a sharp *rat-tat!* of children's voices.

Detecting our presence, the scurrying figures stopped abruptly, then darted through the underbrush. Unable to decipher their excited chatter, I asked Lorenzo, in Spanish, what they'd said. Though born in a Tojolabal village, Lorenzo worked in San Cristóbal and had a primary school education.

"They are being guerrillas," he told me. "They were shooting us, pretending we were soldiers."

Five years later, on January 1, 1994, the guerrillas in the hills overlooking Altamirano were not pretending. Their takeover of highlands Chiapas embarrassed both the Mexican government of President Carlos Salinas de Gortari and state officials, who had maintained until the eve of the operation that "the selva is tranquil, just like the rest of Chiapas."

Even casual observers knew better. Reports that armed militia were practicing maneuvers in the creviced hills beyond recently cleared cattle grazing land were more than rumor.

Both individual cattlemen and cattlemen's associations had requested military presence in the area and their reports had reached and been discussed at the presidential level in Mexico City. A number of coffee growers and agriculturists had complained that "subversives" had been trying to influence their sharecroppers and field hands. They insisted that travel in the thinly populated region was becoming increasingly hazardous.

Some of the smaller landowners formed para-military Ku Klux Klan-type units to invade and terrorize indigena farms and villages, purportedly in retaliation against the natives' increased militancy. Later-to-be-assassinated ruling PRI party presidential candidate Luis Donaldo Colosio, during a visit to Chiapas, advocated the appropriation of special funds to pay for a full-scale investigation of the alleged subversive activities four months before the *Zapatistas* appeared.

For over a year preceding the January 1, 1994 insurrection, Army units from both the 7th and 31st military zones had been making forays into the highlands. Reports circulating in Mexico City, possibly devised as propaganda for the United States, indicated that the soldiers were on drug-search missions, but neither smuggling nor clandestine air strips were prevalent in the area the soldiers were probing. Of more concern to the government was the fact that representatives to a January 1993 convocation of indigena organizations from throughout the highlands had voted, nearly unanimously, that the continuation of the fight for indigena rights should not exclude armed conflict.

According to the INI (Instituto Nacional Indigenista), during the decade that preceded the insurrection, the state's militaristic government had strong-armed the indigena population by ordering state police and vigilante repressions. There was, "a terrible balance sheet of violence for the indigenas of Chiapas during General Absalon Castellanos administration [1982-1988]: 102 assassinations, 327 disappearances, 590 illegal arrests, 427 kidnappings and torture, 407 families forced out of their communities, 12 women raped, 18 cases of homes being destroyed, two attacks on protest marches.

Early in May, 1993, two soldiers from the Seventh Military Zone disappeared while on maneuvers near Altamirano. Searches for them were unsuccessful until some campesinos stumbled across the shallow graves in which they'd been buried. Their killers never were brought to trial, although the military detained (and possibly tortured) dozens of farmers in their efforts to extract information and/or confessions.

A few weeks later, on May 26, a group of armed campesinos killed two soldiers in rugged country near Altamirano. The Army immediately launched a campaign to capture the aggressors and stumbled across a guerrilla training camp that included simulated tanks, bivouac equipment, arms and military clothing. Although state records contained a finding of facts describing the event, both the federal government and the military later denied that the discovery occurred.

In fact, in August, Mexico's Secretaria de Gobernacion, Patrocinio Gonzalez Garrido (who had been governor of Chiapas before being promoted to President Carlos Salinas de Gortari's cabinet) called reports that armed indigena groups existed in Chiapas "false rumors," an opinion confirmed (at least for public consumption) by the commander of the 31st military zone, General Gaston Menchaca Arías.

The week before the takeover, newspapers in Tuxtla Gutierrez reported that both tank and infantry units had launched "expeditions" into the rough country late in December, a clear indication that both civil and military authorities knew that the threat of an uprising was imminent. That same week, a number of individuals called radio station XEWM in San Cristóbal to report that cattle and cargo trucks were being stolen in various parts of the highlands. These notices were delivered to commander of the Seventh Military Zone, General Miguel Angel Godinez, but instead of acting on them he pulled all of his troops into San Cristóbal for New Year's Eve.

On January 1, 1994, the residents of San Cristobal, Ocosingo, Altamirano, Las Margaritas and Chanal awoke to find government buildings sacked, jails opened and armed masked Zapatistas patrolling the streets. A terse communique announced that former governor Absalon Castellanos had been abducted and "put to work" on a tenant farm until he could be tried for crimes against the indigenas. Another communique stated that the EZLN (Ejército

Zapatista de Liberación Nacional), frustrated by government refusals to treat native peoples fairly, had decided "*Basta!*" and taken matters into its own hands.

After burning government records in San Cristóbal de las Casas, the rebels evacuated the city on January 2 but occupied Oxchuc, Guadalupe Tepeyac and Huixlan. Their first skirmishes with Mexican army units left ten or more soldiers dead. More died the following day as Mexican military authorities rushed reinforcements, including helicopters, bombers, field guns and tanks, into Chiapas. Government propaganda insisted that the rebellion was led by "foreign terrorists" — charges which proved to be totally untrue.

A massive military counterattack drove the rebels out of Ocosingo on January 5. The Associated Press reported that newsmen had counted 37 cadavers in the streets of that town of 9,000, all of them apparently rebels. Beside some of them, "the only arms encountered were wooden rifles transformed into weapons by the bayonets attached to them" although a priest who witnessed the confrontation reported that most of the Zapatistas were armed either with automatic rifles or other weapons, including ancient smooth-bore single-shots.

All of the dead were native Chiapans and all wore similar clothing (olive-green pants, brown shirts, red kerchiefs and rubber boots). Some had been carrying backpacks containing tortillas, bread and sugar.

As the insurrectionists withdrew, Mexican army planes and helicopters attacked their new positions in the hills surrounding San Cristóbal and Ocosingo. To save face, both federal and state officials felt it necessary to overlook the unsuccessful military forays and attribute the uprising to "foreign," "ultra-leftist" and "ambitiously self-serving" elements within the indigena communities. When it began to be clear that these charges weren't true, local officials shifted the blame-pointing towards Catholic priests, including Bishop Samuel Ruiz of San Cristóbal, asserting that their pastoral work with the indigena population concealed their encouragement of those who believed in the violent overthrow of the government.

For the nonce, the government re-occupied all of the captured towns except Guadalupe Tepeyac, but sporadic fighting throughout the region drove non-combatants first one way, then the other. Vigilante committees organized by local landowners and caciques ferreted out supposed EZLN "collaborators," many of whom were jailed without trial. Soldiers likewise incarcerated hundreds of Tzeltales, Tzotziles and Tojolabales between 15 and 35 years of age and herded other indigena men, women and children out of the land they had "secured" from the EZLN.

In December 1996, nearly three years after the start of the conflict, a corporal from the 31st military zone disappeared while on maneuvers with his unit in the highlands. Military officials never confirmed whether or not his body had been recovered but a straw boss working with several campesinos near Altamirano reported that several groups of armed soldiers had swept through the indigena communities, detained and tortured several residents and arrested others on trumped up charges.

"Won't they ever learn?" a pro-government spokesman complained as he described this latest indigena depredation against the military.

He didn't reply when I asked back: "Won't you?"

Over the Hills Through Guerrilla Land

Román Juarez was not afraid of danger: He had been a daredevil most of his life. He had walked blindfolded along a fourth-story girder, reached the end and walked back while street vendors, construction workers, sidewalk sweepers, girl Fridays and a traffic policeman or two had gasped, honked, applauded and posted bets beneath him. He had ridden a brakeless bicycle down the Tenejapa hill so fast a pickup going sixty 45 mph couldn't keep up with him.

Not only that. He had leaped from one speeding outboard into another on the Angostura Reservoir — and back again — then repeated the performance for doubled bets when doubters on shore had refused to believe that he'd accomplished the feat. And he had stood on a pyre of flaming brush until all of his clothing was ablaze, then dived into four meters of muddy water to douse the conflagration.

Still, the events of that first week of January 1994 scared him more than he'd been scared in his nearly fifty years of human life. For even in his daredevilishness, Román Juarez was quintessentially practical, an expert at calculating odds (though extremely foolish about money, driven as he was by a need to impress, to rise above the rabble).

It was that need to be liked and admired that put him on the road from Ocosingo to San Cristóbal de las Casas on the fifth day of the Zapatista insurrection, against his better judgment — especially after he realized that he'd miscalculated the odds.

Or been misled into miscalculating them by Francisco Edmundo Martinez.

Like Román Juarez, Francisco'mundo (as Juarez called him) was ebullient, gregarious, preternaturally active, but unlike Juarez he was a committed family man whose wife was a devoted Catholic. He and Juarez were among the first to climb to the top of the steep *cerro* just west of the downtown when low-level attack bombers from the Mexican Air Force began to roar over the city.

But while Juarez had come as a spectator, twitching and wincing as bombs and rockets pummeled the hills outside the city, sending the smells of powder and burning oil across the jet stream-streaked sky, Martinez was on a mission: He had to find transportation to deliver Red Cross medicines to the hospital in Altamirano. He had to do it because his wife insisted upon it, and Martinez wasn't one to disobey his wife.

Had he owned a car, he would have headed for the Altamirano junction just south of Ocosingo with the doctor and the supplies and not asked for help. But he didn't own a car — neither did the doctor, an animated intern who'd just graduated from a medical school in Guadalajara after spending fifteen years as an ambulance attendant, orderly and emergency room nurse.

Juarez did own a car (even though it was about to be repossessed) — a mini-pickup with a rattle in the transmission, but good brakes and adequate tires. Had it not been for the doctor, Martinez probably couldn't have convinced Juarez to plunge through the heart of Zapatista-occupied country, despite his daring reputation.

But the doctor seemed to have some kind of official approval (at least, the way that Martinez presented it) and Juarez, afraid that his friend would think he was chicken, gave in and said yes. And once he'd done that, he couldn't welsh out, no matter how insane the mission became.

He didn't think they'd get to set out soon, since the Army had blocked access to the highways. But Martinez insisted that he knew a "back road" that would allow them to circumvent the patrols.

"Back road! It wasn't even a dirt road, just grown-over car tracks that bumped off the Periferico towards an old rancho." Juarez loved to recount the adventure as he entertained friends and acquaintances in a little bar just off the Zocalo in San Cristóbal de las Casas. It was a performance piece, repeated so many times that the descriptions seemed to leap into existence of their own accord.

"Francisco'mundo wasn't a coleto[6] — he'd grown up in Guadalajara — but he knew every path, stone and ford around San Cristobal. I drove and he sat next to me; the doctor stayed in back hanging onto the supplies loaded in the bed behind the cab.

"Thank God it hadn't rained in days, so the ground was dry and we weren't in danger of sinking up to the axles into anything. Even so, I was fighting dust and rocks and crevices so deep I had to take them one tire at a time. As far as I could see, there was no road — there wasn't even a footpath. 'No!' 'There!' 'Here!' 'Up there!' 'Turn!' Francisco'mundo would shout, pointing this way and that. By the time we'd gone three miles, the windshield was so coated we barely could see through it and every bolt and hinge on the pickup was rattling as if the poor vehicle were coming apart.

"Finally, Francisco'mundo crawled out through the window and stood with one foot on the seat and the other on the fender, waving and pointing as he shouted instructions. Half the time I couldn't hear him and I'd have to brake at the last moment, skid, slam the pickup into reverse, bump forward, swerve, back up again. And all this time the doctor was banging the back of the cab, shouting that this or that was coming loose, or that he heard soldiers, or tanks, or thought he saw guerrillas.

"Finally Francisco'mundo hopped down and took off at a trot in front of the pickup. He is not a big man, but very much a *deportista*; he kept running, motioning 'Here!' 'There!' 'Stop!' 'This way!' 'Follow!' never once slackening his pace. Over hills we plunged, crashing, clanging, scraping the oil pan, hitting the axles. The transmission was making more and more noise — I was afraid it was going to come apart — and the needle on the gas gauge was bouncing around like crazy.

"But listen! That wasn't the worst of it! The worst was not knowing where the guerrillas were. We'd just zigzagged up a slope, half-following an old dry stream bed, when suddenly we were attacked! Rushing, squealing, flapping bodies all around us. I stomped on the brakes. I could hear the doctor screaming as though he'd been wounded, then Francisco'mundo laughing and I realized that it had been a flight of vultures. *Chingada!* My heart was pounding so hard it was bruising my ribs.

"A few minutes later, a gaunt old cow crashed through the brush. I slammed on the brakes and killed the engine; I couldn't get it re-started until

---

6. Residents of San Cristobal de las Casas, Chiapas.

Francisco'mundo and the doctor pushed the pickup over a crest and I went caterwauling downhill, barely missing stumps and rocks and holes the size of bomb craters. I'd just started to relax when I felt the pickup begin to shake.

"I thought the transmission was coming apart. Then I realized it wasn't the pickup: It was a helicopter. It came right over the top of us, making a deafening roar, its shadow swept across us like a blow from a club. We looked up and saw guns pointed at us — lots of guns.

"'They're going to machine-gun us!' I yanked the emergency brake and dove under the steering wheel. Back and forth the huge thing roared, right on top of us. I tried to squeeze out the door, intending to run, then saw Francisco'mundo jumping up and down, waving at the soldiers to land.

"The helicopter made one more pass right over our heads, then veered sharply and headed over the hills. I was trembling so much I barely could get my hands around the steering wheel, but finally I managed to ask Francisco'mundo why in the name of the Holy Virgin he'd wanted the soldiers to land.

"He laughed. 'I did not want them to land — I wanted them to go away. I waved at them to land so they would not land! My God! You know how they are! They never do what you want them to!'

"'Yes, maybe so,' I mumbled but my heart still was pounding. I would have turned back, but Francisco'mundo insisted there were better roads ahead of us.

"For a few miles more we bumped along ridges between ravines, Francisco'mundo trotting ahead and showing me the way. Then as we got closer to the San Cristóbal-Ocosingo highway, the driving got a little easier. Several times we saw little huts, and a few poor indigenas scratching at the soil, but at no time did we see any guerrillas.

"Finally Francisco'mundo got us onto a sort of road that connected two ranchos and the driving was easier, but still there were things that gave me the willies. Like attack planes — little ones — roaring up over a hill and zooming past us. And screams that turned out to be some women and children that we almost ran over when I caromed past their hiding place.

"Finally, for a couple miles, I got to drive on the highway itself. The poor pickup! It rattled and shivered like every rivet had come loose and the gas gauge needle was quivering on the empty side of empty. Where the turn off to Altamirano intersected the highway, soldiers had set up a blockade. They wouldn't let us through. We told them we'd come from San Cristobal de las Casas — they told us to go back. I protested that we didn't have any gasoline and they laughed. 'Use water!' they jeered. 'Up ahead is Zapatista blood, use that!'

"I wasn't in a mood for one-liners, so I kept my mouth shut. We unloaded the doctor's supplies and he sat down to wait for someone with authority to let him go through to Altamirano. Francisco'mundo and I started back towards San Cristobal, but an Army jeep roared up to us. The driver shouted that he'd shoot us if we turned on our headlights.

"I was looking down a gun barrel — the soldier holding it was trembling as much as I was: I would have prayed if I could have thought of anything to pray to. When the jeep roared off, I passed out. Poor Francisco'mundo! He thought I'd died of a heart attack!"

Fortunately, the pair of adventurers detected a light in the distance. It turned out to be a lantern in a little shack set back from the road. Not only did its owner, an indigena who lived there with his wife, two children, and aged mother, let Juarez and Martinez sleep on his floor for the night, he also siphoned enough gas from his ancient truck to get them on their way the next day. After numerous delays, searches and interrogations, they arrived back in San Cristóbal, Martinez to tell his wife he'd fulfilled his Christian obligation and Juarez to cadge a few drinks from his favorite bartender while he worked out the first version of what would become a many-times-told tale of adventure.

Different Faces

Teopisca's shimmering white-washed walls, unpaved streets and sturdy church are tucked against underbrush-tangled forests that grow dense with vegetation during the rain-washed summers but dry into thorny, crackling kindling in the winter. It is connected to the outer world by the highway that weaves down the crest from San Cristobal and speeds along the plateau towards Comitán. Until the insurrection, it was a secure PRI outpost where landowners, indigenas and a sprinkling of outsiders interacted along predictable social lines.

Within hours after Subcomandante Marcos and the band of armed indigenas that called themselves the National Zapatista Liberation Army occupied the government buildings in San Cristóbal de las Casas, Comitán and Altamirano and closed the highway and Teopisca's few functioning businesses on New Year's Day, 1994, correspondents from the world's major television networks, newspapers and wire services descended upon Chiapas, flashbulbs and TV high-intensity lights blazing, microphones, modems, Faxes and cellular telephones flinging words and pictures across mountains and cities and oceans.

"There were more television people here [in Chiapas] than soldiers, guerrillas or the indigenas caught in the fighting between them," Elvira Micaela Amador told me months after most of the media had left and the insurrection had settled into a hostile stalemate between the armed indigenas and the Mexican army. Her thin face twitched and her nervous fingers picked at threads of her clothing as she talked. The walled garden behind the neat little house on the edge of Teopisca was a confusion of neatly maintained divergent colors and shapes. *Ollas* of varying sizes spouted well-watered trees and flowers and shrubs of all descriptions but the garden's overall impression was one of unpatterned coincidence, as though she had been interrupted in the midst of rearranging everything and never returned to complete the job.

Like many other newcomers scattered through the small towns that ring the selva, Amador and her husband, an industrial engineer pensioned for health problems from the aluminum plant in which he'd worked, had settled into a tranquil rural life that imposed few physical demands and provided just enough satisfactions — a garden, trips to nearby San Cristóbal's shops and markets, hunting and fishing expeditions — to keep them occupied. Both she and her husband had grown up in coastal southern Spain and come to Mexico after their children, then both teenagers, had been born. Along with their coleto neighbors, they had heard rumors about secret militia bands in the selva, but had shrugged off the possibilities of an uprising.

"The townspeople joked that the indigenas were too dumb to do anything but drink and have children." A series of minute shivers worked their way through her thin shoulders and her fingers twitched towards her mouth as though to rearrange the embarrassed smile that appeared there. "Oh, now and then someone would hint that guerrillas from Guatemala were hiding out near the Lacandon. Others talked about drug dealers from Columbia, or some secret assault groups the army was training. But no one really thought the indigenas could be a political force."

Their ski-masked appearances transformed Chiapas, Amador insisted. So did the television and news cameras. Minor functionaries who previously had been interviewed only by scripted party officials or *amas de casa* posing as society columnists suddenly had tape recorders thrust under their noses. To give the newspeople the words they wanted, many of these rustic petty bureaucrats exaggerated rumors they'd heard — or made up facts and started their own rumors.

"It was funny, in a way. One of the landowners told a man from the Spanish news service that he'd seen airplanes filled with guerrillas land on his property. 'They were not Mexican!' he said, acting very excited. 'They had hundreds of weapons — big weapons, cannons!' And he said, 'They all put on masks so I wouldn't know they were foreigners!'

"Later he admitted that he hadn't seen the planes, only heard them. Then my husband found out that the landowner only was repeating a story someone else had told him — a story that wasn't even true. By then the Spanish reporter had sent out his story and gone somewhere else.

"Many stories like that were being told. People I knew — one, a woman I'm sure never got out of her house all the time that the Zapatistas were in town — swore that the Zapatistas had taken hundreds of people into the selva and executed them. She said the Army had found them by following the gyres of circling vultures. Others whispered that soldiers were burning the entire selva.

"Oh! But perhaps the funniest was what this *sindicato* leader showed some American cameramen.

"He showed them the jail in, I don't know, Altamirano — or Tres Posadas, maybe — my husband told me the story. This *sindicatero* told the cameramen wild stories about a big gun battle and pointed to bullet holes in the walls and windows of the jail. 'Grind! Grind! Grind!' the cameras went, the television people's head bobbing like corks. But the *sindicatero* left out the part about a fiesta two years ago, when no one was in the jail, and the people celebrating shot it up because they were drunk. That's where the holes had come from, not from the Zapatistas.

"With the truce [in mid-January, 1994], most of the cameras left. I guess most of the stories after that came from the Mexican army. They were very strict about who could go where, and guarded all the side roads leading into and out of the selva. But of course people talked to each other — the coletos to the coletos and the indigenas to the indigenas. Many of the people that we knew were very unhappy about the truce.

"They said the Army should do with the indigenas what Porfirio Díaz did a century ago. He kidnapped and killed the Yaquis and took over their lands and they never were returned. Another popular story was that we all should pass out free aguardiente to the indigenas. 'They will get drunk, throw their weapons away and crawl back to their corn piles!' people argued.

"But of course none of those things happened. The Army just surrounded and cut off the areas that the Zapatistas controlled. The local politicians told us our lives could go back to normal.

"But you see, they couldn't. The way of life had been altered. The way the crops were picked, the way the work was done — all changed. Until then, I hadn't realized what separate worlds we each lived in — the coletos, the indigenas, the outsiders like my husband and me.

"I somehow accepted the way things were without thinking about them. That's the way it is in Chiapas. You see — but you don't see. You try to make things better but inside, you don't change. You focus on your own problems. The indigenas just were there. They were what they were. What they always had been since colonial times.

"My husband tried to...take a stand, but you see, like me, he was confused. In his mind, he's very liberal — intellectually, he supported what the indigenas were trying to do. Intellectually. But it wasn't, really, intellectually that clear. A lot of the indigenas from the town, from Teopisca, were not Zapatistas.

"Others had relatives who were fighting for the Zapatistas, or had friends or relatives who'd been pushed off their little plots of land by the fighting. The women — some of those that I knew — would talk to me, but others only would look at me with a new kind of expression in their eyes. Not hate, not anger, just...I don't know, I'm not sure — possibility, perhaps. The possibility that they could have or would have what I have, and what it would be like.

"And the soldiers, they were here, too. I'd never paid much attention to soldiers before. They occupied Teopisca — they were at every street corner, in front of every store with their helmets and belts and boots and guns. I walked close to them. I looked in their faces. I had never realized how young our Mexican soldiers are. Just children, no more mature than those young people playing football in the schoolyards. Most of the soldiers who were stationed here came from other places in Mexico; they didn't understand the insurrection any better than I did.

"But after the truce there was no need for the soldiers to stay in Teopisca and they moved on to places closer to the selva. Because spring was approaching, some of the indigenas who had been pushed off their little *milpas* by the fighting left to try to cultivate them again. In some places, landowners like the one who lied about the foreign troops landing on his property tore down the remains of some indigena *comunidades* and took over their land. In other places, groups of indigenas had moved in on private property and begun to prepare it in order to grow their corn.

"There was a lot of pushing back and forth — a lot of going to the authorities with charges and counter-charges, a lot of meetings, a lot of quarrels and arguments. Once in a while someone would get beaten up, or cut with machetes, or shot. One meeting took place here in Teopisca. You see, I don't have all of the details — not quite.

"But according to my husband, it started because some of the indigenas who live around here and work around here found out that the federal government had been sending money for various purposes — fertilizer, a school — and the indigenas hadn't received it. They protested through one of the groups or councils that they had formed — there were many of them, all with [identifying] initials, I'm not sure which group this was, but it had way of getting heard in San Cristóbal de las Casas, so the government sent a couple of representatives to listen to the complaints.

"I hardly could believe what was happening. One of the most vocal of the indigenas was a boy — a man, I guess I should call him, but he was very young, maybe still in his teens, he had done little jobs for me the year before, hauling soil and digging and carrying rocks, anyway, he stood up and was very precise — eloquent — in denouncing what the local alcalde had done. I never imagined that he could be that, what should I say? assertive — he always had slid away from me when I'd tried to talk to him, just said '*si'ñora*' and grabbed at the brim of his hat.

"The two delegates — I was told they were state assemblymen — listened to the indigenas and made the usual political promises. They told the campesinos they would 'investigate' the charges, they would audit the municipal books, they would verify which charges were true and which were not.

"But that did not satisfy the indigenas. Some of them — many of them — became very angry. They shouted that they did not want promises. They shouted that they did not want investigations. The boy — man — who had worked for me jumped up and said, 'You have cheated us for years!' and made very specific demands about land. About seed. The delegates repeated that they would do all that the law allowed.

"'The law?' the campesinos shouted. 'The law is what oppresses us!' 'The law is the coletos' law.'

"'No more meetings!' the boy — man — who had worked for me screamed. 'Give us what we want or the Zapatista army will come and give it to us!'

"One of the delegates laughed. That was a mistake. From the front of the crowd a group of men — no, not just men, women too — charged forward. They grabbed the delegates. Oh! You should have seen the looks on those official faces. I've never seen politicians look so scared!

"One indigena — I don't know who — threw a rope around one of the delegates. He slipped and fell and got up shaking his fists — he was so wrought with emotion he was slobbering. 'The other one too! The other one too!' some of the indigenas shouted. The delegate who didn't have a rope around him backed away. I could hear him calling the indigenas '*amigos*' and '*buena gente*' but they responded to each other, not to him. They threw a rope around his waist too and headed towards the alcalde's house tugging the two delegates along with them.

"I didn't know what they were going to do to the delegates — I was afraid for them — but as I watched them I remembered something that happened right after my husband and I came to Teopisca. One of the big landowners accused two campesinos of intruding on his property. He and two of his sons dragged the two campesinos into town with ropes around their waists, then the landowner got on his horse and pulled them along after him.

"They were stumbling and falling — they got scraped up quite badly — but they said nothing in protest and the landowner and his sons laughed. Later, I heard that someone had found the two campesinos hanging by their necks from a tree; but that was later, and I think that might have been just a story. Or that it was something that happened to some other campesinos, not the ones I saw being dragged by the landowner.

"Anyway, it frightened me to see what was happening to the two delegates, but I couldn't help but observe that the indigenas were following a model that the coletos had established for them. And I couldn't help but observe how differently the delegates reacted compared to how the campesinos had reacted.

"The indigenas dragged the two delegates to the alcalde's house and banged on the gate, but no one answered. Some indigenas climbed the walls and came back shouting that the alcalde was gone and so was his car.

"For a few minutes everyone milled around in a state of confusion. Some of the indigenas wanted to hold the two delegates until the alcalde was found. Others wanted to break into the house. I remember that I was surprised that some of the women were taking a very active part in the arguments. Finally, the leaders of the group decided to release the two delegates. They untied them and let them go, but shouted at them to tell the powers in San Cristóbal that the town government now belonged to the indigenas and the state authorities would have to deal with them.

"I think the two delegates were relieved — very relieved — to get away with their lives. They tried to straighten up and appear dignified, but actually they were badly ruffled. They spoke only to each other, and did not respond to the group of indigenas or say anything to any of us who were watching from a distance.

"When the poor fellows got to their car, they discovered that someone had let the air out of all four of its tires. By this time it was dark and they had no great desire to traipse around Teopisca looking for someone to help them. I don't know what happened to them, but I think they must have contacted a coleto somewhere close by and spent the night.

"The alcalde never did return, but I don't imagine that he went very far away. They said he took millions of [old] pesos with him, and kept two sets of books, one that could be viewed officially and the other that would reveal what he really did with the government money that came into the community.

"No one now knows what has happened to either set — if they ever existed. The Zapatistas destroyed a lot of documents. So did the corrupt PRI people — they didn't want their infractions to be made public. I don't suppose anyone ever will know how much was taken, or where it went.

"In the long run, I don't suppose it really will make any difference. The indigenas have their organizations, and what they want, they say, is to govern themselves.

"The landowners now have their own organizations too, and don't have to go through the *alcaldia* to govern. So despite the insurrection, things are slipping back into their old ways. Some people say — my husband is one of them — that the indigenas have learned from the insurrection that they do not have to be docile and passive, that they do not have to be victims, that they can set their own boundaries and not be bought off and that they can revitalize the old religion and discipline themselves away from drunkenness; but I am not sure.

"I do not see the world changing very much. Spain hasn't changed that much — neither, really, has the United States. Different faces, that's all — different personalities — dink around with the same problems that the world has faced forever.

"Or, now, am I sounding too much like a native-born Mexican?"

An Angel on Earth

Stopping to visit Karina Magallon Ahumada was more a duty than a pleasure, despite the fact that I liked both her and her mother and had promised the friend of mine for whom she'd done favors years before that I would make frequent little social calls. Born in the castellar old house surrounded by orchards on the edge of San Cristóbal in which she'd lived all of her life, Karina was crotchety and hypochondriac, an old maid of at least sixty who grumbled unending conversations with herself as she puttered around in the small cold rooms that seldom were lighted and perpetually smelled of old fabric, musty wood and layers of candle carbon.

Her mother lived with her, and each would argue (to anyone who would listen) that she was taking care of the other. Though her fingers trembled and the wrinkles that encased her mouth wiggled like wounded moths when she tried to talk, the octogenarian doña Alma hadn't suffered any diminution of her mental capacities.

She still could cook and read magazines and bring occasional visitors like me cups of boiled coffee. She laughed inwardly and often, kept track of her two married children's coming and goings and she seldom complained about anything except Karina's dog, a beautiful but cowering dalmatian that peed on the floor whenever it got excited.

For all of their involvements with family and friends, their old house and what they felt was the too-rapid growth of San Cristóbal, the two women made all duties and relationships subservient to their one overwhelming joy in life: the Catholic Church and its bishop in San Cristóbal, Samuel Ruiz.

"He is a saint," Karina insisted five years before headlines throughout the world proclaimed him a Nobel Peace Prize candidate for his leadership during the Zapatista insurrection. She did not, she insisted, mean that he would *become* a saint:

"He is an angel on earth. Truly, I mean it literally. He was a man when he came here thirty years ago — a beautiful, kind little man who cared for everybody. Then the man...vanished — the Blessed Virgin called him to Heaven — and the angel appeared in what had been his body.

"One only has to be near him to feel it. At Holy Communion, kneeling before him, I feel lights go on inside my body. When I lift my face I do not see him, only a bright shining. And the Host on my tongue, oh! Roberto! You cannot imagine! It is a deliciousness that this world cannot offer! It is so rich! So sweet! So intensely pleasurable! I walk away from him and I do not limp! Sometimes it is hours before I come back into this horrible shape that is my body!

"I can hardly imagine what powers he must have, yet he is so humble he does not show them. In his sermons he says everything comes from God through the Holy Spirit and we have to let it touch us. You see, you see, he knows! Because, well, for sure he is not a man, although he has to function as one in things of the world; he is an angel carrying that Spirit and infusing everything that is open to him with its beauty.

"If only you would go to him, you would see. Stand close, just look into his eyes and you will see, you will see Jesus!

"I swear, Hailmaryblessedvirgin, that it's true."

Although I saw Bishop Ruiz now and then, and once even returned his gracious nod as we passed each other near the cathedral in the center of town, I did not try to verify dear Karina's claims about him. Nor, with her, did I try to discuss his Liberation Theology and what it really would mean to her firmly conservative values about traditions and property. But I've often wondered if jungle negotiators like Subcomandante Marcos and Major Moises, Manuel Camacho Solis and General Miguel Angel Godinez saw that angel when they looked into his face.

THE DESTRUCTION OF MEXICO

"That morning [January 1, 1994] started the destruction of Mexico," Ruben Gaxiola nodded, confirming to himself what he often had repeated to both acquaintances and outsiders. "No one knew it at the time, but the Zapatistas were surgeons — they cut across the abscess, pulled back the skin and exposed what was inside."

A passionate, obsessive — and intrinsically slow-moving — man of mixed indigena extraction — Gaxiola was one of the few outspoken critics of coleto politics that the entrenched bureaucracy in San Cristóbal condoned, probably because, despite his background, he'd developed what essentially were middle-class habits — photography, vegetarianism, television. Only a few weeks before the takeover, he was present when Chiapas' provisional governor, Elmer Setzer, downplayed the possibility of an insurrection by chiding to Mexico City journalists, "Oh, these indigenas are great jokesters. They love to fabricate stories!"

Setzer, like most coletos, was wrong about the Zapatistas. Their successes badly embarrassed the then popular federal government of President Carlos Salinas de Gortari, who just had negotiated a free trade agreement with the United States and Canada.

"What shocked people was not the takeover, but that indigenas engineered it," Gaxiola maintained. "The President [Salinas], ha! he was helpless. Ambitious? Ah! You see, he planned to be famous, to be important everywhere, a world figure: Going in with troops, crushing the rebellion as other presidents have done, would not have been good for his image.

"But I tell you! What was worse for him was the way the country responded. Support came from all over for the Zapatistas. This 'subcomandante Marcos' in his mask, he became like, like the Robin Hood of Mexico. The poor president was upstaged and people could see that he was just a *perfumado*, not really as strong as he'd pretended to be.

"Then all around him, things leaked out and his supporters — rich men in the United States and other places — pulled away the money they'd been giving him. He had only the money that drug dealers in Columbia were giving him.

"But that wasn't enough. Nothing was enough. The whole country collapsed and the Zapatistas still hadn't taken off their masks.

"Too bad — too bad for all of us. The Zapatistas too. What good have they done for the native peoples, the indigenas? Look around you. Those who are not soldiers in the selva, they still are starving. Still dying. They still have no futures to look forward to.

"And the rest of us, we have this country, this Mexico, that just when it gets back to its feet, wham! we are knocked down again. Our government does nothing for us, and we can do nothing for it."

Ruben Gaxiola said that, like many Mexicans, "I am afraid, because I know there must be change, but I do not know what that change will be."

Chiapas, a Tzotzil shaman is supposed to have told his followers, is "a land of little sky, but much earth." A contemporary Chiapan artist fashioned landscapes that admitted little light, and that from directly above, while merged forms of men and women mingled with old animistic spirit-gods in a tangle of coffee plantation roots beneath the dark trees. For all the sparkling beauty of its landscapes — the plantations, the cloud-crusted mountain tops, the sheer, crystalline waterfalls, the absorptive Lacandon rain forests — Chiapas is a land whose residents dream of the past, when priestess witches could make stones move, and water turn black and snakes swallow themselves whole.

It is a countryside infested with spirits of the night, with ghosts seeking their heritage, with indigenas seeking their culture and their sobriety and their religion. It is a civilization of created coffee plantations and destroyed villages and diminishing natural wonders, a place where the past dominates the present and seems to prophesy a return to a time when time no longer is important, where the sun watches from far away and where the living and the make believe merge into a quiet dynamism of earth-brown and foliage-green.

CHAPTER 11. LAND OF THE MAYAS

SCHEHERAZADE EYES

"You could, of course, compliment my almond-shaped eyes. You could say that Martina Estrada Ruiz's skin has the texture of jasmine petals.

"Ah! You blush! If you're going to stay in Veracruz long, you will have to learn never to give a jarocha an advantage. Even a slightly plump and *thirty-something* one like me.

"Of course, I am teasing. But I owe something to my background. The Estradas once were 'A-saad-ah's — or something like that, and for years after the first A-saad-ah came, God knows from what part of the Arab world or why, he listened for the calls from Mecca. I think, instead, he finally wound up hearing a call from Mandinga and 'embarrassing' some darker skinned temptress.

"We Estrada women pride ourselves on our eyes and skin — my mother used to say we inherited a 'harem look.' Here, let me show you. With a veil I could pass for Scheherazade, wouldn't you say? But not without it — I have a definitely Mexican mouth.

"More coffee? You compliment me, you know, drinking it as you do, like a Cuban. I'm sorry I can't offer you more interesting surroundings. But for your friend Mario and for me, it is easier, being single, to live in apartments, and these are convenient — but the patio is nice, don't you think? And it is hard to find, in these older parts of the city, so close to the beach, protected parking for our cars like we have here.

"He is nice, your friend Mario. I am glad that you've come to visit him. I think he finds me a bit...what would you say? *Loca?* Unconventional. Didn't he say that? Would you tell me if he did?

"See! I thought not! Well, I am jarocha — we're all a bit crazy. And if we're not, well, we act that way — it would disappoint outsiders if we didn't say and do outlandish things.

"Besides, he is from Coahuila — very responsible, he does things the way they should be done, no? He is never late for work, he never goes out without buttoning his cuffs. He is not one who takes a chance on embarrassing himself.

"I, on the other hand...well, I'm not as bad as I was. I nearly drove my parents crazy. My father was very strict — at least he tried to be. He was in the military — an officer; several times he was transferred, but we always kept our house here, in Veracruz. I remember when we went to other parts of the country, no one could understand me, I talked so fast, so jarocha. And I was difficult for my parents — I was not like my sister, 'Miss Goody Two Shoes'; she would do everything to please them and I would throw fits. They thought I was possessed.

"I was. No, really. Finally my father found doctors who diagnosed what was wrong with me. I am what is called a 'manic depressive.' I take lithium. If I go off my lithium, I turn into a hair-tearing witch. Can you imagine? A manic jarocha! I am lucky I was born when I was. A century ago they would have locked me up. Or burned me for being a child of the devil.

"My mother brought me and my sisters back here when I was in *secundaria.* She and my father had decided it would be better for us to live here, and for him to commute to see us until he retired. I just had started taking the lithium, but sometimes I would rebel and refuse to take it. My mother wouldn't know what to do with me but living with us, in a separate part of our house, was an old family friend — a Ruiz, not an Estrada.

"She was a wonderful woman; her name was Aida. I would go up to her room and she would talk to me about women and the world they lived in and about men and their temptations and why they turned bad, as her husband had, and how difficult it was to cope with things when you are young — she would talk about very worldly things.

"Unlike my mother and my father, she did not categorize the things I did into good and bad and she was very patient with me when I'd stop taking my lithium. She was the only one who could make me see a reason to start taking it again.

"She also could tell great stories about Veracruz and what it was like when she was young. Back then, the Ruizes mostly were dock hands and bar owners — they were not like the Estradas, who had land and investments and a few little coffee plantations. Her uncles and cousins used to take her with them to the plaza and buy her hot milk flavored with coffee.

"A sailor one day gave her a parrot and she carried it home on her finger. Another carved an intricate necklace out of hardwood for her: It spelled out A-I-D-A and the letters all were interlocked somehow — it was all of one piece of beautifully polished wood.

"For years I envied her — I thought she had had such a wonderful girlhood, such a wonderful life. Then when I grew up a little, I realized that she had gained her perspective only after suffering a great deal. Her husband — a jarocho — had been a man of great energy, a marvelous dancer and lots of fun, but also he had been fiercely jealous, and he drank a great deal.

"They had had a stormy marriage, filled with accusations and breakups, fights and long separations. He left her with two sons to raise by herself, but he returned to plague her whenever she established a liaison with anyone else. Once he lay in wait and tried to shoot a man who was visiting her. Another time he hired a couple of *pandilleros* to beat up someone else she was seeing.

"I've had my own tribulations, of course. Because of my condition, my going crazy, I felt that I never could marry. That was something that I got from my mother. She loved me and worried about me but she always had made me feel that I was, well, different, that I was dangerous, that I shouldn't — couldn't — lead a normal life.

"So I didn't, really. I always had that excuse — being crazy — to do wild, stupid, different things. I'd quit school. I'd quit jobs. I'd break up with boy friends — even ones that I liked. I'd do things to make my sisters jealous — or angry. Or to make other people angry.

"When my parents moved to a little retirement place in the highlands, near Xalapa, I stayed in Veracruz. I stopped having episodes of going crazy. I learned to understand that with the medication I could be normal — it kept the devil inside me under control — but there's always that shadow, that fear, like it's lurking inside me just waiting to pounce.

"My mother once told me that it was because I was Arab that I was crazy. I told her that I was jarocha — probably there were other things thrown in too. Like a little French blood maybe, or maybe Negro, just to add spice to who I was.

"She didn't like that, but I didn't care. I've had to learn to live with lots of things, like having a devil inside that I have to control.

"I'll make some more coffee...no, please, I have half-an-hour before I go back to work, it would be my privilege. I try always to have some ready for Mario — he is, what do you say? *muy hombre*, he cannot do things for himself, so I spoil him a little bit. In the meantime, you can tell me about yourself.

"Or invent beautiful compliments about my Scheherazade eyes."

Se Habla Pemex

From Tampico and Ciudad Madero in the north, along the thousand-mile coastline curve to Villahermosa and Ciudad Pemex afloat upon the swamps of eastern Tabasco, oil is the force that drives Mexico's economy. Despite the ups and downs of the international market, a huge debt rooted in borrowing on oil revenues that never materialized, union corruption and management by *politicos* more interested in furthering their own careers than developing a national resource, the people who drill for oil, and test it, and transport it, and process it and account for it comprise Mexico's most stable industrial work force.

But "the oil industry created a separate country," insists Veracruz public accountant Jorge Avilez Jimenez. He described a map created by a newspaper satirist that imposed a new state of "Petroleo" on Mexico's east coast. It isolated "the Ancient Kingdom of Veracruz," looped into the Gulf to include "Islas Platformas" and swerved around Coatzacoalcos into the interior of Tabasco and Chiapas.

"There is an accuracy there, in terms of how people feel," Avilez Jimenez outlined the cultural dynamic generated by Pemex, which he called "a business that really is a government unto itself, with its own laws, leaders and wealth."

Although there are second- and third-generation oil workers in Tampico and Poza Rica, the majority of the thousands of new workers pouring into the eastern fields came from other parts of Mexico. The boom began in the 1970s, crested in the '80s and regained momentum in the early '90s.

It brought not only oil drilling operations, but an immense amount of new construction which attracted both experienced and minimum-wage laborers. New cities like Benito Juarez and Ciudad Pemex surged into being and established cities like Villahermosa, Coatzacoalcos and Ciudad del Carmen, in

Campeche, saw their centuries-old provincial isolation become overwhelmed by new ideas, new construction and new problems.

This sudden growth pushed many indigenas — Nashua's, Tectonics, Populaces and Chantal's — off the little *milpas* on which they'd grown vegetables and corn for centuries and destroyed much of the fishing industry.

"There was so much oil in the water," declared Avilez Jimenez, "that you could lubricate a tractor on the squeezing from a *huachinango*."

The surge of money drove prices throughout the oil-producing regions out of the reach of many locals. To them it seemed that the Pemex outsiders demanded grotesque amounts of food, fish, housing, liquor and women and paid for it by polluting the water, scorching the ground and blackening once tranquil blue skies.

As the population of this new state of "Petroleo" increased, the larger landowners along the thousand-mile long stretch of hillsides expanded their holdings in order to hike production of fruit, vegetables, grain and coffee. Smaller farmers and orchardists pushed higher into the hills, uprooting indigenas, harvesting lumber and creating water contamination and erosion problems. Many of the displaced villagers migrated to coastal cities already clogged with new arrivals from the neighboring mountain states, creating shantytown slums around the new boomtowns.

"We weren't accustomed to having to deal with these problems," Avilez Jimenez continued. "This was a very static, very established society, hundreds of years old, with everything defined, everything — everyone — in given roles. Many of the *petroleros* coming in — they essentially were laborers — suddenly had more buying power than schoolteachers and accountants and government workers in Veracruz. At the same time, the old landowners with bigger holdings in the coffee and banana areas lost prestige, as well as some political power.

"Although the oil was coming out of the ground beneath us, the money it was generating — and the political power that controlled it — all was in Mexico City. We weren't ready to become satellites of the chilangos, and we were loath to give up what we felt was a superior way of life."

Unable to compete on the fast track, where money meant power and political fortunes changed day by day, "The Ancient Kingdom of Veracruz" extended its siesta time, repaired its cobblestones and dillydallied with the efficiency of its public services. The other older cities of the region — particularly Villahermosa, Minatitlan and Coatzacoalcos — tried to do much the same thing. In the meantime, the oil industry, triggered by political beliefs that

Mexico would ride out of the Third World into international prominence on the magic carpet of its oil revenues, went plowing full-speed ahead, seemingly without concern for how its drilling affected either the older, established societies or the environment.

Newspaper cartoons depicted Pemex as a devouring monster. In one, a snake uncoiling from Mexico City exposed fangs that were effigies of Jorge Díaz Serrano and Jorge Andres de Oteyza, the heads of the government-run oil monopoly, biting down on a wilting coastline. In another, a chilango with pesos for eyeballs poured oil from a *milpa* filled with oil derricks into a starving indigena's mouth. Still another showed a landscape of ragged Veracruzana Marías holding their abdomens as an army of erect oil derrick penises marched through the charred remains of their coastal city.

Faced with the fact that the new state of Petroleo wasn't going to go away, even when the crash of '82 brought work to a standstill and thrust hundreds of thousands of people dependent on the oil industry out of work, adherents of "The Old Kingdom" accommodated in typical jarocho fashion. The marimbas beat louder during Mardi Gras, the coffee breaks grew longer and the Veracruzanos made fun of themselves, even as they satirized invading outsiders.

A near-the-square Veracruz eatery offered to give Pemex workers special lessons on "how to eat fresh-boiled shrimp out of a folded newspaper." Another parodied "Pemex *pulpo*" (octopus served in crude oil sauce) on its menu. And *Se Habla Pemex* (Pemex spoken here) signs throughout the new development areas lampooned the difficulty that outsiders had with jarochos' dialect.

Anthropologist Gonzalo Aguirre Beltran of Veracruz offers the theory that fate has taken care of "The Old Kingdom" by giving it a charming bay, a place in history and the geological fortuitousness of not having oil deposits immediately beneath the little sway of land it occupies. In fact, one can imagine, in the eternal Carnival that is "The Old Kingdom," old Don Momo, the prototype jarocho, lifting his trident and his cup of rum and chortling:

"In the Old Kingdom one does not need to drive a Continental, build a condominium or have a heart attack to be admired and important. One only has to know how to select a good cigar, to eat *huachinanguito* with spicy salsa, speak about personal and important things in the Alameda,

"And to dance like no one else in the world can dance!"

The Black Disease

Beneath the tinted glass and glistening steel that ring the city of Campeche's historic downtown, away from the diesel smells and throbbing of construction machines that vibrate the discolored, chipped stone walls of its founding, the once placid seaport wrestles the Dr. Jekyll-Mr. Hyde of its suddenly changed personality. One of the oldest cities in Mexico, built on the site of the ancient Mayan capital Ah Kim Pech, it historically has been the jumping off point for trade and exploration, conquest and relaxation.

Cortez landed there before going on to Veracruz to begin the conquest of the Aztecs. Spanish merchantmen built docks and jetties from which to ship hardwood to Cuba and Spain in the early 1540s. For the next two hundred years, the principal occupation of its few thousand residents was to strengthen its ponderous protective walls. Their efforts created a personality, if not protection: English and Dutch pirates attacked, sacked and destroyed the settlement (then called "San Francisco de Campeche") five times between 1597 and 1685.

Left to provincial quietness of fishing, forests and commerce after the last of the raiding corsairs had been driven from the Caribbean, Campeche sidestepped most of the turmoil that accompanied the governmental upheavals of the 19th century. With the same ease that its harbor absorbed the diverse sea life brought to it by winds, rain and tides, the city absorbed all sorts of sailors, travelers, tourists, outcasts and refugees and molded them into a homogeneously relaxed, predominately Catholic, politically conservative community.

The area's few industries turned out lumber and lumber products, food, rope and clothing, including the thigh-length four-pocketed white shirts that the native-born inhabitants scrupulously scrubbed and wore until they practically were in shreds. 19th century visitors described Campeche as a "clean, quiet city clinging to its past." And as "a place where the port town bustle is more cheerful than mercantile."

As late as the 1960s, one could walk for hours along the beaches south of Lerma, Campeche's somewhat trendier suburb, without seeing either swimmers or vendors. (Niched into a protective elbow on the western side of the Yucatan peninsula, Campeche and Lerma face west. The peninsula protects the two towns from torrential rains and hurricanes that sometimes blast the east-facing ports while offering sunsets over Campeche Sound that are astonishments of movement and color.) The swampiness of the isthmus to the south, and the rugged, dry terrain to the west, both of which had separated — and protected — the ancient Mayan civilization from surrounding tribes, would have created an isolated outpost unconnected to the rest of Mexico had it not been for the ease of coastal travel.

For years, ships of all descriptions brought tools and grain, masonry, wool, fuel, meat and packaged goods; others took on cargoes of fruit and lumber, fish and hemp and beans for trips down the coast to the bigger ports of Veracruz and Tampico. Though most of the sea traffic was to domestic ports (including Coatzacoalcos, Carmen and Progreso as well as Veracruz and Tampico), Campeche also was an outlet to Caribbean ports of Central America and to Cuba, Jamaica, Texas and New Orleans.

Each ship's arrival was anticipated by hundreds of speculators, *ambulantes*, curiosity seekers and *amas de casa*. Merchant vessels slid against the piers for "free alongside ship" sales which eliminated unloading and dock hand fees. Hawkers touted the good value and cheap prices of their wares as browsers weaved through stacks of bolted cloth, mountains of bird cages, sacks of grain and nuts and fruit and spices, pens filled with rabbits, sheep and goats, cartons of wristwatches and blue jeans and perfume, cases of vanilla, porcelain, pottery, china and Melmac.

Business probably seemed brisker than it actually was — more shopping went on than buying — but barter was an accepted substitute for cash transactions. Years ago I saw a muscular truck driver trade a gunnysack full of watermelons for a beat-up Remington portable typewriter. Too curious to resist asking him what he was going to do with the machine, I got, in reply, a gap-toothed grin and the statement, "Why, trade it for three times more watermelons there in the interior!"

But 400 years of remaining the same was all that Campeche could manage. The world's need for oil — and the Mexican government's belief that it could enrich the country by filling part of that need — brought an end to *campechano* isolation. A new citizenry surged across the beaches, filled the restaurants, demanded retail goods and built new offices and apartment buildings. Oil tankers replaced coastal steamers in the enlarged harbor. The fish-rich waters filled the beaches with bloated, oil-soaked detritus as offshore leaks darkened the ocean.

The radiant sunsets pulsed through a thickening refinery haze. The vendors disappeared from the docks, and the fishermen from filleting benches. New department stores offered imported goods as highly paid wildcatters sought and bought what local residents neither desired nor could afford. Campeche, like so much of the coast from Tampico east to the Yucatan, became Pemex-land.

Not everyone who followed the oil surge worked for Pemex, or strolled Campeche's streets with bulging wallets, however. Soon after the inland drilling started, a growing stream of displaced campesinos sifted into *colonias populares* on the fringes of the city. Fishermen, driven from their livelihoods along the coast and from the lagoons and bays of the Atasta peninsula and Isla Carmen soon followed. Unable to eke out a living from the fields and swampy waterways ravaged by the search for oil, they forced state and federal officials to seek redress from the powerful monster devouring them.

Pemex agreed to remit 3,117,000 new pesos (approximately $945,00 U.S.) to re-establish some of the displaced workers, and to provide new employments and new environments for them; but the money disappeared soon after it went into the state treasury. The fishermen and campesinos didn't see a penny of it.

Anti-government (and anti-Pemex) manifestations became daily aspects of Campeche life. Fishermen and farmers who'd been forced away from their livelihoods set up picket lines along the Plaza de la Republica, which faced state government buildings. Many local residents — taco and *elote* vendors, children, day laborers, grandmothers gathering to play *loteria* — sifted in and out of their ranks, talking with them, bringing them water, offering advice. *Albañiles* working nearby on building and street projects shared portions of their lunches with them and musicians from the small clubs and restaurants nearer the waterfront drifted by to entertain them.

A few days after a picketing confrontation organized and led by Campeche's most liberal federal congressman had elicited promises of state help (and brought over 500 armed soldiers and policemen to guard the plaza), one of the picketers described what he called "the black disease."

A young man with a round face, he often repeated phrases when he talked, a mannerism possibly provoked by the way that his words originated in the back of his throat, near the aural canals, giving a slurred overlay to his pronunciation. His name, he said, was, "Julio Cesar Bañuelos, Julio Cesar Bañuelos, fisherman."

Like most of the picketers, he had grown up on the shores of the huge Laguna de Terminos, 1,500 square miles of fishable waters whose outlets to the Gulf were on either side of Isla de Carmen, a thirty-mile-long reef that protected the coastal lagoon's thick vegetation and extensive fish and bird life.

"At first we didn't mind, we didn't mind," he described the beginnings of the oil boom. "There were only a few wells, a few roads, and the drillers were men like us, men like us. We could talk to them. And, I'll say the truth, they liked our fish, they bought from us, so it was all right, it was all right what they were doing.

"Then the accidents. First out in the sea, where they built the platforms. Oil — thick oil. You could not touch the water without getting sticky black all over your hands, all over your hands. And the fish? Ah, ask any of these men here, they know, they will tell you, the fish were half dead, oil in their gills, cut them open and you'd find, find globs of oil, of oil in their bellies.

"It got better. But only for a time. Then came more *petroleros*, many more. They came with their equipment — huge trucks, gigantic tractors, cranes, pipes, machines that shook the earth when they drilled. At first they worked around the edges of the lagoon, putting in their holes. Their trucks and tractors ruined land that grew beans, grew corn, beans and corn. Not only that, these machines, these giant machines, tore up all of the roads, the buses no longer could go from town to town, nor the cars, not even the cars.

"The farmers who worked the land, who lived in the little *comunidades* around where their fathers and grandfathers had lived, could do nothing, nothing. The oil, the authorities said, the oil belonged to the state and the state came first, it came first.

"My friend here Montaño, he will tell you, he went out to stop them, hey! With only a machete, he had only a machete to stop the machines! And then, *pues, qué pasó?* They told him the law gave them the right to get the oil, the oil is patrimony, it belongs to all of the people...*híjole!* But the only people, the only people who get the benefits are the *petroleros*, that is why we are here, if the oil belongs to all of the people, all of the people, and the oil is making the people rich, then why have we nothing? Nothing.

"Why have our little habitations, our tortillas, our ways to earn enough to live, why have they been taken away by the oil that belongs to the people, all of the people? Why do the *petroleros*, the *petroleros*, not pay us some of the richness?

"Let me tell you, for us, the fishermen, for us it was worse than for the farmers. Why? Ah! I will tell you, I will tell you. For them, the farmers, for them, when the repayment comes, when it comes the state can give them some land somewhere, there is some land that the *petroleros* have not torn up and spoiled with their machines, and the farmers can build their houses and plow and plant, they will have new homes, new homes.

"But for us, for the fishermen, what? The *laguna* is all oil, all oil. They cannot just give us a new lagoon. They have put platforms in the lagoon, they have drilled in the lagoon, in many places in the lagoon they have put wells. Even the trees, the water plants, are dying, dying. The mangroves which nothing can kill, they have fallen over, they are nothing but black swamps of dying logs.

"And the fish that one could find! I tell you, in half a day I could come back with the boat filled with cervallo, with huachinango, with robalo. Now? Now even the birds are dying. The shores smell of rotting herons, rotting pelicans, dead crocodiles lie on the bank, dead everything, the vultures — imagine! — the water is so bad, the ground is so bad, so bad, that even the vultures that eat the dead bodies, they are dying, they are dying from what they eat. They are dying from the black disease.

"Imagine! The *petroleros* pay us nothing — the government pays us nothing; they take the money that should be ours, that's why we are making demands. But even if they give it to us, when they give it to us, what then? We'll buy little *habitaciones*, maybe, little *habitaciones*, but what will we do? Our children, what will they do? What will they do?

"They say they'll train us, train us to do something else, something else besides being fishermen. They don't understand that this is what we do, what we always have done, what we want to do. They don't understand that it is fishing that we know, it is fishing that we love. They do not understand it at all."

Pressured on one side by the picketers, and by *perredista* legislators pushing for a federal investigation into the disposition of the missing funds on the other, Campeche's state government managed to resolve the problem of the missing indemnifications after publicly explaining that the payments had been delayed because of difficulties encountered in separating, defining and identifying the individuals and families that should receive payments. In the meantime, angry campesinos from the communities that surround the little town of Candelaria, near Campeche's southern border, joined to commandeer, by force, the trucks and cars belonging to a privately financed Pemex affiliate called Comecsa after Comecsa equipment had torn out huge sections of the roads leading to their villages.

Local, Pemex, state and federal police strong-armed the return of the vehicles but a series of incidents, including a mysterious landslide that thrust two bulldozers down the slopes of a steep canyon, prompted Comecsa/Pemex to rebuild the ripped apart roadways. Subsequent retaliations against Comecsa/ Pemex extracted promises of indemnification for irreparably damaged farmland.

Pemex officials discovered a high-powered explosive charge linked to a timing device beneath a truck parked by one of their newly opened wells. The timing device was not set, but a note purportedly attached to it warned that future placement of similar devices would not be so benign.

But even where indemnifications have been paid, the amounts doled out to displaced farmers and fishermen barely enable them to subsist on the lower edge of Campeche economic life, a life that, for years, was satisfying — even beautiful — until the black disease ravaged an environment that for centuries had offered fish-rich waters and arable land, hardwood forests and quiet waterways thriving with reptile and bird life. For Julio Cesar Bañuelos and thousand like him, the future is a frightening empty page.

He and the men and women who picketed with him see families like theirs shoved to the shantytown fringes of the city, working as day laborers, vendors, servants, chauffeurs, *pepenedores*, prostitutes. Even in the "bad times," when layoffs or calamities like the devaluation of the peso disrupt the *petroleros*, the displaced fishermen and campesinos economically remain in their shadows, unable to take advantage of the new ways that swept away four-hundred years of established and satisfying life.

Choices and Gambles

"I wanted to go out with the drilling crews. Hey! Be the first woman to lead a jungle exploration!" Paula Lucero Meza's broad face broke into a grin that transformed downward-turned features into mischievous vigor as she leaned across the glistening formica table in Pemex cafeteria in Poza Rica. "Hey! What did I have to lose? I needed money — I had two kids to support, I figured I was as clever and as tough as any man they could find, and I told them so.

"So instead of a drilling crew, they hired me to read seismograph charts. Thousands of pages of wavy lines. I was only temporary, I was living in two rented rooms, just *albergues*, not even enclosed, with my two daughters. It was hard, but I learned the charts, got into a class, studied seismography. I literally forced my way onto an exploration crew: I threatened, demanded, I wouldn't go away.

"Finally, a supervisor hired me. He was a good man. He warned me that it was going to be hard, that the men in the crews might resent me, or insult me, or make passes. I told him I could handle it: Ah, Mary! When I told him that, I didn't know if it was true or not, but I'd worked so hard to get the chance, and I needed the money, I really did!

"It got me into the Union, that job did. That was important. I moved to a house — the Union subsidized part of the rent. I brought my mother from Santa María del Río to live with me and take care of the girls. After *La Crisis* I got laid off, but only for a few months and the Union took care of me: I worked in their offices.

"Read what you like about the Union, what the government newspapers say about mismanagement or whatever, corruption, believe me, they're the best thing that Mexico has. Without them, I'd've been on the streets. They look after their own!"

"You do have to play their game, though." Lidia Jimenez Mendez rotated her coffee mug between blunt fingers. A strong, compact woman with deep-set dark eyes and a mouth that seemed too small for her wide-set jaw, she spoke with a languor that belied her eyes' sense of urgency.

"I didn't know what I wanted when I came here. I was angry. I'd been back and forth across the country several times. Listen! I was drinking. I was a hellion. I decided that no man could own me or control me. I didn't want to wind up like my mother, beat up and abandoned by the *chingazo* she'd married.

"So of course, what happened to me? I woke up one morning here in Poza Rica, beat-up and abandoned. I was twenty-four years old, I had no home, no place to go back to, no money, no job and no skills to speak of. On top of that, I was mad, really mad. I swore, by God! that I'd make it on my own!

"The first job I got was in a processing plant cutting up chickens. One of the women there said she'd come to Poza to get a job at the refineries but she hadn't finished *primaria* and hadn't been able to pass the exam they gave her. When I got off work, I caught a bus to the personnel office — I didn't even change clothes. A woman there looked at the form I filled out and asked when I'd finished *secundaria*. They were hiring people to pull chemical samples and asked if I wanted to interview. I said yes. I interviewed and they hired me.

"It was hard work. Hot work. There were other women doing it, but I didn't have much to do with them. I liked the men better. I could smoke like they did, curse like they did, drink like they did. Some of them got so they liked me. Accepted me. Treated me like I was one of them.

"For the first couple of years, I transferred around a lot. A couple of times I got my hours cut but I never got laid off. I was passed over for promotion and got angry; then I figured out that you had to figure out who needed you and who could help you. I found out where some money was being siphoned off and sat on the information until I decided which way to go with it.

"You see, I could have cut myself in, or I could have exposed who was doing it. There were risks either way. I decided to play it safe and give the evidence that I had to one of my supervisors. He used it to negotiate a big promotion for himself. When a supervisor's position opened up, he rewarded me.

"That's how it works. You take care of somebody, they take care of you. Sometimes it's a matter of whose team you're on — a couple of times I've been on losing teams. But that's okay, you keep sharp, you do your work, sooner or later another opportunity comes up.

"Once one of my immediate supervisors got arrested for hit and run driving: He wiped out somebody riding a bicycle. He abandoned the car and reported it stolen; I told the police he'd been with me at a hotel restaurant at the time of the accident. A waiter there vouched for us, a Nahua; we didn't have to pay him a *centavo*. My supervisor slipped the family a few hundred thousand [old] pesos and the case was closed.

"Except, of course, for me. He knew he either had to get rid of me or reward me. I think he decided that to reward me was safer, so I wound up with a raise and a promotion. That's the way it goes. You work hard, but you keep your eyes open to what is going on around you.

"You make choices and gamble on who's going to win and who's going to lose."

Used Up

"Bad? Things are bad, yes, you can see, can't you? It is very sad the way the children here in Tahdziu live. And the parents. But what are they to do? Leave? To go where? To Tekax, *sí*. To Peto. Some even go far, very far, *sí*, to Cancun. That is why, you can see, can't you? why there are few young men here. They have gone. Gone.

"To be a good place, a town needs its young men, *sí*. Look, here what do you see? Old women like me. No, señor, to lie to me, it is not necessary, I am old. Perhaps in years, not so old as you, perhaps, but in other ways, *sí*, I am old. I am like this town, this Tahdziu that you see, I am used up.

"You can see, can't you? Once cars came here — more cars than these few that you see barely able to run on these streets. Come on, I'll show you. The roads, then, years ago, when I was having my children, my three children who now are grown, were not like this. The roads then were level, the water when it rained drained along the gutters and into the arroyo. Every week men worked on the streets — worked on all of them. Now, no. You can see, can't you? Now there is no money to pay for the work, so the work is not done.

"There, around the corner, look beyond that building there. Once, that building was important, a big store that sold a lot of things, tools and wire and nails and the metal to make gates and grillwork with. There on the other side, see, that was a place to play baseball, with the places for people to sit — all broken now, like an old skeleton.

"Things were built when I was younger, a lot of things in Tahdziu...how long ago? Four presidents ago, I don't remember. It was here, a place to play baseball. Do you see young men running and throwing and hitting the ball now? No, only little pigs rooting around, what do they find to eat? Only God knows. And those calves, look, how much meat would you get off of them? Their bones show through their skins.

"I tell you, stranger, there is nothing here, nothing in Tahdziu. No, what is here is worse than nothing, worse. This street, like the other we came down, look, we who live here, we have become used to the broken things, the garbage, there is no one to pick it up, no one to haul it away, like we used to have. Yes, at one time we had those things.

"And a school. There is still a school, yes, and sometimes a teacher. The good teachers we had went away because they did not get paid. Yet the children learn, yes, many can read and can write, at least some, but most of them, see, like those over there, most of them work. When there is nothing else, they go through the hills looking for scraps of wood to sell so people can make little fires.

"Hsst! You, little one, tell the stranger...no, see, she will not talk to you, she is afraid, afraid because you are different, you are not from here. Look at her feet, look at her fingers, have they ever been clean? And her clothes — you can see, can't you? Would you call them clothes? No, rags, nothing more. For her there is no school; there are many like her, too many.

"Look, down this street, I'll show you. See? Here the telephone used to be, yes, one of the telephones in Tahdziu, in this place behind these walls that are broken now. In Tahdziu now we have no telephone, not even in the store. Look, that is the store. That! Come, I will take you inside, hsst! Chino, this stranger, he wants to buy things, things to eat, good things.

"What? This is what you have? Is this all? Milk in a can, look! The can is dented, how do I know that what is in it is good? And these, stale *galletas*, ay! How long have they been here? And these? You call them platanos? The pigs in the street there, not even they would eat them, and you would sell them to this stranger here? You would take his money for these?

"He doesn't even sell tortillas. Imagine! A store without tortillas! Not only does he not sell tortillas, there is no store in Tahdziu that sells tortillas. There is no little factory to make the tortillas, no little tortilla machines.

"Once there was a place with a tortilla machine...what? Yes, the Chino is right, there were two. Two tortilla machines. Come, I'll show you, this way, no, down this little street. You can see, can't you, that the people who live on this street never sweep in front of their houses. They used to — even though the street was dirt, the people swept. There were no droppings from the animals everywhere; in front of the houses everything was clean.

"Here, look here. Inside there, that was a tortilla machine, the tortillas came down there, people stood here, where you are standing, to buy them. Hot, they would be hot. Ah! Little ones — the children — would stand close just to watch, just to smell.

"But now? You can see, can't you, that it is broken, there hardly any parts of the machine left. Now we women make our own tortillas, pat-pat! pat-pat! every day. We make them, if we have *masa*. If we have corn to grind up to make *masa*, we make our own tortillas, pat-pat! pat-pat! Like our grandmothers used to do.

"Ay! It is very sad the way the people of Tahdziu live. There is the church. It is like the rest of Tahdziu, it is old. It is like me and all of the other old women here, it is old and used up. No one takes care of it. No one brings flowers like they used to do.

"And there is no priest. Oh, yes, from Peto one comes, on Saturday he comes to say mass, but that is all. To be a good place, a town needs a priest. A priest could tell us to do the things we need to do. Once we had a priest, a priest who lived here and took care of us and took care of the church. He conducted my marriage and baptized my children. Now? Well, you can see, can't you? There is nothing here that is as it used to be.

"There are no new houses — only two or three — and everything comes from Peto. The electricity, it comes from Peto, through wires from Peto. Only sometimes it does not get here, something happens to the lines; then we have no lights. Sometimes the electricity comes back, sometimes it does not — not for days. Then those who have wires into their houses are no better off than those who do not. We light candles and do not watch the televisions. Watching television is the only entertainment that some people here have.

"No, do not go down that way. Why? It is not good. Down that way there is something in the ground. It is where the water goes after the rain and carries things with it and where they kill animals and the smell is very bad. Here, down this way. The things we see on television are different from what we see in Tahdziu. There are those who say that the television is bad because the people we see on television don't live as we live here and that makes us unhappy.

"But I don't believe that. The way we are, we would be just as unhappy without television. The way we are, we would be happy with some money to spend. Some money to buy the little things that we need."

The roads that connect Tahdziu and other isolated and forgotten villages of Yucatan's *cono sur* ("southern cone") with the larger towns of Peto and Tekax are passable, but trips over them are arduous and slow. The eroded countryside which once yielded lumber for Spanish sailing ships now is covered by dense scrub, the majority of which seems to be dead or dying.

The tourist influx that energized other parts of Yucatan and the beach-side resorts of Cancun and Cozumel did not bring prosperity to the southern cone. (The state of Yucatan is triangular in shape. A long, rugged coastline occupies the top of the triangle; the bottom, or "southern cone," is wedged between Campeche on the west and Quintana Roo on the east.)

Even a thousand years ago, during the expansion of the Mayan culture from Yucatan southwestward into what is now Campeche, Tabasco and Chiapas and southeastward into Quintana Roo and Guatemala, the southern cone was sparsely inhabited, a source of lumber and perhaps a hunting and grazing grounds. The cities and temples of the great Mayan civilization follow a semi-circular curve across the northern part of the peninsula (Uxmal, Chichen-Itza, Tulum) and another semi-circular curve across the jungle belt from Palenque on the west to Chetumal on the Caribbean coast and south into Guatemala, leaving the cone — as it is today — essentially undeveloped.

Until the 1970s, when the oil boom triggered new construction throughout Mexico, "the Yucatan" was a poor, distant cousin of the industrialized Central Spine. ("The Yucatan," in popular terminology, differentiates the peninsula, which includes Campeche and Quintana Roo, from the state of Yucatan, which occupies only a third of the peninsula.) Like Chiapas, which once was part of Guatemala, the Yucatan functioned as a more or less separate entity under Spanish rule.

Dissatisfaction with the upheavals ripping the federal government (and federal treasury) apart in the mid-19th century prompted the governor and state assembly to petition the United States for admission to the Union, a move that was regarded favorably by certain expansionists connected with the Confederacy. But the South lost the Civil War and with it any dreams of creating a Caribbean Republic.

In the latter part of the 19th century, the uncovering of more and more Mayan ruins brought a steady stream of American and European tourists to the peninsula and to Merida, which sits on a high dry plain some 25 miles inland from the Gulf of Mexico.

The Spanish chose Merida as the capital of the peninsula because it occupied high ground on a relatively fertile plain accessible to the coast and the harbor at Progreso and because an indigena center, Ichcaanzho, already was situated there. From Merida the conquistadors launched their conquest of the Yucatan. (The "conquest" was more a declaration than an occupation, however; the natives raided forestry operations, attacked and destroyed Spanish outposts and refused to submit to either administrative or ecclesiastical rule.)

The city remained a tiny rural headquarters for almost 100 years, when pirate raids along the coast prompted the construction of fortifications in 1633. Later, to protect against native insurrections, Merida became a walled city, complete with its convent, church, market and government buildings.

Until the Mexican government decided to push tourism (in part as an alternative to the petroleum industry as Mexico's only attraction for foreign investment), Merida remained the sleepy capital of a placid and essentially out of the mainstream province whose leaders, problems and accomplishments impinged only slightly on national life. There was little immigration out of the rural Yucatan into urban areas; *curanderos* were as respected as doctors and locked doors were an unheard-of (and unnecessary) precaution.

In other parts of Mexico, to refer to someone as a *yucateco* meant calling him a hayseed or a hick. Even so, residents throughout the rest of Mexico envied the *yucatecos* for their cleanliness, honesty and tranquil ways.

Few Mexicans — and even fewer non-nationals — knew of or had heard of the beaches of Quintana Roo until the Mexican government decided to exploit Cancun and Cozumel. In many ways, it was a logical choice for the government to make: The beaches rivaled anything the Caribbean islands could offer, and Yucatan had its by-now world-famous Mayan ruins as well. Equally logically (if aesthetically and environmentally damaging) was the decision to build an international airport capable of handling the world's largest jets in Merida, which not only is closer to the eastern half of the United States, but to Europe.

Those decisions yanked the Yucatan into the Twentieth Century. The rapid expansion brought employment, much of it basic labor: clearing land for the runways, clearing land for the hotels, putting in road beds, installing breakwaters and marinas, providing lumber, hauling the rock used for construction, cutting trees, raking beaches, putting in new drainage systems. Farm workers from throughout the Yucatan flocked towards Merida and the resorts to earn extra money.

Many of them returned to their home villages to plough, plant and resume family life, bringing with them things valued by the more urban cultures they'd come into contact with. The prosperity that Mexico enjoyed in the '70s brought government expenditures. Ambitious projects authorized the building of schools and *casas de cultura*, power stations, roads and bridges, machinery of every kind.

Unfortunately for places like Tahdziu, the money didn't keep coming. As the building boom waned, the resorts hired fewer and fewer new people. The wave of prosperity, pipelined through the PRI, became over-extended, both financially and bureaucratically. Towns like Tahdziu, far from urban centers, were the first to feel the financial desiccation.

One by one schools, businesses and markets closed. Local political figures, entrusted with the distribution of funds, often pocketed the money, or shifted it to projects that benefited business interests, rather than people who needed sewers, roads, fertilizer and medical care.

Many of these people, like Marina Cota, wound up worse off than they would have been had the boom never come to the Yucatan. A community built around what its own labor can produce and provide, even though it is isolated and victimized by hard times, contains within it the means, and the energy, to renew itself. Its young men and young women work, court, wed, parent, build houses and cut trees, plow, plant, hunt, fish (and drink, fight, have affairs, break things, and run away, but all within the context of the community as a community).

The flight of youth changes the balance of communal living; the integrated process of birth, nurturing, aging, death that once was taken for granted becomes impossible. The barely distinguishable images sent towards television screens in town after town from the stations in Campeche and Merida are as shadowy and unreal as the lives that their residents live in forgotten corners of the Yucatan.

They grow grayer and grayer. Soon they will disappear.

The Passing Suns

Oil is not the only intruder threatening the traditional lifestyle of the jarochos. Projected plans for creating efficient "new cities" to divert the over-crowding of Mexico City, de-centralize the bureaucracy and create investment and industrial production target Mexico's east coast for meteoric expansion. Change, when it comes, may not be as abrupt as that created by the oil discoveries, but it will supplant orange and coffee groves, fields of corn, hillsides covered with flowers. As the oil industry brought new laws, new standards, new landlords, the projected industrialization — even that which is fiber-optically "clean" and environmentally progressive — will bring new rules, new values and new standards of behavior.

It will enrich, and it will displace, it will alter and it will destroy, just as the Spaniards' arrival enriched and altered and destroyed, and the Aztecs' conquests before that, and before that the Toltecs and the Mayas. Looking down from his holy place in the hills south of Macuspana several years ago, a Chontal shaman shrugged off the furor of the economic tides that had thrust coffee growers' bulldozers higher towards his refuge in the mountains, brought lumberjacks' saws and trucks and the imperative thuds of oil excavation crews, and said, simply, that such changes were like the passing of suns that had come and gone since the beginnings of the Chontal world.

The Mayans had come — and now were gone; the Spanish had come — and now were gone; epidemics had come — and now were gone; why shouldn't he expect that the oil, the foresters, the coffee, the Mexicans wouldn't come and go as well? And in the end, overlooking the green forests (or the devastated stumps), why shouldn't he expect that the rhythms of Chontal life, which had begun soon after time began, shouldn't be as they always had been, before the changes began?

On the edge of Lago Catemaco, a wiry wild-haired woman who laughingly called herself "*La Bruja*" (but whom most residents of the little village close to newly re-routed, re-banked and re-paved highway 180 called "The Caiman Lady") used to stop motorists speeding past by waving wild reptiles at their windshields. The tiny ones she sold for a few pesos, the larger ones for more.

To those who stopped, The Caiman Lady offered to treat them to the spectacle of seeing her wrestle the largest and most ferocious of the primordial swamp creatures. "Stay longer!" she'd purportedly add, "and I'll cut one apart and sew you a suitcase from its skin!"

The alligators, of course, paid little attention to her — as they pay little attention to visitors who seek them out today. Wallowing through the ooze created by centuries of alluvial back flow, they occasionally open their heavy-lidded eyes and seem to say, like the shaman of the Chontales, that the world has endured innumerable changes since the first of their species crept out of its shell 200 million years ago and undoubtedly will continue to change as the centuries roll over each other, leaving behind their residues of flesh and metal and clay.

Printed in the United States
33773LVS00003B/71

9 780875 862156